Advance Praise for
For Land and Culture

"In this work on the Turkmen Council Movement of 1979 in Iran, Peyman Vahabzadeh offers a unique phenomenological approach, inspired by Hannah Arendt's writings on council democracy and radical mobilization by workers, into an otherwise unexplored world-historical movement of a marginalized people within Iranian modernity. Vahabzadeh's careful analysis of the Turkmen movement in Iran and their fight for land and cultural sovereignty, and his introduction of the concept ancestrality, offers an important and timely dialogue with other grassroots, participatory, decolonizing, anti-imperialist, and justice-seeking indigenous global movements of our time."

—Daniel Ahadi, School of Communication, Simon Fraser University

"An engaging yet scholarly counter-history of the Turkmen council movement – the remarkable experiment in radical democracy repressed and vilified by Iran's Islamic regime, and largely ignored by left scholars. Vahabzadeh meticulously probes the struggle for land, culture, autonomy and the commons, placing it in a transnational context and exploring it's profound lessons for those interested in collectively creating change from below."

—William K. Carroll, professor of sociology, University of Victoria

"Revolutions are not just about the change of regimes and state institutions. They are also expressed at the base of society — in schools, farms, factories, and families. This original study highlights one of the most neglected aspects of the 1979 Iranian revolution — the peasant council movement of Turkmen Sahra. By underlining its struggles for land and cultural revival, Vahabzadeh brings the Iranian experience into a productive conversation with the current indigenous movements around the globe."

—Asef Bayat, Bastian Professor of Global and Transnational Studies, University of Illinois Urbana-Champaign

For
Land
and
Culture

For
Land
and
Culture

The Grassroots Council Movement
of Turkmens in Iran, 1979–1980

PEYMAN VAHABZADEH

Fernwood Publishing
Halifax & Winnipeg

Copyright 2024 © Peyman Vahabzadeh

All rights reserved. No part of this book may be reproduced or transmitted in any form by any means without permission in writing from the publisher, except by a reviewer, who may quote brief passages in a review.

Development editor: Fiona Jeffries
Copyediting: Amber Riaz
Cover design: Jess Koroscil
Text design: Brenda Conroy
Printed and bound in the UK

Published by Fernwood Publishing
Halifax and Winnipeg
2970 Oxford Street, Halifax, Nova Scotia, B3L 2W4
www.fernwoodpublishing.ca

Fernwood Publishing Company Limited gratefully acknowledges the financial support of the Government of Canada through the Canada Book Fund and the Canada Council for the Arts. We acknowledge the Province of Manitoba for support through the Manitoba Publishers Marketing Assistance Program and the Book Publishing Tax Credit. We acknowledge the Nova Scotia Department of Communities, Culture and Heritage for support through the Publishers Assistance Fund.

This book has been published with the help of a grant from the Federation for the Humanities and Social Sciences, through the Awards to Scholarly Publications Program, using funds provided by the Social Sciences and Humanities Research Council of Canada.

Library and Archives Canada Cataloguing in Publication
Title: For land and culture : the grassroots council movement
of Turkmens in Iran, 1979-1980 /
Peyman Vahabzadeh.
Names: Vahabzadeh, Peyman, author.
Description: Includes bibliographical references and index.
Identifiers: Canadiana 20240352823 | ISBN 9781773636658 (softcover)
Subjects: LCSH: Turkmen—Land tenure—Iran—History—20th century. |
LCSH: Land reform—Iran—History—
20th century. | LCSH: Peasant uprisings—Iran—History—20th century. |
LCSH: Collectivization of agriculture—Iran—History—20th century.
Classification: LCC HD3532.56.A4 V34 2024 | DDC 333.3/155—dc23

This book is dedicated to three world-historical towns:
Gonbad Kavus, 1979
La Realidad, 1994
Kobanî, 2015

Human action, like all strictly political phenomena, is bound up with human plurality, which is one of the fundamental conditions of human life insofar as it rests on the fact of natality, through which the human world is constantly invaded by strangers, newcomers whose actions and reactions cannot be foreseen by those who are already there and are going to leave in a short while.

— Hannah Arendt, *Between Past and Future*

Contents

Acknowledgements xii
    A Note on Transliteration and Translation xii
    List of Abbreviated Sources xiii
    List of Abbreviated Names of Organizations xiii

Introduction: Against Oblivion 1
    Back to the Watershed 2
    A Movement of Our Global Future 8
    The Road from Here 11

1 Historical and Conceptual Preparations for the Study 12
    A Glance at the Grassroots Councils in Europe 13
    Hannah Arendt's Councils: Acting in Concert 19
    The Social Question 23
    The Ambivalence of Strikes 27
    Councils and Iranian Modernization 30
    Workers' Councils in the Revolutionary Period 37
    The People's Fadai Guerrillas: A Brief History 46
    Conclusions 53

2 Dispossession, Appropriation, and Repressive Development 55
    From Traditional Landownership to the Modernization Threshold 56
    The Pahlavi Initiative: Modernizing Property Rights 61
    Royal Land Appropriation 64
    Land Reform and Its Consequences 68
    The People's Fadai Guerrillas and Land Reform 75
    Conclusions 79

3   Land Is Life: The Prolonged Dispossession of Turkmens 81
   Situating Iranian Turkmens... 82
   Turkmens Between the Constitutional Revolution and the Rise of Reza Shah . . 87
   The Appropriation of Turkmen Lands 89
   Transference and Aggressive Privatization 93
   A Glance at Turkmen's Traditional Life 98
   The Impact of Land Reform 99
   Cultural Hegemony 102
   Conclusions.. 108

4   The Turkmen Council Movement: Advent, Challenges,
    and Thriving 109
   Turkmen Activism in the 1970s.. 110
   The Advent of Councils and Leading Turkmen Organizations 116
   Fadaiyan's Dilemma.. 126
   The Provisional Government and Complications 130
   The Spring of Councils: The "First War" of Turkman Sahra 135
   Expansion of the Councils 144
   The Spring Wheat Harvest Festival... 146
   Conclusions.. 158

5   The Councils and Collective Life: Expansion, Repression,
    Assimilation... 162
   The Structure of Councils... 164
   The Bloody Summer of 1979: The State's Show of Force 168
   New Developments in Turkman Sahra....................................... 174
   The Organization of Iranian People's Fadai Guerrillas and Its Program..... 180
   The Autumn of the Councils 184
   Women's Participation in the Movement................................. 191
   The Winter of the Councils: The February Clash 193
   Aftermath: Decline and Assimilation..................................... 206
   Conclusions.. 213

Conclusions: A World-Historical Movement 216
   A Transnational and Anticipative Movement............................. 217
   From Arendt to Gramsci and Back 221
   Ancestrality and Collective Democratic Life 223
   (Re-)Collecting the Past 225

Appendix 1: Reports from Turkman Sahra Villages.................. 227
    Tatar Olya 227
    Report from the Rural Council of Tatar Olya............................ 231

Appendix 2: The General Principles of Self-Governance Plan
(July 1979)... 232
    The General Principles of Self-Governance Plan 232

Appendix 3: The Fadaiyan's Minimum Program (February 1980)... 234

Bibliography 238

Index 247

Acknowledgements

WHILE THE IDEA BEHIND THIS BOOK and my eagerness to engage with the subject of the Turkmen council movement in Iran had simmered for some time, the motivation for writing it emerged from a conversation with friends around 2020. I would like to thank Mohsen Saffari, Mohammad Safavi, and Siyamak Ghaffari for their friendship and our conversations on matters of mutual interest, namely the unfinished and threatened project of social and ecological justice in Iran. I would like to especially thank Arne (Amin) Goli who provided me with substantive materials without which this research could not have its present shape. Mr. Goli and the Turkmen Study Centre in Sweden have done a remarkable job in creating the unique archive of Turkmen history and social life and making it publicly available. I would also like to thank the Department of Sociology and Steve Garlick, Chair of Sociology, for providing me with the much-needed research time to complete this monograph. Thanks also to Mandana Karimi and Sajjad Kaveh Shaldehi who assisted me with translations of two of the appendices. As well, I acknowledge the assistance provided by Mandana Karimi in uncovering and obtaining some of the sources necessary for this study. I would also like to thank the anonymous reviewers of this monograph whose useful and encouraging comments helped me improve the manuscript.

Last but certainly not the least, at Fernwood I would like to thank Fiona Jeffries, Anumeha Gokhale, Lauren Jeanneau, Brenda Conroy, and Sanna Wani, for their professionalism and amicable process through the submission, review, marketing, and publishing process. I thank copyeditor Amber Riaz for her marvellous job and the designer of the book's cover for the captivating cover image.

A Note on Transliteration and Translation

In transliterating proper names in Persian, I used the common spelling instead of the existing scholarly rules. My intention was to simplify the Persian words or names for the purpose of smooth reading. I have only used two typographical marks. The inverse apostrophe indicates the letter *ain* (as in Shi'i) except when the *ain* is the first letter in which case I dropped the typograph (as in Ali). The backtick indicates the letter *hamzeh* (as in Reza`i). The English names of towns and places in the Turkmen region are mostly done in accordance with Google Maps.

With respect to translations, I have tried to primarily stay with the contextual meanings. There are some polysemic words in Persian with more than one English equivalent. Of particular importance to this study is the Persian *khodmokhtari* which literally means "self-autonomy" or simply "autonomy," but also "self-governance," but in the Iranian context at the time it implied federalism. I translated *melli* as "national" but contextually pertaining to nations, not necessarily the nation-state, and *sarasari* as "nationwide" in political sense and as "plenary" in organizational sense. In cases of ambiguity, I have always put the Persian word in parentheses.

List of Abbreviated Sources

(full citation in Bibliography)

DCM1	Arne Goli (ed.), *Documents of the Council Movement of Plains of Turkmen, Vol 1*
DCM2	Arne Goli (ed.), *Documents of the Council Movement of Plains of Turkmen, Vol 2*
THD	Arne Goli (ed.). *Turkmens in the Historic Documents of Qajar and Pahlavi Periods (1878–1978)*
LSTP	CPCTP (Cultural-Political Centre of Turkmen People), *The Life and Struggles of Turkmen People*

List of Abbreviated Names of Organizations

CHCPT	Central Headquarters of Councils of Plains of Turkmen
CPCTP	Cultural-Political Centre of Turkmen People
IRGC	Islamic Revolutionary Guards Corps
OIPFG	Organization of Iranian People's Fadai Guerrillas
PFG	People's Fadai Guerrillas

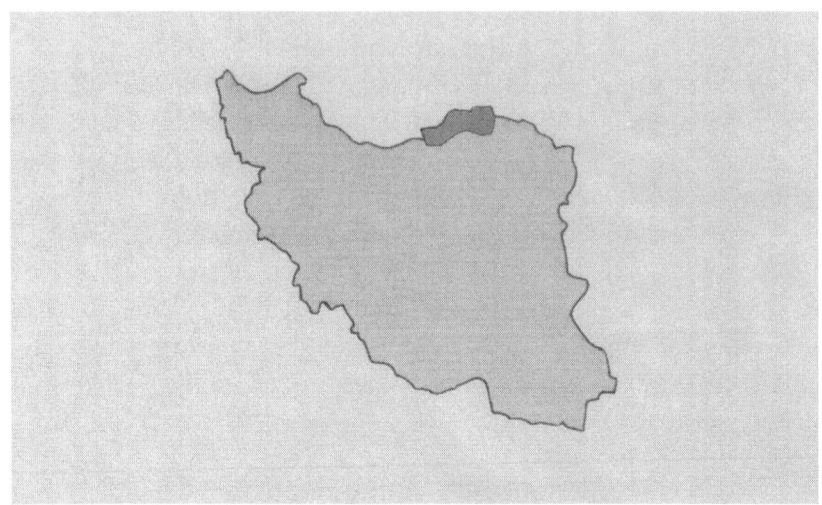

The Plains of Turkmen and Turkmen populated region in Iran

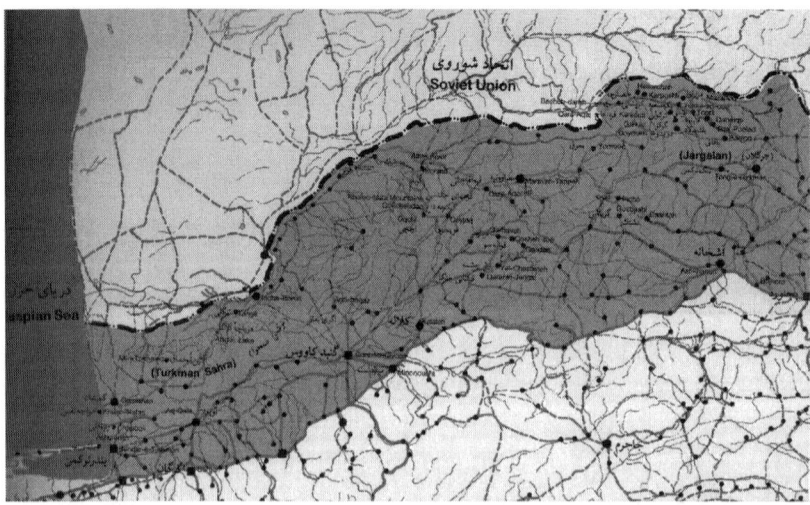

Cities and towns of the Plains of Turkmen, 1979 (image courtesy of Arne Goli)

Introduction

Against Oblivion

What the Turkmen people want are the natural rights of every nation and minority. To deny our demands is to deny our very existence.

— Cultural-Political Centre of Turkmen People, 1979

AS WE CELEBRATED NAWRUZ (MARCH 20), the Persian New Year of 1979 in Tehran, the bitter news of an armed conflict in the Plains of Turkmen in the north broke out. Having participated as a very young man in the revolution that had toppled the monarchy just a month prior, I had experienced a true sense of freedom — not in the sense of controlled, legislated "freedom" under a state, but freedom as if all the invisible tentacles of power and control had been cut off, not just from my limbs but also from my mind. Since then, I have never felt free and have been longing for a unique experience: the freedom to be able to give birth to the impossible. The impossible dream of many in my generation was to build a better Iran, a country built on freedom and social justice, a truly livable Iran for all. While the retrograde Islamists were busy consolidating their power, Iranians from different walks of life were experiencing flourishing grassroots social experiments everywhere the people had congregated to forge their own communities, unions, and councils: in neighbourhoods, schools, universities, factories, farms, government offices, even barracks. The country was blooming with novelty.

The news from the Plains of Turkmen — and a similar armed conflict in Kurdistan — was disheartening, an ominous sign of what to expect in the months to come while we were still mesmerized by the fresh air of the "Spring of Freedom" (as those months were called) as it caressed our souls and imaginations. But the conflict made me a firm supporter of the movement. I remember calling friends about it. A bunch of us met in front of the University of Tehran in the city centre and joined hundreds of others with different political proclivities who were participating in heated sidewalk debates about the causes of, and solutions to, the armed conflicts in the Plains of Turkmen and in Kurdistan. It was another expression of true freedom.

Since then, I have admired the Turkmen's novel approach to egalitarian communal life, their efforts toward collective land ownership and in cultural and linguistic revival, their resoluteness and tenacity in the face of adversarial forces that were multiple times stronger. I find myself fortunate to be able to historicize and theorize in this book what I felt with my heart more than four decades ago. This book is therefore owed to the magnificent women and men who had created the shining Turkmen peasants' council movement. They brought the impossible to this world. The Turkmen people gifted to the rest of the country an alternative, just society that Iran never became. For that I am — indeed we are — grateful.

Back to the Watershed

In February 1979, the seeds of a unique social and cultural movement in Iran were sown by the Turkmen peasants and activists who have been the ancestral inhabitants of the fertile plateaus, known as the Plains of Turkmen (in Persian: Turkman Sahra; note different spelling of Turkmen/Turkman) — a region stretching from the southeastern coast of the Caspian Sea to the northeast. This self-governing, council movement, primarily and mainly of Turkmen peasants but also of different social groups and non-Turkmens of urban dwellers, workers, fishermen, high school students, and professional sectors was launched at a historic moment: the dawn of a brief but life-altering "Spring of Freedom" in 1979–1980 when Iranians were gradually grasping the enthralling, if challenging and precarious, reality of a post-monarchical era, on that shone with incredible possibilities for a better Iran, before the Islamists consolidated the state power that equipped the rising ruling oligarchy with the necessary apparatuses to brutally suppress social movements and spread their clerical black robe all over a diverse, colourful nation. For the duration that this historic moment lasted, however, "Iran" was the floating signifier of unrivalled, creative, and imaginative social experiments — namely, experiments in participatory self-governance and semi-autonomous social organization (as opposed to hierarchical, colonial, and dominating power structures). In the transitional period when one dictatorship had collapsed and the next had not yet harnessed its imminent heavy hand, workers, teachers, university students, state employees, peasants, and national minorities reverted to the most authentic form of grassroots self-governance: the councils.

This book offers a counter-history: the tremendous experiment of Iran's Turkmens has been relegated to historical oblivion in the past four decades. By funding and promoting garden variety "research" works that regurgitate state propaganda, the Iranian regime derides the movement as an insignificant ethnic disturbance instigated by sly Marxists (Khajehnejad 2020; Naderi 2011; PSRI nd), often calling this popular experiment using derogatory terms like "intrigue" or "sedition" (*gha'eleh* or *fetneh*; PSRI nd). As in any ideological historiography, the starting point of all sources sanctioned by the security apparatus of the Islamic Republic is the self-righteousness of the Islamists and their Islamic state, thus rendering all efforts to build social justice–oriented social imaginaries, democratic alternatives, and legitimate resistances against exploitation and autocratic rule to the alleged, self-defeating defects of these movements and foreign conspiracy. This historiography simultaneously justifies and minimizes the state's murderous measures taken against the post-Revolutionary movements.

On the other hand, the Iranian left has not afforded to the Turkmen council movement the attention and analysis this tremendous experiment deserves. There have been only a few, albeit important, memoirs of the Fadai cadres and Turkmen activists involved in the region at that time, and even then, they mainly focus on the two episodes of armed conflict, allowing these episodes to overshadow the entire year-long movement (Fatapour 2023; Hamidian 2004; A. Hashemi 2016, 2021; Mahfuzi 1984). Some of these accounts narrate history backwards, as their accounts of the past are tainted by their present-day values and stances (Hamidian 2004; Mahfuzi 1984). This is an example of memory erasing itself in the interest of current-day political correctness or values. These memoirs are also coloured by the fact that the movement was vanquished: no one wants to be the bearer of the legacy of a defeat.

A welcome and refreshing exception to this trend is the recent two-volume set of documents pertaining to the movement, edited by tireless Turkmen researcher Arne (Amin) Goli and published in exile by the Turkmen Research Centre (DCM1, DCM2). True embodiments of a labour of love, these volumes (and others on Turkmens edited by Goli) must be regarded, by any party involved, as original sources that contain the documents, reportages, interviews, and press releases pertaining to the Turkmen council movement. Turkmen organizations, newspapers, government press releases, and analyses of leftist and Islamist groups should all see these volumes as invaluable. Like this study, these volumes position themselves as resisting oblivion, as a bulwark against the discounting of the movement of a marginalized people within mainstream historiography of modern Iran. These volumes allow me and other researchers to gain a valuable view from the inside of the movement and its contributions to, as well as how it was received in, public and state-run media at the time. However, there are very few sources in any shape or form about the inner challenges of, and disagreements within, the movement, or about the movement's assimilation by the Islamic Republic. As such, any study of this kind potentially runs the risk of reconstructing this movement in rather monolithic ways, which I have tried to avoid to the best of my ability and in as much as my sources allowed, by cross-referencing and triangulating the various accounts. In the end, I too construct a narrative about the movement, based on my research, but I emphatically note that no one can ever say the last word in history. History is open to interpretations, and as such it lives on, inspiring future generations to partake in the unfinished projects of past generations. I hope this book will do the same for the younger activists in Iran.

The transformative months following the 1979 Revolution provided the Turkmen minority in Iran with a rare historical opportunity to realize its long-held dream of national self-assertion as a people, a movement aimed at cultural self-expression and linguistic revival as well as a particular mode of self-governance that was based on both Turkmen tradition and modern values that promoted participation, inclusion, negotiation, and above all, a better, collective life. As such, it turned out to be a movement simultaneously for cultural revival and for social justice, with land at its heart. The Turkmen council movement represented everything that the Islamic Republic was not and could have never been. This movement stands out in recent Iranian history due to, first, its sheer size and reach, and second, the radical, sophisticated, all-embracing vision.

Both features render the neglect of this movement by scholars all the more astonishing. In fact, scholars of modern Iran have evidently played their part in relegating this movement to oblivion. In some of the most widely read general histories of modern Iran, references to the Turkmen council movement do not exceed quick notes in passing (Amanat 2017, 773, 780, 817; Keddie 1981, 258, 261), if not nil (Abrahamian 2008; Ansari 2019), although one these historians clearly advocates minority rights (Amanat 2017). More interestingly, in a book dedicated to the history of the Iranian left, only a paragraph-long quick overview of this movement is offered (Behrooz 2000, 108). The only exception to this trend is an article published during the movement's activity in *New Left Review* (Azad 1980). It is fair to say that the continued scholarly empirical neglect and disregard imposes silences on this and other movements that did not register with the (often orientalist) epistemic frames of mainstream historiography.

This omission has clear pedagogical consequences. I wonder how such silences will tint the views of students of Iranian history as well as their understanding of the dynamics of change in a country known — to this day and under a brutally repressive regime — for its people's tireless defiance of authority. Modern Iran is the land of undying, albeit changing, social movements for social justice and democracy. Such omissions are partly because historians of Iranian politics have largely dwelled in a particular epistemological gaze that directs scholarly focus toward formal and institutional sources of political power as represented by the modern state. These studies have been fascinated by, and focused on, the state as the privileged agent of change. Hence, the generative power of social movements has always been subsumed by the study of formal institutions. Of course, the works of Asef Bayat (1987; 1997; 2017) provide refreshing exceptions to this trend. This book resists the dominant and long-rooted lure of concentrating on formal institutions as privileged sites of power and invites the readers to focus on the original makers of politics — social movement activists — and their initiatives.

An important note is in order: the present-day Iranian nation-state contains several nationalities that have lived alongside each other, at times peacefully and at times not, on the Iranian plateau for centuries and millenniums. By all accounts, therefore, the country named Iran — whose current international borders are fixed by imperial and colonial legacies of powerful states (such as Russian and British Empires) — is an irreducibly multinational and multicultural country, though it has never been "colonized" in the classical sense of the term. In the twentieth-century political lexis of Iran, the word *melli* (national) often refers to both the Iranian nation and the minorities that regard themselves as nations.

In English, the terms "ethnicity" or "ethno-national" are used to distinguish culturally distinct peoples from the nation within a nation-state. As I have argued elsewhere, Iran has no "ethnics" (Vahabzadeh 2022a), only national-cultural groups. As such, in this study and depending on the context and on par with the original sources of this study, I use the term *nationwide* (*sarasari* but also, depending on context, *melli*) mostly to refer to the Iranians within the nation-state and the term "national" (*melli*) to refer to national-cultural claims of peoples within the nation-state. The word "people" or *khalq* is also used to refer to national-cultural groups. Likewise, I have decided that "self-governance" is the most context-sensitive translation for the polysemic Persian word, *khodmokhtari*, which can also be translated as "autonomy." The latter term implies secession, which was not the case in the political imagination of post-Revolutionary movements in Kurdistan and the Plains of Turkmen.

While regional, the Turkmen council movement was closely associated with Iran's most popular Marxist political party, Organization of Iranian People's Fadai Guerrillas (henceforth, OIPFG, or Fadaiyan, the plural of Fadai; see Chapter 1) even though the exact relations between the two is a subject of unending disagreements and debates, which this book will critically probe. Undoubtedly a left-leaning movement, what distinguished the Turkmen council movement from many other post-Revolutionary alternative movements, while associating it with the workers' (and other) council movements in revolutionary Iran, was its vast grassroots mobilization, sophisticated organization, and cultural-linguistic aspect.

Never studied prior to this book, the Turkmen council movement lasted for a year before it was crushed by the new, hostile regime that had been actively seeking to destroy this movement right from the start. The process of eradicating this experiment by the state entailed two imposed armed conflicts, continued hostile encroachment in the region, and then a long process of forced assimilation.

Modern Iranians are no strangers to councils and other organizational forms of self-assertion and self-governance. Most studies of councils are actually in Persian and written by activists and scholars of the left. Although it has a history that spans more than a century, *showra* (Persian/Arabic for "council"; also spelled as *shura*) as a form of grassroots and direct democratic participation in Iran has appeared in the English-language scholarship, but only few works have attended to it

(Afary 1996; Bayat 1987, 100–141; Bayat 2017, 49–67; Jafari 2021; Rahnema 1992). In the period that led to the foundation of the modern Iranian state as an agent of authoritarian modernization (Atabaki 2018) and "repressive development" (Vahabzadeh 2010), as well as in the periods of relaxed state repression and control, we witness the (re)surfacing of *showras*, these expressions of alternative, participatory, and democratic modernization.

The last point brings us to yet another oversight caused by epistemological blind spots. With the aforementioned analytical focus on institutional politics and the state in mind, one notices that the amount of literature dedicated to this aspect of Iranian modernity — that is, centralized, institutionalized politics and programmes — overshadows and pushes to obscurity the extent of council experiences and experiments in contemporary Iran. Therefore, a conceptual neglect has been afforded to the forms of power from below, the power of "acting in concert," à la Hannah Arendt, as the source of political life in social movements. By and large, social movements have been investigated mostly in relation to the state and its policies, and thus in a secondary fashion, not in their own rights. They have been studied from the top down, not from the bottom up. The study of *showras* was also generally affected by such epistemic tendency, which also explains the above-mentioned erasure of the Turkmen council movement from mainstream historiography.

But there is further complication: the Pahlavi dynasty founded the modern state by identifying Iran and the Iranian state with Persians and the Persian language, interestingly through a self-orientalizing gaze (via the Germans) that revitalized ancient Persia as the foundation of the postcolonial Pahlavi state (Dabashi 2015, 8). This has affected the aforementioned epistemic gazes — in a dual fashion, in the case of the Turkmens, as a *movement* of a *minority* — such that the movements of national minorities have been treated only in relation to the larger contexts of Iranian politics and history. The movements by national minorities — Kurds, Azerbaijani Turks, Baluchis, Turkmens, Arabs, and others — have been and are, of course, situated within the general context of the nation but still deserving particular attention. Fortunately, this trend seems to be changing with emerging scholarship (see, for example, Jahani Asl 2017).

These preliminary remarks shed light on the approach of this book and my acute epistemic awareness of and resistance to, the lures of generalizations, subsumptions, orientalizations, and omissions. On par with my previous books (Vahabzadeh 2010, 2015, 2019a, 2022b), this book offers a bottom-up view of the Turkmen council movement and situates it within a transnational context. Simultaneously, the book represents a work of scholarly advocacy of movements for a better life. This particular research tries to showcase the contexts, struggles, visions, challenges, successes, and failures of the Turkmen council movement, but also and with emphasis, its contributions to present and future movements in Iran and in the world. It tries to register how a particular novel, grassroots experiment of the Turkmen national and cultural minority in Iran can be regarded as a potentially universal watershed moment for an alternative social self-organization based on principles of social justice. To that end, what I particularly wish to communicate in this book is a nuanced reading of the Turkmen council movement: one that incorporates facts and existing interpretations but intends to go beyond. As with my previous studies, I achieve a nuanced reading by projecting a phenomenological gaze on it. In a phenomenological manner, this research tries to bring out the concealed from that which has been revealed already. This can be done primarily by going back and (to use phenomenological terms) "reactivating" the "sedimented" origins of the movement.

One last but important note: my lack of knowledge of the Turkmen language imposes a limitation in terms of an inability to access publications in Turkmen, just as I might have misspelled some Turkmen proper nouns. This should have an impact on the cultural aspect of the research. Fortunately, though, the majority of documents pertaining to the Turkmen council movement — the original sources of this study — were published in Persian.

A Movement of Our Global Future

This research has been like a puzzle: it needed to weave together events with ideas within a particular context and through contested narratives with incredible detail. I aim to show the originality of the Turkmen council movement's initiatives — a pathway not specific to Iran but shared by many land-based movements around the world, especially in this age of simultaneous global-capitalist domination and decolonizing movements across the world and the recognition of the rights of indigenous peoples.

To those who did not actually live through the movement, like me (but possibly even those!), the unenviable task of unearthing the movement appears to be a demanding one. As mentioned earlier, at the time the Turkmen council movement was unfolding, I was a young supporter of Fadaiyan in Tehran who followed the events in the Plains of Turkmen with great enthusiasm and supported the movement morally and politically. Aside from the movement itself, my interest was also boosted by what we erroneously called — and unfortunately continue to call — its "ethnic" (*qowmi*) element — a term that has emanated from the colonial mindset at the time of the formation of nation-states and still lingers in our conceptualizations.

I was born in Tehran to Persian and Azerbaijani parents. My mother tongue is Persian, and my father spoke Azeri Turkish to his many siblings, but never to his children. Instead, he taught his children English and French. I ended up publishing my first English to Persian translation (an article from *The Reader's Digest*) at the age of 14. I was already a transnational teenager! My father was a dissident intellectual, vocally critical of the Shah and a supporter of militant resistance to monarchy, but he still had a "modernist" mindset, like most of his contemporaries, that privileged "international" (implicitly, colonial) languages to the national ones. I picked up my paternal language, though, by listening to my father's conversations with others and by listening to Turkish songs, but I could not master it. In my teen years, I had intuitively learned the power of assimilation into Persian. But, thinking back, it really did not have to be this way. In this context, when decades later I entered academia in Canada, I realized that while Persian was my ancestral language and the country's largest lingua franca, it was also a means of state power to forge its ideal citizens. That said, I feel content to have been born into the Persian language, and I soon developed great passion for Persian classics, poetry in particular, which I read voraciously from a very young age to this day; I have read all major poetry divans as well as the complete works of key modern poets. My world is indeed a Persian world. However, in my teenage years I realized, without being able to utter the experience, that assimilation deprived me of parallel worlds of other languages native to my homeland. During high school, I had Kurdish, Turkmen, and Armenian friends and became aware, again intuitively, of how they would feel at home in their own mother tongues. Iran speaks in many languages. So, reflecting back, my interest in the Turkmens' movement was also in part cultural, an unconscious attempt perhaps for recovering what I had lost: being multilingual in my homeland. I remember attending the folk music festivals of Fadaiyan, where the music from Azerbaijan, the Plains of Turkmen, Mazandaran, and other regions felt like breeze in my soul. I purchased cassettes of these concerts and enjoyed listening to them until the repressive machinery of the Islamic Republic finally reached my home and I had to destroy my entire library and collections to survive, a trauma that pierces my heart to this day.

I have been an uninvited guest, living on the ancestral lands of the Indigenous Peoples of the West Coast of Canada for more than three decades. My home and the University of Victoria, where I work, are located on the unceded territories of ləkʷəŋən peoples, the traditional lands of the Songhees, Esquimalt, and W̱SÁNEĆ peoples on the southern tip of the so-called Vancouver Island (a colonial name). A complex struggle for decolonization has been going on around me, and in my courses, I try to contribute, in a small way, to this ongoing struggle. This island is a mysterious and charming place that allows those who are still able to *feel* the meta-humans — trees, animals, birds, boulders, rivers, and the ocean — a spiritual connection to this place. I was thrown here as a refugee and an exile and miraculously found myself a humble denizen of this land.

Given where I stand, the story of the Turkmen council movement that I tell, in historical and analytical ways, is indeed coloured by my experiences. I am not (cannot be, nor do I want to be) the detached scholar who aims to produce impartial accounts for academic consumption in an extractive way. Thus, this book offers an advocate-scholar's account whose interpretive foundation is the movement itself and the literature it left behind. I show that the Turkmen council movement was a movement of ancestral inhabitants of the region for land and culture, and unbeknownst to the activists and participants, it had an organic affinity with the struggles of 350 million indigenous peoples across the world. I show certain organic, worldview affinities of the Turkmen council movement of four decades ago with today's autonomous movements such as the Zapatistas in Chiapas, Mexico, and Rojava (Autonomous Administration of North and East Syria) in Syria. I register that the Turkmens wanted the fundamental right to live as a people on their ancestral lands, and that is essentially what links this movement of yesteryear to today's growing movements of peoples for self-governance in a world that is rapidly disintegrating ecologically, economically, politically, and socially. I hope to show that a movement of the past contains lessons, and that it offers a model of participatory, democratic self-governance for land-based movements of today. Theoretically, I suggest a concept, in addition to indigeneity, in relation to the existing land- and culture-based movements of the world today: *ancestrality*.

The Road from Here

Chapter 1 offers the theoretical foundations and historical accounts that are necessary for this study. It briefly refers to the history of modern councils, before offering a reading of Hannah Arendt's concept of councils as grassroots, egalitarian, and participatory political formation of a people. The chapter then offers a short history of councils in modern Iran and a quick history of Fadaiyan because the group played an important role alongside the Turkmen council movement. Registering the historical complexities of landownership and the peasant conditions in Persia, Chapter 2 discusses the process of dispossession and appropriation of land in the course of Iranian modernization and state formation in the twentieth century and under the Pahlavi dynasty. It offers an analysis of capitalist encroachment through the 1960s land reform that aimed at the proletarianization of Iranian peasantry. Chapter 3 provides a history of Turkmen people in the region and how throughout the twentieth century they were adversely affected by Pahlavi transformation of landownership. State-sanctioned cultural assimilation also affected Turkmens as a national and linguistic minority. Chapter 4 attends to the formation of the Turkmen peasant council movement and goes through its activities in the face of the oppressive Islamic state. By registering sufficient detail, this chapter speaks of the March 1979 armed conflict and traces the subsequent activities of the movements from the Revolution's victory until the Summer of 1979. Chapter 5 narrates in due detail the movement's expansion and its politics until the second armed conflict in February 1980 and the movement's repression. This chapter also speaks of how the councils were gradually dismantled. The conclusion discusses the concept of ancestrality and offers a multilayered reading of the achievements of the Turkmen council movement and the lessons of this movement for today.

Chapter 1

Historical and Conceptual Preparations for the Study

In the birth of each [hu]man this initial beginning is reaffirmed, because in each instance something new comes into an already existing world which will continue to exist after each individual's death. Because [s/]he is a beginning, [a hu]man can begin; to be human and to be free are one and the same.
— Hannah Arendt, *Between Past and Future*

IN ORDER TO SITUATE THE THEORETICAL and historical significance of the Turkmen council movement within the study of social movements, council movements, and the myriad of transnational struggles of peoples for social justice and freedom past and present, I engage in this chapter with several relevant literatures that help us braid history and theory together and contextualize the movement at the heart of this study.

The Turkmen council movement was the brainchild of leftist activists associated with post-Revolutionary Iran's most popular leftist organization, the Organization of Iranian People's Fadai Guerrillas (OIPFG). I begin with a brief overview of the formation of workers' councils in the modern European history of rapid, colonial-capitalist industrialization. It is well-known that prior to (globalized) capitalist modernization, collective decision-making was present in many cultures across the world. But modern workplace councils have their roots mostly in Europe, which is a reaction of disenfranchised classes against capitalist exploitation. While councils had undeniable affinities with socialist and workers' movements, the very idea of council as a democratic and participatory political body exceeds the leftist tradition. Therefore, it is necessary to probe the foundational essence of councils, and thus, I offer a glimpse of the theoretical propositions of Hannah Arendt who regards the councils as the most authentic form of human political life and exercise of freedom. This section is followed by some debates around the "social question" and the working-class action. Then, I situate the emergence of councils with the advent of postcolonial, political modernity in Iran, beginning with the Constitutional Revolution. Next, I attend to Iranian workers' and others' councils and the push for unionization during 1979–1981 and offer conceptual clarifications. Lastly, a brief history of the Fadai Guerrillas is offered to foreshadow the complex relationship between this group and the Turkmen council movement, before some concluding observations are added.

A Glance at the Grassroots Councils in Europe

The struggle of the emerging and expanding working class during the period of rapid industrialization in Europe (and elsewhere) was concomitant, in due time, with the drive toward creating grassroots, collective bodies of workers' self-assertion. The advent of labour unions and workers' councils in the early twentieth century attests to struggles for social rights that were and are still systemically excluded from the formal constitutional rights within modern European nation-states as the institutional ancillary to ruling capitalist classes in the liberal democracies.

It is difficult to speak about the councils in Europe and not fall within ideological debates or theoretical expectations. However, keeping my topic in mind and avoiding Eurocentric views, instead of providing a survey of, or rationale for, council experiences in Europe, I want to highlight their importance at certain historic junctures as grassroots, activists' self-organizations that challenge the modern, capitalist-state institutional edifice.

As is known, there was a wave of European (and non-European) workers' councils in the early twentieth century that connects these experiences conceptually if not historically to that of the Paris Commune and the 1905 Russian revolution (Gluckstein 2018, 35; Muldoon 2018b, 3). Although lasting only for just over two months (March 18 to May 28, 1871) and defeated brutally by the military, the Paris Commune of 1871 was a pioneer in council-based autonomous self-governance. It took place in the context of the Franco-Prussian war (1870–1871) and the collapse of the Second Empire in France (1852–1870). Having been placed under siege, the commune's socialist, feminist, and anarchist activists, residents, and workers managed to set up a participatory municipal democracy that held up principles of social and economic justice. Karl

Marx analyzed this experience in *The Civil War in France* (1871). For Marx, the Paris Commune represented the emancipatory, working-class self-government that created a federal authority through local districts in which council delegates were under permanent recall. He believed that as a new form of government this system could be implemented at the national level. The council system represented simultaneously the executive and legislative powers, just as it was a working-class government (Popp-Madsen and Kets 2021, 165). It was indicative of the fact that a genuine workers' government bore no resemblance to the hierarchical system of modern state or representative government, and that the bottom-up form of participatory, popular control was indeed possible.

The 1905 Russian revolution took place in the context of the Russo-Japanese war (1904–1905) and Russia's humiliating defeat. Protests pressured the government for measurable reforms, and workers and soldiers set up soviets as bodies of democratic self-organization that, notably, directed strikes or mutinies. The revolution eventually led to a new constitution and parliament, but of course, failed to deliver the social democratic expectations or radical change. Nonetheless, it showed the possibility that under the conditions where the crushing force of the state is slackened, people are capable of setting up instruments of self-governance. Remarkably, an earliest influence of the first Russian council experience appeared in Iran's 1906 constitutional movement.

I wish to point out that both the Parisian and Russian experiences took place in the context of wars and weakened state control. Consequently, councils "arose in countries as far apart as Russia, Germany, Britain, Hungary, Ireland, Austria, Indonesia and Italy" (Gluckstein 2018, 33). Particularly in Europe, the failure of the socialist parties and labour unions against the imperialist war contributed to the emergence of grassroots councils (Gluckstein 2018, 36–37). These movements' emergence was *overdetermined* by complex elements:

> If we turn our attention to another period of radical mobilizations by workers — that of the workers' council movements in Italy and Germany at the end of the First World War — we see that they too have at their base an overdetermined set of circumstances: the collapse of the social order following the war, the militarization of the factories, the beginnings of Taylorization, the transformation of the role of skilled workers in production. (Laclau and Mouffe 1985, 157)

The level of workers' specialization is an important factor that should not be missed: in a majority of cases, metalworkers were council pioneers because, in the age of rapid industrialization, they produced diverse ranges of products for all economic sectors. Thus, according to Donny Gluckstein (2018, 37) "Although council structures spread right across Russia, Germany, Austria, Britain, Hungary and Italy, they almost always began in centres of metalworking. These included Petrograd, Berlin, Glasgow, Vienna, Budapest and Turin."

In the Russian revolution of 1917 these conditions were present, just as they variably were in the German and Italian cases. Here, the workers' and soldiers' councils took shape quickly following the February revolution. Their role in the revolutionary process was undeniable, contrary to official Soviet historiography, as the "soviets arose and assumed de facto power alongside the Provisional Government in March 1917 during a period of dual power before the October Revolution" (Muldoon 2108b, 3). After the February revolution, the impending assault of bourgeois counter-revolution motivated workers to mobilize and set up (in the summer of 1917) their soviets (Mandel 2018, 155). At this time, the soviets were democratically elected and expanded to town and neighbourhood councils. Of particular significance were the Saint Petersburg (Petrograd) workers' councils in 1917–1918 (Mandel 2018). The Bolsheviks did not regard the soviets in the same way the council participants did. During the revolutionary months of 1917 the Bolsheviks propagated the motto, "all power to the soviets" because within the councils dwelled their own party's constituency's power, but after the consolidation of their power, they tried to centralize the soviets and bring them under state control (Rees 1987, 12–13, 19), a move contrary to the grassroots Soviet's raison d'être. The rest is history: factory councils became extensions of the Bolshevik Party and their democratic structure was transformed into a top-down bureaucratic one.

In Germany, too, workers' and soldiers' councils (*Arbeiter- und Soldatenräte*) flourished in November 1918, "following a sailors' mutiny at Kiel, which led to the abdication of the Kaiser and a political struggle over the future form of the German state," which included, inter alia, the introduction of the eight-hour workday and women's suffrage (Muldoon 2108b, 3). This council movement led to a national revolutionary period. The workers' and soldiers' councils held a congress in Berlin in December attended by local *Räte* delegates from across the country, the vast majority of whom were supporters of the German Social Democratic Party. According to Brian Peterson (1975, 113) "This *Räte* congress also approved of democratic elections in January 1919 for a National Assembly which would write a new constitution and take over as the sovereign law-making body."

However, the problem was that the socialists did not view the councils as alternative to a bourgeois parliamentary system. Ben Fowkes (2014, 43) shows that "Most of them viewed the councils as a temporary and regrettable phenomenon, considering that they would cease to have any function at all once a properly constituted parliament-based government had taken over, which happened in February 1919." Yet the movement, in part, translated into the formation of the Communist Party of Germany (1918), and its radical splinter, the Communist Workers Party of Germany (1920). These events marked the advent of council communism, a position rejected by Lenin and the Bolsheviks. The revolutionary period in Germany (1918–1919) was marked by the government's move to push back against the councils and the revolutionaries trying to oust social democrats from local *Räte* leaderships. The "response of the national government was to send in *Freikorps* (bands of proto-fascist soldiers organized by the [Friedrich] Ebert [Social Democratic] government) and army formations to crush the local *Räte* and turn local power over to a municipal government elected by all classes" (Peterson 1975, 114).

Just like their counterparts in Russia, Hungary, and Germany, following the crises unravelled through the First World War (Amadori and Brunetti 2020), Italy (northern, industrial Italy to be exact) woke to its two Red Years or Biennio Rosso (see Bertrand 1982). Massimo Amadori and Giuliano Brunetti (2020) show that "A vast and militant mass movement which began in the spring of 1919 lasted until September 1920 only after several of the large factories in Northern Italy had been occupied." The "factory councils" took off in Turin in 1919, expanding to a national movement. Workers occupied the FIAT factory, the pinnacle of Italian industry. Militant workers and the Marxists within the Italian Socialist Party (like Antonio Gramsci) who founded the Italian Communist Party in 1921 played crucial roles during the Red Years (Gluckstein 2018, 42). Also important was the formation of fascism within the Socialist Party by Benito Mussolini and Alceste De Abris (National Fascist Party was founded in 1921). Already in 1917, inspired by the Bolshevik revolution, insurrectionary land occupations in northern and southern regions had taken place. Meanwhile, the radicalization of workers translated into the growth of Socialist Party membership "from 24,000 members in 1918 to over 200,000 in 1920" (Amadori and Brunetti 2020). Labour unions membership also grew: "the Italian General Confederation of Labor (CGIL) could count on almost two million members, while the anarchists of the Italian Syndicalist Union organized no less than 800,000 workers" (Amadori and Brunetti 2020). Not surprisingly, then, "In 1919 alone there were more than 1,800 strikes, involving more than 1.5 million strikers" (Amadori and Brunetti 2020). Factory occupations also created their Red Guards: the armed detachments of workers as units of popular self-defence. In Italy, it was the state's military occupation of Turin that ended the council movement.

The council movement experienced a sharp decline following WWI, but it also reappeared, curiously, during the Prague Spring (Dolack 2018). These councils had a living experience of the short-lived workers' councils in Czechoslovakia after the Second World War as well as the Yugoslavian model of self-management in the prior two decades. But unlike the Yugoslavian model, the Czechoslovak "work councils" at this time rose from a grassroots movement (Dolack 2018, 32–33). Note that the 1945 workers' councils took place in the context of Czechoslovakia's transition to communism, and yet, they were removed in 1949 as the country switched, under pressure from the Soviet Union, to the doctrine of "one man management" (Dolack 2018, 34). The internal context of the 1968 councils in Czechoslovakia was the push for reforms within the Communist Party under the leadership of Alexander Dubček that began in January 1968 and ended with the Soviet invasion in August. Oriented toward decentralization, the envisioned reforms entailed promotion of democratic rights and economic restructuring. In this context, the councils indeed played a role in decentralization and democratization of the top-down communist rule. Pete Dolack (2018, 32) points out that "Czech and Slovak workers began implementing workers' control in factories, wrote statutes and organized a national conference of councils at which one-sixth of the country's workers were represented." Trade unions organized two-thirds of over 200 councils, and the local chapters of the Communist Party also helped organizing councils (Dolack 2018, 32). Interestingly, despite the Communist Party push back, the number of councils grew from 19 at the time of Soviet invasion to 260 by the end of 1968. The councils continued in 1969 (Dolack 2018, 45–46).

When Dubček was removed from party leadership in April 1969 and replaced by pro-Soviet Gustáv Husák, the purges of reform-minded party members and workers began, followed by recentralization policy (Dolack 2018, 49–50).

The above cases of European council movements, only touched upon here, are witness to grassroots and participatory self-governance and self-management in an organizational model that contrasts the hierarchical, power-over system of modern capitalism and the bourgeois (liberal) state. The major movements of the past should not veil the continued council movements around the world. In fact, today's "factory commoning" model (Rappaport 2021) shows the rise of worker-owned factories and cooperatives, at times through expropriation, as a means of workers' empowerment and economic equity.

From their inception, workers' councils stirred up endless definitional disagreements within the leftist traditions. This is due to the undeniable fact that the councils were irreducible to theoretical principles and ideological norms. I argue that what Robin Wagner-Pacifici (2017, 105–106) observed about the "representational uncertainty" surrounding the Paris Commune applies to most grassroots, council movements: the "ambiguity" and "multivocalism" of these movements cannot yield to particular epistemological or ideological expectations. Consequently, there have been three conceptions of councils. The first, that of Lenin, regarded the councils merely as insurrectionary bodies, instrumental for dismantling the ancien régime but incapable of governing (Popp-Madsen and Kets 2021, 160). In fact, as early as 1905, the Bolshevik Central Committee appraised the Saint Petersburg Soviet "as a needless distraction" (Gluckstein 2018, 35). Not surprisingly, "After the Bolshevik conquest of state power, Lenin argued that the councils were never meant to become a permanent political form of self-governance" (Popp-Madsen and Kets 2021, 166). No wonder the genuine soviets of 1917 were transformed into meaningless appendages to the state.

The second conception "favored by the interwar council communists, stresses the ability of workers' councils to democratize the workplace, providing the germs of economic democracy" (Popp-Madsen and Kets 2021, 160). This is best represented by the Italian and German councils. The council movement in Germany and the Netherlands led to the emergence of "council communism" within the Second International. The proponents of council communism rejected Soviet-style management of workers and instead "adhered to a principle of the self-emancipation of the working class and advocated the establishment of workers' councils" (Kets and Muldoon 2018, 51). As such, they were indebted to Marx instead of Lenin because they regarded the workers' councils as (1) political instruments of revolutionary change; (2) workplace bottom-up structures; and (3) consciousness raising among workers and masses (Popp-Madsen and Kets 2021, 168–169).

The third conception of the councils arises from the works of Hannah Arendt (but also Cornelius Castoriadis's "council democracy" [Muldoon 2018a; Popp-Madsen 2020; Popp-Madsen and Kets 2021]). Arendt regarded the councils as genuine alternatives to representative democracy and the formative moment of democratic politics. In this tradition, the councils configure a project of democratization through decentralization and grassroots self-management and self-government (Muldoon 2108b, 2). Her position has provoked many critical responses, especially from the left, but it is fair to state that she offers "an original new dimension to the council tradition" (Lederman 2018, 162).

Due to her focus on the councils as the formative moments of political life, Arendt's concept of councils informs this study and sheds light on the Turkmen council movement. So, I now attend to her work.

Hannah Arendt's Councils: Acting in Concert

The preceding must be positioned within the framework that seeks to step back phenomenologically from the aforementioned traditions and movements in order to unravel the formation of the councils as springing from the human ability to act collectively and thereby to understand the councils in relation to political foundation — an approach that explains today's grassroots movements for self-governance and self-assertion. Stated differently, unlike their (largely) organizational and mobilizational significance within the socialist tradition, the councils *potentially* signify the emergence of a *people* as the founders of (collective) political life, according to Arendt. It is important to note that "Heinrich's experience" was important to Arendt's conception: her husband, Heinrich Blücher, had participated in the soldiers' and workers' councils in Germany in 1918–1919 as a young Spartacist — member of the Spartacus League, a social revolutionary faction founded by Rosa Luxemburg and Karl Liebknecht in 1916 that was transformed into the German Communist Party in 1918. A self-didact socialist and philosopher (in exile in America, a professor at Bard College), he reflected on his hands-on experience with the workers movements and councils and his ideas about councils had a deep impact on Arendt's conceptualization. Equally important was Arendt's admiration of, and impression left on her, by Rosa Luxemburg (Lederman 2018, 151) for whom she wrote an admiring biographical account (Arendt 1955, 33–56). In short, this was not an abstract subject for Arendt. This line of inquiry contributes the necessary conceptual clarifications, as I show in subsequent chapters: according to my nuanced reading and analysis, the *seeds* of the Turkmen council movement were Arendtian, as the movement emerged by deploying the councils as the grassroots mobilization of Turkmens as a people.

In 1963, Arendt published *On Revolution*, a comparative, theoretical treatise on the American and French revolutions. This book succeeded three foundational books — *The Origins of Totalitarianism* (1948), *Between Past and Future* (1954), and *The Human Condition* (1958) — and preceded a conceptual and polemical engagement, *On Violence* (1970). A certain theoretical concern pertaining to, and an increasingly refined conceptualization of, the nature of political foundation runs through all these works.

Her phenomenological engagements with the issues of power and violence relate to the human condition, and they yield sophisticated conceptualizations. For Arendt, the councils are braided with power and natality at the origins of the foundation of a body politic in a free and egalitarian manner. The very act of *founding* denotes the moment of *liberation* (from tyrannical rule) and represents human *freedom*. This unique ability of humans to found something new is due to the "miracle of birth" — that is, the human condition of "natality" (Arendt 1963, 211; 1970, 82). Concerned about the growing militancy within the African American and student movements in the United States in the 1960s, Arendt aptly dissects the seemingly equivalent terms of power, strength, force, authority, and violence. We need not discuss her taxonomy here and should focus on her concept of *power*. According to her, "power" captures the humans' "act[ing] in concert." Power, therefore, "is never the property of an individual; it belongs to a group and remains in existence only so long as the group keeps together" (Arendt 1970, 44). In contrast to the common parlance that deploys the term "power" to designate the wielding of institutional might or traditional force, for Arendt the source of power, in its original pre-institutional configuration, emanates from human individuals congregating around the common concern of how to govern themselves in a participatory fashion. She tries to capture the foundational moment of the formation of a people before it is tainted and *instrumentalized* by institutional politics. Power as such resides with praxis; institutionalized power belongs in toto in the rank of fabricating things (society). I have discussed Arendt's theory elsewhere extensively (Vahabzadeh 2019b); here, it is important to note that this foundational movement requires the assembly of the people who, in acting together, recognize *diversity* and *equality* among them. I have termed this the assembly of "divers equals" (Vahabzadeh 2019b, 44). Both of these qualifications — diversity and equality — are modern phenomena. In particular, equality of humans ties modern revolutions to the secular age (Arendt 1963, 40).

To summarize, power only resides with the collective and arises from collective action toward creation of a new body politic. The dissolution of the collective translates into the dissolution of power (and its replacement with authority, force, and violence). As acting in concert, power is by definition nonviolent. The power of the collective represents a genuine political existence, which we may appreciate further if we contrast it, via Arendt, with life under a totalitarian, "classless" state, "a highly atomized society whose competitive structure and concomitant loneliness of the individual had been held in check only through membership in a class" (Arendt 1958a, 317). Totalitarian states create the lonely human incapable of praxis and thus at the complete mercy of fabricating through labour — a human without freedom. Therefore, Arendt's interest in the revolutionary tradition stems precisely from the manifestation of power in the councils, the only genuine outcome of the revolutionary tradition. In Arendt's view, councils represent the most promising human congregation in face of totalitarian states (Arendt 1958b, 216).

Readers of classics in political philosophy recognize a certain affinity between Arendtian conception and Rousseau's "social pact," in that the decisions of diverse equals to create a new body politic stands outside of the law, or, their collective action will be "lawmaking." This is the truly revolutionary moment in all revolutions: a point in history that Arendt seeks to conceptually isolate to phenomenologically reflect on the action of united people that start something new in a nonviolent fashion. Precisely because of beginning something new, this moment of *constituting* is suppressed by the subsequent institutionalization of politics. Arendt (1963, 203) is cognizant of the *paradox* of constituting — the word "constitution" simultaneously means the act of constituting and the result of that act. The paradox lies in the problem of perpetuation: that the newly founded body politic based on nonviolent "acting in concert" ends up resorting to the state's instrumental violence that brings stability and durability (Arendt 1963, 223–224) while betraying the original act of participatory foundation.

In revolutionary periods, when the force of the state is diminishing and when authority has faded in the minds and mannerisms of the people, or, phrased differently, in the moments when a collective becomes *ungovernable*, the councils blossom as the embodiments of the collective will. In her study of modern revolutions, Arendt identifies these institutive moments: in the town hall meetings of the American revolution aiming to create a confederation and write a new constitution (she misses the fact that this happens on a colonized land and at the expense of indigenous peoples); in the 1905 workers' soviets and the 1917 "workers', soldiers', and peasants' councils" in Russia; in Arbeiter- und Soldatenräte in Germany in 1918–1919 demanding a new constitution and in the short-lived Bavarian Räterepublik or Soviet Republic of 1919; and in the Hungarian revolution of 1956 (Arendt 1963, 118, 145, 262, 266, 112). One can add to this list the short-lived councils during the Spanish Revolution (1936). The common denominator of them all? Councils as bodies of collective "self-government" (Arendt, 1963, 262).

The amazing speed with which the councils spread across the country in such cases attests to people's "faculty to begin something new" (Arendt 1963, 34). The most striking aspect of these spontaneous developments is that in such instances it took these independent and highly disparate organs no more than a few weeks, in the case of Russia, or a few days, in the case of Hungary, to begin a process of coordination and integration through the formation of higher councils of a regional or provincial character, from which finally the delegates to an assembly representing the whole country could be chosen (Arendt 1963, 267).

Arendt's idea of democratic participation shines in these lines: that a people, liberated from the grips of institutional politics and imposed states, has the collective ability to create a new body politic "from the few to the many" (to quote Iranian revolutionary Mostafa Sho'aiyan). The *spontaneity* of council formation rests precisely in the unique human ability of *natality* — of starting something new, a universal human experience. This perspective of Arendt is unique as it transcends particular ideological and theoretical proclivities that inform specific council or autonomist movements, allowing for a unified concept that is rooted in the human collective and can capture a variety of specific council experiences. As such, Arendt allows us to treat particular council and autonomous movements *not* as exceptions taking place in exceptional circumstances, but as a universal human faculty. The numerous instances of councils in modern history illustrate that when left to themselves, peoples are capable of collectively governing themselves, and that is the moment of foundation of a new *people*, or put differently, the "emergent publics" (Angus 2001).

There is an unuttered streak in Arendt's worldview that implies that humans are endowed with and capable of egalitarian participation and self-governance. Once in place, the councils grow almost contagiously and create power from the bottom up. They are incompatible with the top-down, hierarchical, power-over forms of ruling — one-party dictatorship or liberal democracy. So, Arendt observes, the designation "Soviet Union" was a lie (Arendt 1963, 258). Observing the "equality" within Greek *polis*, Arendt discovers *isonomy* as "a form of political organization in which citizens lived together under conditions of no-rule, without a division between rulers and ruled" (Lederman 2018, 158). Councils provide not only inalienable political rights but also the political body for participation and decision-making. This *genuine* praxis that resides within human collectives creates "spaces of freedom" that defy the controlled or ideological "ready-made formulas" of political parties (Arendt 1963, 263–264).

The Social Question

Arendt's depiction of the council as the foundational *moment* of a new body politic is interestingly permeated by an Aristotelian notion of politics and is thus impacted by an intentional self-limitation: she excludes the "social question." For her, want cannot be the basis of the individuals' free and egalitarian action. She is cognizant of social inequalities, while remaining concerned about deep political inequalities (Lederman 2018, 158). This observation is driven by her comparison of the French and American revolutions, where, in France, poverty, indeed food riots, led to revolutionary conditions. The "tragic failures of the French revolutionary tradition," which includes the Bolshevik revolution (Arendt 1963, 66), stem from having the revolutionary praxis motivated and organized around the question of poverty and need. In contrast, she states, in the American revolution, misery did not constitute the principle of constituting something new (Arendt 1963, 68), and the partial reason for this, she submits, is because the American colonists were basically "subsidized" by slave labour (Arendt 1963, 70–71) and, I would add, occupation of Indigenous land. Details about the leaders of the American revolution being slave-owners abound (Losurdo 2014). Emphatically, one cannot escape the observation that the freedom of American colonists came at the expense of slaves and indigenous peoples. Therefore, for Arendt, freedom and need are two different things, and addressing need does not necessarily usher freedom. This is because a revolution driven by poverty cannot change the relations between the ruler and the ruled (Arendt 1963, 74). Unending want fails to found free and egalitarian relations.

Arendt's position on the "social question" makes many who would otherwise find her advocacy of the councils insightful uneasy. Her position goes against the early twentieth-century council movements through which the workers' councils tended to "overcome the division between the political and the economic by instituting workers' control over the production process" (Muldoon 2108b, 3). Based on his study of councils (Persian *showra* or *shura*) during the 1979 Iranian Revolution and the 2010s Arab revolutions, sociologist Asef Bayat seeks to contrast these experiences with Arendt's conception: "But far from the Arendtian *polis*, the square life of this sort [e.g., Tahrir square] is a liminal reality, a kind of transitory egalitarian community that navigates between utopia and reality," Bayat (2017, 118) argues. "Reminiscent of the carnivals of late medieval Europe, these square lives resonated more with Victor Turner's notion of *communitas* than Arendtian agora, representing an egalitarian community of equal individuals who break away temporarily from the everyday norms and structures of power to operate in an ad hoc state of liminality" (Bayat 2017, 118). Point taken. However, the fact that in the Arab revolutions the grassroots councils where liminal and short-lived, cannot eliminate the possibility that these forms of "acting in concert" could have *potentially* grown into the basis of a permanent political body. This position is consistent with Bayat's thesis that the revolutions of our time do not entail the subversion of the existing order as was the objective of old revolutionary models from 1789 France to 1979 Iran. Revolutionary movements, Bayat holds, in fact push for reforms within the existing system, which Bayat calls "refolutions" (2017, 209).

However, it seems unnecessary to stress (twice within one passage) the "transitory" and "temporary" character of these Middle Eastern collective actions to annul Arendt's point. The transitory character is indeed written into the experience of councils as foundational moments, unless the actors decided to embark upon constituting something new, which clearly was not the case in the Arab Spring but has been the case in the Plains of Turkmen where spontaneous councils (transitory, Bayat would say) grew into a system of democratic self-governance for one year. According to Bayat (2017, 139), "It is equally unhelpful to reduce politics, as Hannah Arendt does, to town hall meetings, organized civic activism, or mass demonstrations where conscious deliberation for freedom occurs, dismissing the realm of life, labour, and work as simply apolitical struggles for survival or apolitical endeavours." Again, nowhere in Arendt do we see any attempt at the reduction of politics to the councils that embody "acting in concert" by diverse equals. Au contraire, she does raise the question of permanence when she argues that the word "constitution" means both an *act* of constituting (a historical moment) and the *outcome* of that act (institutionalizing a new political structure). Bayat (2017, 139) contends "One wonders where Arendt would place activities and institutions like factory *shuras* [*showras*] in the Iranian revolution of 1979, the Zapatista movement in Chiapas, or the Saudi women's initiative of 'push normal' to augment gender equality, all of which navigate through life, labor, and politics." In other words, Bayat argues that people are capable of creating the new in their daily lives at revolutionary movements. This argument implies a critique of the social question.

I am aware that Arendt's position on the social question in combination with her concept of councils seems incongruent with the history of working-class councils. Note that Arendt speaks of *both* the town hall meetings and workers' soviets. This point is important. She does not categorically reject that workers' specific economic demands exclude them from her model of politics. On the contrary, as long as the workers councils seek self-assertion and autonomy, they indeed stand at the threshold of beginning a new body politic. The *showras* of Iranian workers, which Bayat (2017: 49–67) discusses elaborately, did have the potential of a new beginning. The Soviet Union (a lie, Arendt called it) and the Islamic Republic of Iran both founded new regimes by destroying the "acting in concert" of free individuals. The Iranian regime destroyed the Turkmen councils by assimilation after military occupation (which I discuss in more detail in Chapter 5).

Here is where one needs to expand on Arendt's theory through Ernesto Laclau and Chantal Mouffe's concept of *articulation* as "any practice establishing a relation among elements such that their identity is modified as a result of the articulatory practice" (1985, 105). So, it is possible to establish through political practice a particular configuration of the social question such that the question of need is transformed into a praxis of political reconfiguration altogether. Take Podemos in Spain, for example, in which the issues of class and neoliberalism (economic issues) were translated into a left populist movement (Errejón and Mouffe 2016) that sought, *potentially*, to reinstitute politics en masse.

Arendt did not live to see the brilliant and significant contemporary examples of councils in the Autonomous Rebel Zapatistas Municipalities in Chiapas, Mexico, a successful experience in indigenous self-governance. The Zapatistas have been governing a quarter of a million peoples, mostly indigenous Mayans, since 1994 through a participatory system in which every decision must be discussed and ratified by every community (Debray 1996; Holloway 1998; Mentinis 2006; Subcommandante Marcos 2001). The six activists who clandestinely went to Chiapas in 1983 soon learned how to articulate the issues of racial discrimination and economic deprivation of Mayan peasants into a well-conceived, autonomous, egalitarian, and participatory political formation. Arendt did not live to see the case of Rojava or Autonomous Administration of North and East Syria, a polynational, democratic confederalism of two million peoples (Kurds, Arabs, Assyrians, Turkmen, Armenians, Circassians, and Yazidis) who have been living according to an elaborate, four-tiered council system based on the principle of gender equality, 40 percent minimum membership of either gender in each council, and co-chairing (a woman and a man) of all councils. This system, located in one of the most belligerent regions in the world, has been in place since 2012. Significantly, in Rojava, the decisions of the higher council are not binding for lower councils (Strangers in a Tangled Wilderness 2015). This is how Kurdish activists, inspired by the works of Abdollah Öcalan, who was, in turn, inspired by the work of American anarchist Murray

Bookchin, articulated continued ethnic discrimination of Turkish and Syrian regimes against the Kurds into a council-based autonomous political movement.

The Turkmen council movement, as I show in this book, also translated the issue of land (a question of want for Arendt) into a politically viable and sustainable council system of self-governance.

These discussions will allow us to highlight the radical lessons of the Turkmen council movement in the concluding remarks.

The Ambivalence of Strikes

It would be fruitful to bring Arendt's philosophical propositions to a virtual conversation with a certain tendency in early twentieth-century European socialism, so that I would not leave the impression that the two approaches are mutually exclusive. My aim, instead, is to show that Arendt's discovery of the foundational essence of the councils can be traced in those moments in the workers' and socialist movements when the theorists sought to push the movement back to its epoch-making power, the idea that Marx originally had in mind. To this end, let us focus on the concept of "strike" as the formative moment when the workers go beyond common, concrete grievances and converge, act in concert, and exercise power from below. The strike is the highest form of collective action of workers — a potentially political act.

Georges Sorel ([1908] 2004, 56), a self-proclaimed anarcho-syndicalist, finds this formative moment in the general strike. There are various ways to approach Sorel, since his work simultaneously entails critiques of capitalism, parliamentary socialists, and systemic violence of class society. In *Reflections on Violence* (orig. 1908), written in the aftermath of the 1905 revolution in Russia, Sorel attends to the way the proletariat must *envision* revolutionary change beyond capitalism, one that inevitably entails "violence," which for Sorel captures the "acts of revolt" (2004, 171) that are distinct from capitalist "savagery" or "brutality" (2004, 118, 190). Since the proletarian revolution inexorably involves the destruction of the existing capitalist order where a minority imposes its will and interests on the rest of society (Sorel 2004, 171), it remains violent. This is the moment to which Marx alluded but did not conceptualize, Sorel argues. He captures this pure and violent moment in the "myth of general strike, ... a phenomenon of war" (2004, 274), a moment that is not reducible to any particular workers' strike but embracing them all. Why is the general strike a "myth"? Because it provides an image, a *vision* of the emancipated proletariat that precedes the *act* of revolt. Stated differently, for liberation, as a "social movement," to materialize, the proletarian movement must "always picture their coming action as a battle in which their cause is certain to triumph." He calls these "constructions" (or "pictures") "myth," exemplified by "the syndicalist 'general strike' and Marx's catastrophic revolution" (2004, 41–42). The task of revolutionary syndicalists is to bring about that moment. These revolutionaries are distinct from parliamentary socialists who wish to reform capitalist savagery and thus lack a revolutionary vision (Sorel 2004, 120, 78). This contrast allows us to understand the myth. I have previously discussed the importance of "myth" and "violence" in Sorel (Vahabzadeh 2019b, 78–84; 2022b, 26–29); so here I want to focus on the historic moment of change.

A close reading reveals that this moment is in fact the *generative* moment of proletarian "acting in concert" through which the proletariat emerges to embody all of humanity in an entirely new social order. Because the proletarian action entails leaving the present reality behind, it needs the myth as the means of rendering a liberated future *intelligible*, or in Sorel's words, "the *framing of a future, in some indeterminate time*" (Sorel 2004, 124; original emphasis). Because the proletarian struggle is a fight for the future of humanity, the myth serves the proletarians as a cognitive and educational tool, a normative horizon that unifies all particular proletarian strikes and purifies the movement of the general strike from those who feign the proletarian identity (parliamentary socialists). Accordingly, the myth captures the possibility of not only proletarian self-constitution but also its self-assertion such that in acting together as a social movement, the proletariat arrives at its very own ontological possibility of emancipation, supersedes its own class particularity, and re-emerges as a new people representing humanity emancipated from class divisions. Clearly, the concept of councils is absent in Sorel, and his vision of the proletariat remains abstract and unspecific. And yet, in conceptualizing the *violent* moment captured by the *myth* of the general strike, he envisages a moment of beginning, of constituting a new people in a new order akin to Arendt's theory. To reiterate, the general strike is a formative moment. Arendt was right in the epigraph to this chapter: the ability to create something new attests to human freedom. The fighting proletariat is already free, even though still unliberated. Sorel's "myth" was emphatically a discovery: that Marx's scientific determination of the proletarian revolution (historical materialism) was insufficient for the formation of the workers' movement, indeed for the proletariat to embark upon an epoch-making revolutionary praxis. The proletariat needs a unifying vision that may be realized through collective action. Sorel's myth, therefore, is not dissimilar to Walter Benjamin's messianic moment (1968).

Inspired by workers' soviets in the 1905 revolution in Russia, Rosa Luxemburg wrote *The Mass Strike* (orig. 1906). Arendt wrote a sympathetic intellectual biography of her fellow countrywoman, reminding the readers that the Bolsheviks, with whom Luxemburg felt great affinity, eradicated her critical legacy in post-revolutionary Russia. Arendt hoped for Luxemburg's "belated recognition" as a political thinker (Arendt 1955, 55–56). Note that Arendt never agreed that trade unions could be bodies of revolutionary organization (1958b, 216–217).

Standing at a crucial juncture in the history of workers' unions, Luxemburg was concerned about the purpose of labour unionism in Germany because she realized that the strike, as "the external form of the class struggle" (2005, 21) and the unifying praxis of the working class, was ultimately ambivalent since it could arise "mechanically" (French and Italian syndicalists) or "objectively" (Russian Social Democracy; Luxemburg 2005, 18, 20). For the syndicalists, trade union activism was important because it represented the "direct action of the masses" (Luxemburg 2005, 18). We can see how "direct action" is conceptually and practically related to the workers' councils that in due course led to the Red Years or Biennio Rosso (1919–1920) in Italy. Following mass strikes, the workers' councils, by armed workers' occupation of factories, implemented self-management, exercising the Arendtian "power." But Luxemburg refutes the anarchist notion because of its "unhistorical" and speculative models (2005, 18–19). Interestingly, while rejecting syndicalism, her concern is nonetheless similar to Sorel's (a syndicalist): how can it be ensured that the mass strike, as the genuine collective expression of the working class, leads to the emancipation of the workers. We can see that Luxemburg has a deeper concern: how the strikes of particular groups of workers can lead to the "mass strike" as the revolutionary action aimed at dismantling capitalism. The strike, in other words, must rise above and beyond economic interests and become a political and transformative action, she believes (2005, 71). For this to happen, workers need a social movement, or to be precise, "a people's *movement*" through which "the widest sections of the proletariat must be drawn into the fight" (Luxemburg 2005, 66; original emphasis). The transformation of the particular strike into the universal mass strike (and mass mobilization) constitutes Luxemburg's theoretical concern.

The theoretical propositions of Sorel and Luxemburg reaffirm Arendt's concept of councils. They both discover not only the power of "acting in concert" but also how this power can become the basis of an all-embracing, revolutionary transformation. These revolutionary socialists moored their discoveries of the "strike" to a normative pier of the proletarian revolution — the "myth" (Sorel) or the "objective" political action (Luxemburg). As such, the strike was indeed instrumental in their thinking. Arendt was utterly suspicious of normative signposts, observing that all future systematizations of the councils entailed the destruction of the people's genuine power (recall Arendt: "the Soviet Union was a lie"). As such, she would not reduce the councils to instruments, although by virtue of "constituting" something new, the councils both acted in freedom and created a constitution that curtailed that freedom.

Councils and Iranian Modernization

Councils, in the modern sense of the concept, emerged alongside the Constitutional Revolution of 1906, Iran's first democratic revolution, which "propelled, if not inspired, the Young Turks' revolution of 1909 and Egypt's nationalist movement after World War I" (Chaqueri 2001, 29). This was a revolutionary period that marked Iran's entry into political modernity at the turn of the twentieth century. It is imperative to situate modern councils in this historic junction because the epochal norm of classical national democratic revolutions in this period entailed the formation of nation-state with the state's all-powerful agency in institutionalizing capitalist modernization. The fact that councils emerged at this particular historic junction, as Arendt would say, attests to the potential power of the people in trying to determine their own future at the grassroots level. However, the formation of the strong state, with the founding of the Pahlavi dynasty in 1925, put an end to such grassroots efforts. One could observe that there were dual origins to the councils at this time: Iranian social democracy and labour movement, on the one hand, and the grassroots congregations in the cities during the revolutionary period, on the other (Afary 1996). The dual origins cannot be separated, and it can be said that they were mutually influential and crossbreeding.

In terms of its historical context, the Constitutional Revolution was a political reaction against the corrupt and declining Qajar dynasty that, in the age of concession colonialism, had commissioned Iran's natural resources to European entrepreneurs to finance the Royal Court's lavish expenditure, while the Iranian populace lived under a despotic state, suffering from disease, malnutrition, ignorance, and prolonged poverty. As such, "the nineteenth-century development in Iran should be characterized as colonial and dependent" (Afary 1996, 19), if one can even call it development. After the devastating defeats in two Russo-Persian wars (1804–1813 and 1826–1828) and the loss of significant Iranian territories in the Caucuses to the Russian Empire, a sense of national soul-searching by Iranian intellectuals — who were often in exile — spiked. Paving the way was the Tobacco Protest of 1891–1892 against the state's monopoly concession of tobacco to the British that led to a massive boycott of tobacco and forced the Shah to rescind it. The Constitutional Revolution's immediate context included waves of protests against imposed tariffs and the subsequent merchants' solidarity protest after the bastinadoing of two Tehran merchants for price fixing. Taking sanctuaries in shrines or foreign legations, Shi'i clerics and protesters demanded a "House of Justice." In August 1906, the ailing Mozaffar al-din Shah Qajar agreed to a Constitutive Assembly and signed the Constitution Decree on December 31, 1906, just before his death that occurred a mere three days later. Iran now had an elected parliament or Majles that later wrote Iran's first constitution. But the ascending Mohammad Ali Shah (January 25, 1907) was against constitutionalism and his relations to the parliament quickly deteriorated. With the military support of the Russian Cossacks, in May 1908, Mohammad Ali Shah launched an attack on the parliament and repressed the constitutionalists. The period of imprisoning and killing the constitutionalists had begun. This threw the country, now under occupation by the Russians and the British (officiated in the Anglo-Russian Convention of 1907), into a civil war, which began with the resistance in the city of Tabriz in July 1908. Long story short, through armed resistance, the constitutionalist forces from the north, including the social democrats, and constitutionalist tribal forces from the south, finally pushed back the state and Russian troops and triumphantly entered Tehran on July 16, 1909, forcing Mohammad Ali Shah to take sanctuary in the Russian embassy and later leave for exile in Russia. It is in this context, in particular during the civil war, that the grassroots councils or *anjomans* became de facto governments, managing cities and public affairs in liberated areas and acting as bodies for popular mobilization against dictatorship.

In the immediate years prior to the waves of protests leading to the Constitutional Revolution, there had been organizing efforts by Iranian migrant workers in the Caucasus. Under the influence of the Russian Social Democracy, Iranian workers and activists created the organization named Hemmat in Tbilisi and Baku in December 1904 and January 1905 (Afary 1996, 81–82, 87). Hemmat's program was radical and progressive. It demanded free and secret elections; freedoms of press, expression, assembly, and individuals, and to strike; confiscation of Royal land and distribution of landowners' lands among peasants; eight-hour workday; graduated, progressive taxation; and mandatory public education (Jazani 2009, 144). Hemmat was followed by the formation of the Secret Society (Anjoman-e Makhfi) on February 17, 1905, and the Social Democratic Party-Mojahed (Ferqeh-ye Ejtema'iyoun-'Amiyoun, Mojahed, FEAM) in early 1905. According to Ahmad Kasravi (2013, 407), when constitutionalism broke out, Ali Mussiyo, Haji Ali Davaforush, and Haji Rasul Sadaqiani translated the program of FEAM, started the Mojahedan, and set up a Secret Centre that managed affairs during the revolution, all in Tabriz. Following Tabriz and the Tehran city council (*anjoman*), another pioneer that began meeting as early as February 1905, the *anjomans* began to be formed in most cities in January 1907, after the Constitution Decree, and spread to the countryside and among national and religious minorities.

There is ample research on the role of Iranian social democracy and workers' organizations in this period including two outstanding works by Janet Afary (1996) and Cosroe Chaqueri (2001). While at this time the Iranian working class was very small in size, peasants and nomads constituted the majority of the population, about 80 percent (Afary 1996, 38). The nascent working-class movement, coinciding with the Constitutional Revolution, made significant strides in raising class consciousness. For example, the first recorded organized labour action in the country took place between November 21 and December 15, 1906. The "fishermen at the Caspian port of Anzali protested against the low prices of Russo-Armenian concessionaire Lianazove paid them for the catch" (Chaqueri 2001, 90). In attacking the protesting fishermen, government forces killed one person. Then came the general strike of the telegraph workers in March 1907, right after the ascent of Mohammad Ali Shah to the throne, and amazingly, the Shah met their demands (Chaqueri 2001, 91; Kargar 2011). As a result, "Strike fever spread to other sections of society ... [including] the workers at government military workshops and banks" (Chaqueri 2001, 91). The fact that labour and social democratic movements sprouted in the northwest is because, according to Bizhan Jazani (2009, 130), "Geographically, Azerbaijan and Gilan were Iran's gateway to Europe and economically Tabriz and Rasht stood as two important trade centres of Iran." From these regions also spread armed, constitutionalist resistances to Mohammad Ali Shah and ushered back parliamentary democracy in 1909.

It is in this period that the *anjomans* burgeoned in the country. In the absence of labour unions, the number of *anjomans* formed as grassroots associations grew exponentially among workers. This link is important: Iran's *anjomans* were influenced by, and resembled, the workers' and peasants' soviets that formed during the 1905 Russian revolution. Iranian migrant workers and social democrats brought back the idea to their homeland, although this claim probably cannot be documented. This inference is based on the way workers created the *anjomans* that functioned like labour unions. Among others, Iranian servants working for foreign residents in Iran created their own *anjoman* (Chaqueri 2001, 91). According to Cosroe Chaqueri (2001, 91), "The formation of *anjomans* along professional and vocational lines was at this time the order of the day." But *anjomans* had greater capacity and did not just emulate union, guild, or group associations to advance the interests of specific publics: they soon realized their political potential as autonomous bodies of self-governance, akin to Arendt's concept, in the absence of a strong or legitimate state.

Growing into autochthonous phenomena, these *anjomans* were the grassroots organizing bodies behind resistance to the Shah's autocracy and played a decisive political role: "By mid-1908, there were at least seventy *anjomans* in Tehran alone, with an estimated five-thousand armed fighters. Best known among them, Anjoman-e Azarbaijan, acted as a political party and a paramilitary force, and was the political agent for the influential provincial council in Tabriz known as Anjoman Ayalati [provincial] Azerbaijan" (Amanat 2017, 345). In Tabriz, the *anjoman* functioned as a de facto state. According to Kasravi (2013, 195–196), "In Tabriz the freedom-seekers (*azadikhahan*) were victoriously active. Outside of the anjoman (or as they called it, National Assembly) and clandestinely, the Secret Centre managed the affairs …. Anjoman had taken the place of both Justice [Ministry] … and the governor, seeing to the security and order in the city." I must emphasize that the social democrats played a key role in Tabriz resistance through their Mojahed brigades that defended constitutionalism alongside the forces of popular Tabriz revolutionary leaders, Sattar Khan and Baqer Khan. During the civil war, the Azerbaijan Provincial *anjoman* played a pivotal role in spreading resistance and despite the presence of the first Majles, it was a de facto governing power, and the Rasht *anjoman* and the Azerbaijani *anjoman* of Tehran also functioned accordingly (Jazani 2009, 127).

The *anjomans* were diverse in terms of their constituents: there were "official" *anjomans* that functioned like governing bodies as well as "popular," group-specific ones that pushed for changes, but in many cases (like the Anjoman Melli in Tabriz) the distinction was not always clear (Afary 1996, 79, 80). In general, "popular *anjomans* were formed along existing professional lines. While this development reflects the continuity of the traditional element in the society, it also reveals the introduction of the sublating aspect in this continuity" (Chaqueri 2001, 110). The urban anjomans were diverse in terms of class and social backgrounds (Afary 1996, 38). In this particular context, the women's *anjomans* in this period stand out (Afary 1996, 177–208; Jazani 2009, 128–129). Among other things, women contributed to the establishment of the National Bank of Iran as an anti-colonial move aimed at freeing Iran from hitherto operational colonial banks (Afary 1996, 179). Some women's councils were more radical than others; for instance, the women's councils of Isfahan demanded the Isfahan council arm the women so that they would fight against the Russian troops (Afary 1996, 206). According to Chaqueri (2001, 111) "On the whole, the *anjomans*, collective leadership, and cooperation were the hallmarks of this period."

After the victory of the Constitutional Forces, a curious period appeared in the country. While Majles was in power, the state was weak and the last Qajar king, Ahmad Shah, had little interest in ruling the country, spending a lot of time in Europe. Popular grassroots associations, the *anjomans*, were shunned by the emerging institutional politics. They did not transform into political parties either (Amanat 2017, 364). Ahmed Kasravi (2013, 591) speaks of declining *anjomans*, some of which became corrupt and sources of political opportunism and exploitation, to the extent that even the Shah's cronies created their own *anjomans*. He refers to the "useless anjomans of Tehran" while praising the Secret Centre (Kasravi 2013, 408), suggesting that not all *anjomans* were revolutionary in spirit. With the victory, some constitutionalist heroes became state officials (e.g., tribal Bakhtiari chief, Sardar As'ad, became the Minister of Internal Affairs and Yeprem Khan, commander of the Armenian Brigade, became Tehran's Police Chief), while others (most prominently Sattar Khan) were disarmed, marginalized, and relegated to oblivion.

This period, characterized by a weak central government and the erosion of the *anjomans* that had kept the cities safe and running, witnessed insecurity and disorder. The First World War spelled disaster for the country: widespread famine and the Spanish flu caused massive deaths and significant reduction of population in a short span of time. In this context, Cossack Brigade officer Reza Khan rose first to War Ministry (1921–1923) and then to Premier (1923–1925) under Ahmad Shah, before he staged a coup with the assistance of the British in 1925 and subsequently founded the Pahlavi dynasty. The British involvement stemmed from fear of Bolshevik influence in Iran and a response to the socialist Gilan Republic (1920–1921) that Reza Khan, with the assistance of the British and the consent of the Bolsheviks, had destroyed (Vahabzadeh 2019a, 92–95). Intent on rapid, authoritarian modernization of the country, the strong state was finally in place.

With the transitioning of the country into political modernity, the Constitutional Revolution led to the formation of the modern state, but it failed as an anti-colonial movement represented by social democracy (Jazani 2009, 291). The labour movement was not propelled into organized labour. The first attempt at creating a National Federation of Trade Unions in 1921, originally out of nine unions and growing, was eventually suppressed after Reza Shah's ascent to power (Abrahamian 1982, 129; Rahnema 1992, 71).

Reza Shah ruled with an iron fist. Upon their occupation of Iran, however, the Allied powers forced Reza Shah to abdicate in favour of the 22-year-old crown prince Mohammad Reza in September 1941. Foreign occupation and the political elite's lack of support for the young Shah inadvertently gifted Iranians with a 12-year period of unprecedented, but fragile, freedom and democratic participation. Political parties, free associations, labour unions, and free press burgeoned until the 1953 coup engineered by CIA and MI6 finally consolidated the Shah's power.

This period witnessed the formation of labour unions. By 1945, as Abrahamanian (2008, 109) shows, "[the] Central Council of Federated Trade Unions had thirty-three affiliates with more than 275,000 members. This constituted 75 percent of the industrial labor force with a presence in most of the country's 346 modern industrial plants." The Central Council's membership included, "45,000 oil workers, 45,000 construction laborers, 40,000 textile workers, 20,000 railwaymen, 20,000 carpet weavers, 11,000 dockers, 8,000 miners, and 6,000 truck drivers" (Abrahamian 2008, 109; see also Abrahamian 1982, 347–371).

The Central Council was affiliated with the pro-Soviet Tudeh Party of Iran. So, one can observe that between 1941 and 1953, the Tudeh Party's vision and influence effectively transformed the council movement into workers' syndicates. Of the legacy of the Constitutional Revolution nothing was left and labour organization was understood in syndicalist terms as approved by Soviet Marxism.

After the coup, labour unions were subject to continued repression and harassment. Although various job actions spread across the country, these were not sufficiently organized. After the Shah's reforms — called the White Revolution — the state began taking initiatives in organizing labour to direct the working class in tandem with the state's policies and impede its radicalization. The state promoted labour organizations as bodies of collective contract, much in a classical corporatist manner. According to Asef Bayat (1987), the state pursued three interrelated objectives: building hegemony in a Gramscian sense, linking workers ideologically to state-promoted nationalism, and mobilizing workers for purposes like state rallies. The number of state-run syndicates grew from 397 in 1971 to 1,023 in 1978. Accordingly, "In 1976 the state amalgamated a number of unions and established the Organization of Iranian Workers, which along with the employers' organization joined the Rastakhiz Party, Iran's single party after the Shah abolished all other existing political parties. According to the official figures in 1976, the Organization consisted of 845 syndicates and twenty trade unions with three million workers" (Bayat 1987, 60).

However marginal and repressed, labour activism continued in various shapes and the state did not succeed in totally hegemonizing industrial workers. In his noteworthy memoirs, Yadollah Khosrowshahi (2019) speaks of his experience as a worker-activist in the oil industry in the span of three decades (late 1950s to mid-1980s), speaking of challenges and objectives, his arrests and hardships. Another case pertains to SAKA (Revolutionary Organization of Iranian Communists): a small group of socialist workers that had created council-style, clandestine "red cells" that lasted, under different designations, from 1946 until 1971 (Vahabzadeh 2011). Also, Jalil Enferadi and Eskandar Sadeghinezhad, members of the guerrilla team that launched the Siahkal operation (see the next section), were active members of the Ironworkers and Mechanics Union (Vahabzadeh 2010, 220). The list goes on.

The early councils in modern Iran represent both grassroots self-assertion and the transitional collectives to be absorbed through state building. The organic connections of workers' councils to the labour union movement also reveal a long tradition. The Turkmen council movement unwittingly rode on this tradition. Unfortunately, the "state-centric approaches have rendered the showras invisible" (Jafari 2021, 253). This is precisely the epistemological screen that we need to shed.

Workers' Councils in the Revolutionary Period

Within the recent past, it was in the months leading up to the February 1979 revolution that the tradition of councils resurfaced as a social force, refashioned thanks to several decades of capitalist and industrial expansion in the country (especially in the gigantic oil sector) and the growth of leftist imagination. The consensus is that the workers' councils emerged mostly out of the "strike committees" in late 1978 and early 1979 (Asefi 2018; Bayat 1987, 94; Goodey 1980, 5; Moghadam 1985, 17; Rahnema 1992, 69, 72; Salour and Salour 2020), most notably in the oil sector (Jafari 2021, 252) whose general strike contributed immensely to the demise of the monarchy. These councils were instrumental in the victory of the revolution and constituted "the apex of the labor movement" (Salour and Salour 2020). Despite differences, this wave of the Iranian council movement "may be unparalleled in the Middle East" (Azad 1980, 14) and arguably "was among the first major examples of its kind in the Third World" (Rahnema 1992, 70) — a "first," of course, only if we ignore the early grassroots councils or *anjomans* of the Constitutional Revolution.

While particular council experiences are significant for understanding the movement itself, they also reveal the dynamics of civil society — a point sadly missed by many observers because of their epistemological partiality that regard labour activism to be distinct from civil society activism. Iranian civil society has always been under siege by monarchy, and the Islamists have been trying to nearly choke it; the grassroots council movement indeed showcases how such assemblies create the necessary space for civic and civil rights activism, among other things, that challenge the strong state that has been the plague of modern Iranian society.

The literature pertaining to the councils is rather lean when one considers its vast reach in 1979. The prominent exception is Asef Bayat's *Workers and Revolution in Iran* (1987), a detailed and analytical account of the workers' councils based on his fieldwork. Personal narratives of lived experiences of grassroots mobilizations at this time are also rare, the exception being Mohammad Safavi's personal recollections of the unionization movement of project-seasonal workers of the oil industry in Abadan in 1979–1980 (Safavi 2017). Moreover, the council movement was not limited to the workplace; neighbourhood councils, university student councils, and even the Council of Air Force Servicemen are often highlighted (Bayat 1987, 96, 136; Rahnema 1992, 86; Salour and Salour 2020), but a larger list of councils includes "factories, countryside, schools, hospitals, army bases, government offices, press, [and] radio and television" (Azad 1980, 14), many of them short-lived. Soon after the revolution, a government's decree banned all councils in the army (Azad 1980, 19). It seems that these councils have not been studied. I found an allusion to peasants' councils in Iranian Kurdistan and the Turkmen region (Abrahamian 1982, 527; Azad 1980). For the purposes of our study here, aside from an article (Azad 1980), the Turkmen council movement is almost never discussed. I surmise that the nearly exclusive focus on the labour movement, and the gaze that privileges movements of nationwide significance (*jonbeshha-ye sarasari*) over the regional ones might explain this inattention. In short, I want to emphasize that the experiences of *showras* are more extensive than acknowledged within published literature, be it scholarly or popular, that is almost exclusively dedicated to workers' councils.

To avoid unnecessary Persian semantic complications, it should be mentioned that council and union, *showra* and *sandika* (from

French *syndicat*) have had overlaps in practice, at least in the inceptive moments, within the working-class history and shop floor activism. Naturally, though, there is a conceptual and therefore practical distinction: a council could be regarded as the original, participatory formation of a movement within a congregation (factory, neighbourhood, etc.). In societies where labour unionism has not been legally institutionalized, the council could be worked out toward creating a future union, the formalized and institutionalized body that theoretically strives for and entails (if successful) a legal status. In Canada, there are formal and legal processes of application, approval, and implementation of a new union. So, one cannot really speak of councils in this context. When such legal prerogatives are not present, the councils as the grassroots association of activists find prominence. They constitute the primary collective that can develop into new bodies for shop floor control across classes (workers and managers), or alternatively, into other, formal organizations like unions. In the Iranian cases, we sometimes notice that the distinctions between the two are not clear in practice. Within the oil industry, in "the absence of genuine labour unions, the showras articulated oil workers' socioeconomic demands, particularly regarding wages and housing conditions, and campaigned to realize them. They were, however, much more than labour unions" (Jafari 2021, 257). Mohammad Safavi's (2017) recollection of unionizing Abadan's project-seasonal workers shows the conceptual and practical overlap of council and union as bodies of collective action. We can witness councils that function like unions because the state does not fully or legally recognize the latter.

For this study, I stay focused on the councils instead of the unions or syndicates — the latter constituting a more vast experience and being better researched. Still, the blurred difference between Iran's councils and syndicates in practice is evidenced through Bayat's fieldwork and study of the council movement in 1979. The Iranian working class mostly comprises of "semi-skilled without education" (Asefi 2018). Bayat shows that Iranian workers had developed multiple conceptions of councils and/or syndicates: a trade unionist conception (a minority view); a universal conception that regards *showras* as being responsible for the interests of the country that unlike unions holds a trans-class conception; and as a democratic body for workplace control and supervision (the majority view; Bayat 1987, 148–150).

Given the context of the emergence of *showras* in Iran, the most vivid episode when the councils flourished was in the months following February 1979: "The *shuras,* or factory committees (or councils), were a particular form of workers' organization that emerged in Iranian industry following the overthrow of the Shah," argues Bayat (1987, 100). Accordingly, "They were shop floor organizations whose elected executive committee represented all the employees of a factory (blue- and white-collar) and/or an industrial group, irrespective of their trade, skill or sex. Their major concern was to achieve workers' control" (Bayat 1987, 100).

Consistent with the distinction I draw between unions and councils, Bayat (1987, 100) differentiates the councils that were concerned with "offensive control" in this period from the "shop-steward movement" as well as "from syndicalism which fought a political battle to change the social structure through industrial activities." The Iranian *showras,* Bayat submits (1987, 100), "lacked a clear political objective" and "were not influenced by the outside left political tendencies and did not act as a vehicle for social change." Instead, they wished to exercise power from below in the industry (Bayat 1987, 100). The claim, however, that the councils were not influenced by the left is not entirely accurate. One can rightly observe that unlike "Russian *soviets* that were fundamentally political institutions challenging state power, Iranian *showra* are economic institutions concerned with the immediate process of production" (Salour and Salour 2020). However, the contrast does not hold: regardless of their self-perception, Iranian *showras* emerged as political forces with leftist tendencies. The Turkmen council movement is certainly a case in point. Here we witness an intentional association of the peasants' councils with the Marxist Fadaiyan (OIPFG; see next section). The peasants' councils in Kurdistan were supported by the Democratic Party of Iranian Kurdistan (DPIK) and the Toilers' Organization of Iranian Kurdistan (Komala; Azad 1980, 15) that were socialist and Maoist, respectively. To varying degrees, in most factory *showras,* members or supporters of Marxist Fadaiyan, Peykar Organization, the Tudeh Party (although it rejected councils and advocated a "nationwide workers' syndicate" [Azad 1980, 23]) and certainly smaller Marxist groups, as well as radical Muslim People's Mojahedin (OIPM) were present. For instance, as early as April 1979, reflecting the workers' council initiative in a certain factory, Fadaiyan encouraged all factory workers to create their workplace councils (*Kar* 1979e, 1, 5). Indeed, the relationship between Fadaiyan and syndicate and council movements in this period (Azad 1980, 17, 22) can be the subject of independent research. There was evidence that many council members within the industrial sector were supporters of leftist political parties (Rahnema 1992, 86; Salour and Salour 2020). This is why one could state — with some stretch of the term — that the councils constituted the "socialist element of the Iranian Revolution" (Azad 1980, 14). These facts do not mean that the leftist organizations actually organized the councils. Rather, it appears that once "the showras had been established, nearly all of the communist organizations supported them enthusiastically … without having a clear understanding of their potential, and without proposing a concrete strategy for them" (Jafari 2021, 261). Simultaneously, though, all shades of the Iranian left were challenged by councils because despite their different views they still could not properly conceptualize *showras*. For the most part, they simply viewed these councils as the instruments of workers' or popular control. The association of the councils with leftist and political parties explains in part why the new regime was unwaveringly intent upon destroying or assimilating the councils, just as it attacked the universities and purged leftist and dissident students and professors in the name of the Cultural Revolution in the spring of 1980. Due to this association, the council movement was also negatively impacted by the fate of leftist parties — above all, by the major split in Fadaiyan's ranks in June 1980 (between a majority that shortly after supported the ruling Islamists and a dissenting minority; see Chapter 5).

Bayat (1987, 100–102) offers a view of the short history of the councils in four periods. The first period (February–August 1979) was "characterized by control from below." The new state was still weak and the workers' revolutionary zeal at its highest. The workers questioned the "legitimacy of capitalist relations." This period ended with the first heavy-handed wave of repression in August 1979 when opposition political parties, the Kurdish movement, independent newspapers, civil society associations, and factory councils were attacked by the regime's forces or thugs, a process that had started much earlier (see *Kar* 1979f: 1, 5). The second period (September 1979–July 1981) witnessed the solid "return of management from above" and the gradual weakening of the councils, imposing on them a defensive position. Liberal-minded Muslims who had manned the Provisional Government were removed by the hardliners supporting Ayatollah Khomeini, and the already diminishing freedoms faced even greater limitations. This period anticipated the assimilation and Islamicization of the factory councils in the third period (June 1981 to mid-1982) in which the regime's all-out assault on opposition and the bloody repression of activists emptied the councils of their original activists, replacing them in greater numbers with pro-regime workers. In this period, all councils were officially banned by the government and replaced by workplace Islamic Associations (Bayat 1987, 100–102).

Peyman Jafari (2021, 264–265) also offers comparable stages, pointing out judiciously the war with Iraq (beginning in September 1980) as an important factor (Jafari 2021, 253, 266). To bring *showras* under control, in August 1980 the Ministry of Labour finalized Resolutions of the Islamic *Shuras* that incorporated the councils under the ministry and nullified workers' control, although given the precarity of the provincial government, workers or the management did not accept the resolution (Bayat 1987, 113, 115).

A few points are important regarding this periodization. First, there is no doubt that the Islamic Associations (Anjomanha-ye Eslami) in the factories were tasked with bringing down independent councils. They were agents in the multipronged approach of the ruling Islamists to the councils: depending on the situation, the state used infiltration, provocation, and repression to weaken the councils between 1979 and 1981. Second, repression became systematically bureaucratized. For instance, within the National Iranian Oil Company the purging of activists started in the 1980s with the installation of Dismissal Committees (Hey'at-ha-ye Paksazi), which consisted of "representatives of the provincial governor, the revolutionary prosecutor, the factory management, the ministry of labour and an elected employee" (Jafari 2021, 279). Similar committees mushroomed across the country within the next two months. Interestingly, such committees were originally demanded by the oil workers' councils after the revolution for the purpose of purging the managers and supporters of the ancien régime. But now these committees were turned against the originators of the idea — dissident and leftist workers. In the oil industry alone, about 5,000 employees were dismissed or forced into retirement by the end of 1983. The dismissal of managers and workers, Jafari (2021, 279) observes, provided "an opportunity for upward mobility into managerial positions for hundreds of Islamic activists." But dismissal was not enough: one account holds that around 500 worker activists from *showras* of different sectors were killed by the regime (Salour and Salour 2020). The state used every crisis to further repress dissidents. Bayat (1987) offers a concrete case: in July 1981, the Iranian parliament voted to dismiss President Abolhassan Bani Sadr on Khomeini's orders. Street clashes broke out immediately, as thousands of supporters of the People's Mojahedin combatted state forces. During these days, according to Bayat, the Revolutionary Guards or Pasdaran (Islamic Revolutionary Guards Corps; IRGC) swarmed the Iran Khodro car assembly plant and began arresting council and other factory activists based on the blacklist the factory's Islamic Association had produced. Bayat (1987, 157–158) shows that "In one day, 73 workers were taken away. The *shura* leader, a proMudjahedin worker, had already been kidnapped at the factory gate, and a few days later I found his name in the daily paper in the list of executed people of the day."

By 1981, the regime no longer tolerated any association that did not fully conform to its rule. The state enacted a physical liquidation policy designed to eliminate worker activists. During the Provisional Government, run by liberal-minded Mehdi Bazargan, legal limitations were imposed on the councils, but after Bazargan's resignation in November 1979, the liquidation policy gained momentum. The first wave of repression in August 1979 was followed by the second wave after the Cultural Revolution in the spring of 1980 and then shortly after July 1981 (Bayat 1987, 164).

Bayat (1987, 130) delineates three types of councils based on their objectives. The "full control" councils succeeded in running their workplace according to their own views and policies without effective control of appointed management. Jafari (2021, 268) reports that in Pars Oil Company (refinery) near Karaj, a *showra* of seven people representing 503 employees "took over almost total control of production and administration." Bayat contrasts these councils with the syndicate-types that were inherently defensive bodies. The "militant interventionist" type of councils was driven by class struggle and challenged the state-appointed management in defending the workers' rights but did not exert control over production. Councils of this type exhibited different degrees of militancy. Lastly, the "corporatist" or "universal view" councils were made up of workers and management loyal to the Islamist state and dedicated their struggle to enhance the state's glory. These councils would challenge liberal or leftist tendencies within their workplace.

Reflecting on this remarkable experience, scholars have flagged two critical points about the councils. Bayat (1987, 136) suggests that the workers' councils "acted both as the organs of democracy (in terms of work organization and political considerations) and as instruments of repression at the workplaces where the corporatist committees were dominant," that they were limited to workplaces and did not extend to "the whole community." His first point suggests class struggle. With respect to the second, Bayat seems to suggest that the councils' expansion might have brought it greater social force in the face of imminent state repression. This is a noble idea. As mentioned previously, there existed student and neighbourhood councils (the latter were fairly short-lived). The alliances among them, which would have strengthened civil society, never happened. According to Saeed Rahnema (1992, 85–86), the councils could not transcend the workplace because they had no organic relations with neighbourhood councils as such. Lateral relations between councils of different constituencies, thus, did not materialize. Still, different workers' councils did try to expand. The oilers did create a national council consisting of one representative per every 1,000 employees (Jafari 2021, 269). A report also holds that thirty-four councils and strike committees in Gilan Province unified as late as April 1980 (Peykar 1980, 3, 5; see also Azad 1980, 22). In short, the idea of building alliances did exist, but the conditions changed so rapidly the councils could hardly develop such ideas. As we see in Chapter 5, the Turkmen council movement took actual steps toward unifying the councils.

The other major criticism is offered for the distinct purpose of a sweeping, categorical refutation of councils: "The defeat of the council movement in Iran adds yet another example to the countless cases of the failure of the notion of councils and worker control …. If the councils are to substitute democratic organizations — trade unions at workplaces at the economic level, and regional and national parliaments at the political level — they will undermine democracy and thus are doomed to failure" (Rahnema 1992, 90). Opposing councils and "democratic organizations" simply reveals the author's presuppositions. This institutional understanding of workers' activism (as assigned by the scholar) seeks to blame the workers for their "premature initiative" that "was doomed to failure" (Rahnema 1992, 69, 70). The failure of the councils is attributed to "the weaknesses of the Iranian working class and the left" (Rahnema 1992, 69). Surprisingly, the single most important factor in the "failure" of the councils, which was the brutal repression of the Islamic Republic, appears only in a passing remark (Rahnema 1992, 72) and without analytical significance. This helps with the reasonable but indeterminable advice that the "working class should be powerful and sufficiently well organized" before experimenting with councils (Rahnema 1992, 89). This suggests that the scholar will tell when social movements can engage in activism!

It is important to remember that the "source of legitimacy of the *shuras* was … the dynamics of class struggle and the balance of forces in society" in a revolutionary situation (Bayat 1987, 115). According to Jafari (2021, 253–254), the *showras* had five distinct features: (1) "direct democracy"; (2) "self-activity" through collective action; (3) control over production process; (4) potential to expand activity beyond a sector; and (5) having to "relate to state power in one way or another." These features enable us to appreciate the councils in their own terms, not in terms of our theoretical expectations.

History works curiously — the councils have now returned, notwithstanding the above criticisms. After the Iran-Iraq war that ended in 1988, Iranian authorities unleashed a savage neoliberal policy of privatization of economy through a rentier state populated by corrupt cronies. Thirty years later, in addition to the international economic sanctions, neoliberal policies have resulted in the impoverishment of a vast majority of Iranians. Mohammad Maljoo (2017) illustrates that by transforming permanent jobs into temporary contracts and cancelling benefits through the swelling private "human resource" sector, these policies are meant to "unmake" the Iranian working class. The good news is that in the past decade workers, teachers, nurses, transit operators, and retirees have challenged these policies through their persistent collective action led by their councils or unions, despite the state's reprisal. As evidence, compare "the 365 instances of strikes, sit-ins, work stoppages, and protests by workers in 2014 to the, at minimum, 1,300 such instances in 2019–2020" (Salour and Salour 2020). Observers contend that these sectors, the working class in particular, are returning to the council experience of 1979–1980. Thus, according to Nasrin Salour and Sam Salour (2020), the council experience has been transferred from one generation to the next "through the word of mouth from parents to their children, from worker to worker, through the writings of radical thinkers, pictures, and internet stories…. The memory of 1979 manifested itself in the uprisings of 2017 and 2019, and it has been a constant source of inspiration for labor movement activists in their attempt at forming workers' councils."

An outstanding example is the workers' unrelenting movement at Haft Tappeh Sugar Cane Complex against privatization of the company through what the movement's leader called "the formation of independent and democratic workers' councils" (quoted in Asefi 2018). The Haft Tappeh union's slogan in 2018 was "Bread, Work, Freedom, Council Governance." The workers' grassroots council/union movement prove to be the only means of stopping privatization (Asefi 2018). As such, the councils seem to reflect workers' class consciousness (Azad 1980, 16).

The *showra* experience and experiments represented grassroots initiative in popular self-control during the revolutionary period when the state was weak. The councils also represented another creative, though not theoretically coherent, attempt by the Iranian left as the bastion of social justice. Afshin Matin-asgari (2017) shows that in advocating social justice, the left has contributed notably to the expanding of civil society in the country. The council movement signifies an outstanding collective effort to that effect. That said, important as it is, scholarly focus on the workers' councils reports a certain epistemological preference (possibly if not obliquely informed by Marxism) on the class associated with the industrial sector.

I am hoping my work on the Turkmen peasants and hopefully future research on other councils will shed light on this liberating experience. I therefore echo Jafari (2021, 252) in that "the *showras* became an important part of the political power struggle that emerged in 1979, and reflected the radical reimagining of social and political possibilities among significant sections of the urban workforce." The *showras* left a legacy that still contributes to today's struggles of the working people and the working poor for social justice and participatory democracy even after four decades of repression of activism and eradication of memory.

The People's Fadai Guerrillas: A Brief History

The 1953 coup in Iran overthrew the democratically elected government of Dr. Mohammad Mosaddeq, the head of the National Front (Jebheh-ye Melli-ye Iran), who had led the legalist and popular movement of national liberation by nationalizing Iranian oil and enforcing the constitutional restrictions on the Shah's powers. The coup ended a 12-year period of relative political openness and the nation's dreams for self-assertion and democracy. Shah Mohammad Reza Pahlavi returned with a heavy hand to rule through political repression and social and economic development over the next 25 years, a curious phenomenon I have called *repressive development* (Vahabzadeh 2010). The authoritarian state launched Iran into the periphery of world capitalism, which required rapid infrastructural and social modernization, but foreclosed on political modernization that required democratic institutions and participatory citizenry. This is because the state in Iran, under the Shah's absolute control, emerged as the uncontested agent of modernization, but capitalist development in Iran was not concomitant with democratic participation. Needing funds to implement his ambitious structural reform plans, the Shah turned to the United States for loans, and was forced by the Kennedy administration to hold free elections. Dr. Ali Amini, a US favourite, became the Premier and allowed the National Front and a few other legalist parties to return to politics. The student movement grew back, and clerical opposition became more vocal and confrontational. But this period of controlled "open" politics that had started in 1960 finally ended with the crackdown on clerical opposition in June 1963, followed by the suppression of all parties and movements. Since these processes have been extensively discussed by scholars (Abrahamian 1982; 2008; Amanat 2017; Ansari 2019; Keddie 1981), I refrain from offering detail and analysis. However, it is within this particular historical context and experience that the militant opposition was embryonically formed. The roots of Fadaiyan go back to the conclusion — reached by certain student activists in the early 1960s — that legalist opposition and challenging the Shah's autocratic state through constitutional means was no longer viable, nor even possible. I have extensively researched the OIPFG, to which I refer the interested reader (Vahabzadeh 2010, 16–77; 2022b). The following is a synopsis that relates to our study.

The People's Fadai Guerrillas (PFG) emerged on the Iranian political scene in April 1971 as two underground militant groups unified. The groups unified in the aftermath of security raids that were conducted after a small but daring operation popularly called the Siahkal operation — this was an attack, led by a handful of Marxist militants, on the Gendarmerie Post in the village of Siahkal in the Caspian region on February 8, 1971. The origins of the older founding group of PFG are, interestingly, traced to university student activists who, as teenagers, supported the pro-Soviet Tudeh Party in the early 1950s but had been disillusioned with the party when the Tudeh leadership took no action — despite the party's popular base and its clandestine Officers' Organization — against the 1953 coup, fled the country, and left its rank-and-file supporters at the mercy of the state. Bizhan Jazani (1937–1975) was a Social Sciences graduate who started a secret cell in 1963 along with three comrades to organize armed struggle. They were soon joined by Hassan Zia Zarifi (1939–1975), a lawyer. Jazani and Zia Zarifi were both university student activists who were loosely associated with the student body of the Second National Front in 1960–1963. After the crackdown of 1963, they concluded that, to create a popular movement, it was necessary to break the mood of defeat in popular imagination, and that armed struggle would show the masses that the regime was vulnerable. In 1967, the group internally published a small pamphlet that asserted armed struggle had become inevitable. By this time, a network of twenty militants had been formed and partitioned into three sections. Among these militants were the commander of the Siahkal operation, Ali Akbar Safai Farahani (1939–1971), and the future legendary leader of the PFG, Hamid Ashraf (1946–1976). Security forces exposed the group in Fall 1967, and Jazani, Zia Zarifi, and a majority of the group's members were arrested, tried, and sentenced heavily. A handful of surviving members, including Ashraf, began rebuilding the group, which, by the summer of 1971, had over twenty members. Nine militants of this group, under Safai Farahani's command, carried out the Siahkal operation. The arrest of these militants and their support network led to the rushed trial and appeals process by military court. Thirteen militants were sentenced to death and executed on March 18, 1971. A handful of the group's members survived security raids, among them Ashraf who then cofounded the PFG.

The other formative group of PFG came from a younger generation: they were high school students during 1960–1963 and associated with the Islamic activities of the time. Massoud Ahmadzadeh (1947–1972) and Amir Parviz Puyan (1947–1971) moved from their hometown of Mashhad to enter university programs in Tehran, where they met Abbas Meftahi (1945–1972). Coming from religious backgrounds, they created a reading circle and gradually leaned toward Marxism-Leninism. These young men were impressed by Latin American revolutionary literature: Che Guevara and the Cuban revolution, Brazilian Carlos Marighella, Uruguay's Tupamaros, and French Régis Debray. They managed to create a large network of activists in 1969 and debated the possibility of launching guerrilla warfare. Puyan wrote an influential polemical pamphlet (Spring 1970) that concluded that armed struggle had become inevitable under the police state. Ahmadzadeh wrote a treatise (Summer 1970) that theorized armed struggle. Influenced by the experiences of Latin American revolutionaries, this treatise became the uncontested guiding theory of PFG during its first three years. Meanwhile, as the group grew to include up to fifty members, the security raids of late 1970 exposed the group, forcing the surviving members to go underground. The crackdown on both founding groups catalyzed their unification.

Thus, the PFG was founded in April 1971 by Ahmadzadeh, Meftahi, Puyan, and Ashraf. Marxism-Leninism was declared its ideology and urban guerrilla warfare its strategy. Ahmadzadeh and Meftahi were arrested within a couple of months of PFG's founding and executed in 1972. Puyan was killed in a shootout in Spring 1971. Once again, Ashraf survived the raids and became the group's capable, elusive, and loved leader until his death in June 1976. He was Iran's most wanted man for six years. The arrests and deaths of PFG members caused its near eradication by 1972, but thanks to the growing support of PFG by Iranian students and intellectuals who supplied finances and joined Fadaiyan, the group bounced back. A leaner, more efficient, well-funded, and well-trained PFG took the upper hand in its psychological warfare against the regime between 1973 and 1975 (Behrooz 2000, 63). During this time, the group changed its designation to Organization of Iranian People's Fadai Guerrillas (OIPFG) and gained the financial and campaign support of the Confederation of Iranian Students–National Union abroad, as well as logistical and financial support from Libya, the Democratic Republic of Yemen, and the People's Front for the Liberation of Palestine. The PFG carried out a number of bombings of the military, police stations, and powerlines, but its most spectacular operations were a number of assassinations of key military officers, a security agent, and a capitalist mogul. The most high-profile operation was the April 1971 assassination of Lieutenant-General Zia Farsiu, Chief Prosecutor of the Military Court, who had penned the death sentences of the Siahkal militants. A change in security methods and the use of wiretapping finally spelled disaster for the Fadai Guerrillas, leading the police to the meeting of OIPFG leadership in southern Tehran on June 29, 1976, where Ashraf and nine leading members were killed. The few surviving members went into hiatus: the group's activities ceased, and their support network was lost.

As stated earlier, Ahmadzadeh's treatise on armed struggle was the guiding theory of the OIPFG until 1973. He proposed that since the objective conditions of revolution were at hand, armed struggle would break the psychological barrier and soon instigate a popular uprising against the regime. He did not live long enough to revisit his theory, but three years into urban guerrilla warfare, many Fadaiyan activists were beginning to have reservations about his hypothesis. While in prison and sensing the theoretical gap in the OIPFG, Jazani wrote some key treatises on the relationship between armed struggle and popular uprising. In his view, armed struggle was only the initial step toward the political mobilization of the people. His works reached Ashraf in OIPFG leadership and influenced the group's new directions by 1974, which involved creating unarmed OIPFG cells that were, in turn, tasked with creating workers' cells in the factories. The OIPFG terminated its spectacular operations and began taking the initial steps toward this reorganization, but the security raids of Spring 1976 and the death of leadership annulled all plans. The few rank-and-file surviving members went deep underground, trying to survive in the absence of support networks and financial resources.

In Fall 1977, the OIPFG finally resurfaced through a declaration that announced Jazani's ideas as the group's guiding theory. This basically meant a shift away from a mere guerrilla group and toward an organization that would lead popular resistance against the regime, peaceful or otherwise. But at this time, there were no theoretically capable persons within Fadaiyan's ranks. Ashraf and the highest-ranking members of the OIPFG were killed in June 1976; prior to their deaths, two key theoretical figures of Fadaiyan, Hamid Momeni (d. February 1976) and Behrooz Armaghani (d. April 1976), had also been killed (see Vahabzadeh 2010, 51). The surviving members — none of them previously high-ranking or trained theoretically — gradually recovered the lost contacts with the isolated, surviving teams and revived the group after several months. With the pressure of the Carter administration in the United States that emphasized human rights, the Shah released political prisoners in 1977 and 1978, as the initial waves of the revolution surfaced. With veteran Fadai prisoners out of prison, the existing leadership decided on a "special recruitment" of former prisoners who were known for their theoretical competence. This allowed the group to remedy what it lacked in theory and strategy. This effectively took the group away from being merely an underground, militant group, as most Fadai activists at this time no longer believed in guerrilla warfare. The speed of revolutionary movement in effect forced the OIPFG to follow the events rather than take initiatives in regard to the popular movement that overthrew the Shah in February 1979. Between 1977 and 1979, the OIPFG carried out a small number of bombings and assassinations. On February 10, 1979, it was the OIPFG supporters who took their Siahkal commemoration rally to Tehran's east side and joined the mutinous air force technical personnel (*homafaran*) in their barracks and staged the armed uprising that terminated monarchy in just under two days. Between 1971 and 1979, 237 Fadai activists lost their lives (Vahabzadeh 2020, 257–259), while dozens of OIPFG members and thousands of supporters received various prison terms.

After the Revolution, the OIPFG emerged as Iran's most popular leftist organization, despite the fact that the group's actual membership did not exceed a few dozen people. The Fadai Guerrillas had been loved by hundreds of thousands due to their selfless dedication to the cause of liberation. Thanks to their audacity and devotion, as depicted in the arts and literature of dissident intellectuals and literati, Fadaiyan had captured the imagination of secular Iranians, gaining the status of mythic liberators (Vahabzadeh 2022b). They emerged from the Revolution as the defenders of social justice and the rights of minorities, workers, and urban poor. They also rose to variably support democratic-secular values of the professional and educated middle class. One unconfirmed account holds that in the country's first and only free parliamentary elections in March 1980, the sixty-four OIPFG candidates across the country together gained 10 percent of the total ballots cast (OIPF-M 2010). Fadaiyan's popularity was registered by the May Day parade of 1979, invited by an OIPFG-led coalition: on this day, hundreds of thousands of people took to the streets in Tehran alone (*Kar* 1979d, 1–2; Peygham-e Emrooz 1979, 1–2). Similarly, on March 7, 1980, as the regime had begun to take harsher steps to descend on opposition with a heavy hand, a mass demonstration organized by the OIPFG brought hundreds of thousands of people who filled Tehran's Azadi Square (*Kar* 1980h, 8–9). The OIPFG's weekly, *Kar* (*Labour*), had a circulation ranging between 100,000 and 300,000.

Other leftist parties significantly lagged in popularity: the oldest, the Tudeh Party, had been absent from the Iranian political scene since 1953, and now its leaders had just returned from exile after the Revolution only to support the Islamists. Rah-e Kargar (Organization of Revolutionary Workers of Iran) was a PFG offshoot founded after the Revolution by former Fadai prisoners who had rejected armed struggle. The group offered important and fresh analyses of the new clerical regime, but it mainly remained an intellectual group. Peykar (Organization of Combat on the Path of the Working Class) was created in 1979 by leaders of a Marxist-Leninist faction that had violently branched out of the liberationist Muslim People's Mojahedin in 1975. This was a small group with cells in universities, high schools, and factories, and despite its size, it published extensively. Peykar, too, was too small to effect measurable policies. With its deep connection to Kurdish peoples and tribes, the DPIK was a highly popular Kurdish social democratic party that pursued a negotiated semi-autonomy for Kurdistan within a federated Iran. But soon the Kurds experienced the repressive measures of the Islamists, and a civil war was imposed on them that lasted for several years. Komala (Revolutionary Organization of Iranian Kurdistan's Toilers) was a Maoist Kurdish group second in popularity in Kurdish regions.

This quick description shows that the OIPFG was uniquely situated in the post-Revolutionary period. Alongside the Muslim People's Mojahedin that constituted the largest party outside the state orbit (and later clashed with the clerical regime), the Fadaiyan enjoyed the sufficient popular support base, resources, and capacity to enact meaningful change. Of course, the wisdom granted by retrospect confirms that the state was already intent upon eradicating all opposition eventually and planned to achieve it cunningly and calculatingly. Like most other groups in the opposition, the OIPFG had participated in the Revolution and emerged in post-Revolutionary Iran having very little idea about, or analysis of, the new clerical ruling class. In short, the OIPFG was in its prime in the first year after the Revolution, driven not so much by ideology but by unrelenting love for and commitment to oppressed and marginalized peoples. The OIPFG policy in this period is certainly subject to criticism, and its gender blindness and failure to firmly stand by the women's rights movement reveals a major lack. Fadaiyan's prime came to an end by the May 1980 fateful schism within the OIPFG that pushed the majority toward the Tudeh Party and the shameful policy of supporting the clerical regime and the minority toward an unclear policy of opposing the regime that cost its members dearly.

In any case, having abandoned Jazani's theory and still unable to offer an analysis of its own during this period, Fadaiyan's leaders gradually turned to worn-out Leninist class analyses to decipher the nature of the Islamist state. The group appraised the Provisional Government as a shaky alliance between traditional petit-bourgeoisie of clerics around Ayatollah Khomeini and the nationalist bourgeoisie represented by political personalities around liberal-minded Muslim Premier Mehdi Bazargan. This analysis was dead wrong; it caused the OIPFG to regard the radical clerics as potentially within the ranks of the people (*khalq*) and ignore their ominous and systematic encroachment on rights and freedoms of minorities, women, workers, and the marginalized. In contrast, Fadaiyan wanted to expose the Provisional Government because they were bourgeois. So, the OIPFG ridiculed and shunned the Bazargan government's attempts at steering the Revolution away from the retrograde clerics. This disastrous policy, enabled by ideology and blinded to reality, led the OIPFG away from its democratic and secular responsibilities.

From 1979 to 1981, the OIPFG split into several factions. Some factions opposed the new regime and launched militant resistance against it in various ways, although to no avail. Other factions ended up shamefully supporting a repressive and theocratic state. As if factionalism was not enough to devour a once proud and shining group with significant moral weight in Iranian collective conscience, all the factions were ruthlessly supressed between 1981 and 1988. Hundreds of Fadai activists lost their lives in the dark decade of the 1980s, or sustained prison terms under inhumane conditions, while thousands were forced into exile.

Conclusions

An Arendtian approach to councils as the participatory and democratic origins of modern politics allows us to analytically situate the councils within international and Iranian histories and understand the deep and shared, albeit always context-specific, human drive for genuine self-governance. In short, Arendt allows the understanding of the common ground — within the human ability to collectively create something new — among the council movements across different cultures and times. The long and diverse experience of councils — in particular as they pertain to the working-class movement within the age of rapid industrialization, socialist revolutions, and revolutionary movements — indicate the connection between production self-management and political self-organization. Through anarcho-syndicalist and communist visions in the first half of the twentieth century, the workers' councils did arise as the epitome of participatory and democratic self-assertion relating to the process of production, eyeing *in potentia* the emancipation of labour. The Iranian workers' councils in 1979 and later indicate the continuation of this long global tradition. As elsewhere and as the means of democratic self-governance, the *showras* in Iran offered the possibility of opposing the top-down colonial-capitalist power, enforced by the state as the sole agent of development.

The association of councils with workers' movements, while historically factual, need not block our view into the greater, far-reaching possibility of councils as a way of participatory self-governance. In this respect, Arendt's insights remain almost unparalleled. Her views can be adjusted to accommodate the "social question" (contra Arendt!), which, in my view, is a necessary step for advocating councils in today's world. The advent of *anjomans* during the Constitutional Revolution — as Iran transitioned to political modernity through a painful process filled with major setbacks — attests to the fact that councils do go beyond the socialist- and anarchist-inspired workers' movements and traditions. These grassroots *anjomans* proved to be both transnational and local, a testament to the fact that the council movements transcend national boundaries or regional differences. In 1906 Iran, city, neighbourhood, women's councils, as well as workers' councils, proved beyond any doubt the *institutive* essence of council movements, what Arendt would call the "birth" of a new body politic. In this respect, Janet Afary's 1996 study (however unwittingly) stands out and is on par with Arendt: when left to themselves, people often tend *not* to choose hierarchical systems and, instead, act in unison as free individuals. This is what Turkmen peasants and intellectuals chose to do: land takeover, establishment of new commons, and revival of culture and language through an elaborate council system.

The historical and theoretical preparations in this chapter allow us to focus our attention on examining the way Iranian capitalist modernization entailed dispossession of land and the reshaping of rural Iran through repressive development (Chapter 2), so that we can measure the impact of modernization and land reform on the Turkmens' ancestral lands and ways of life (Chapter 3).

Chapter 2

Dispossession, Appropriation, and Repressive Development

> *The Turkmen has a historical pain, one that you would not understand unless you read history with fairness, and if you have already read history with fairness and understood it, [you realize that] learning about pain is not the same as feeling it. You have to stand alongside them [the Turkmens], in their midst, and share their pain so that you experience a feeling that is horrifying.*
> — The National Front of Iran (May 1, 1979)

THE TURKMEN COUNCIL MOVEMENT HAS BOTH a long and a short history; to understand its "long history" in this chapter, it is necessary to properly situate Iran's state-championed capitalist modernization and attend to landownership in this process. My intention is to register how the 1979 Turkmen council movement was a response to long processes of economic dispossession and cultural marginalization and in particular to capitalist encroachment on land. Moreover, I propose that legal land registration has been the colonial-capitalist means of simultaneous land appropriation by a rising ruling elite under the Pahlavi monarchy and dispossession of the original inhabitants of their ancestral lands in certain regions within the country — namely in the Plains of Turkmen.

This chapter begins with a glance at the age-old landownership in the Iranian plateau and then offers a brief but focused overview of the question of landownership and its economic significance and transformation under first the reign of Reza Shah and then through the land reform carried out by Mohammad Reza Shah. These processes indicate that the land issue in Iran was connected to the state's push for developing resources for the country to enter the world capitalist orbit as a peripheral player. Next, the chapter focuses on the historical context of dispossession of the Turkmen's ancestral lands and its privatization by the state. In forging a modern nation, the Pahlavi state launched an authoritarian push for the Persianization of the multinational and multilingual Iran. This issue will also be briefly discussed to illustrate how this process had an impact on national minorities, including the Turkmens. Consequently, cultural revival was concomitant with addressing the land question during the Turkmen council movement.

I would like to note that Iran has experienced an irreducibly multifaceted, complex, and transcultural modernity with transnational influences that shaped contemporary Iranians as a postcolonial nation (see Matin-asgari 2018). My focus in this study is *modernization*, or strictly, building the infrastructures and institutions and creating the necessary laws so that the modern state would rise as the unrivalled (and monotonal, imposed, and heavy-handed) agent of nationwide projects of capitalist modernization. So, in my subsequent discourse, by *modern* I mainly refer to economic modernization and infrastructural, institutional, and legal development under the auspices of an autocratic state, instead of Iranian *modernity* as a simultaneous cultural, social, political, and economic movement. I acknowledge, though, that the two processes were indeed intimately interweaved. Significantly, both processes were also heavily gendered and racialized (or ethnicized).

From Traditional Landownership to the Modernization Threshold

In contrast to European feudalism where the transformation of landownership led to the emergent capitalist system through what Marx called primitive accumulation, in Iran such transformation largely resulted from colonial impact and the role of the Pahlavi modern state — as the uncontested, self-acclaimed, privileged agent of capitalist expansion — in registering property ownership and subsequent land reform that facilitated the country's entry into world capitalist periphery. By the same token, capitalist development in Europe was advanced by an emerging and independent bourgeois class that, due to its need for political representation, pushed for parliamentary-representative institutions that would serve its interests. In Iran, the rising ruling class's wielding of state machinery to champion colonial-capitalist development rendered the Iranian state highly centralized and authoritarian — a state that issued laws and decrees that served the ruling class. There is a common misconception regarding the traditional Persian agrarian system, which identifies it as "feudal"; this is due partly to the inept and schoolish application of Marx's brilliant theory of capitalist development in Europe to Persia and partly to the celebration of land reform propagandized as the "abolition of the landlord and peasant system" by the Pahlavi state that implied feudal relations.

As is well-known, the system of landownership of the nobility, called *manorialism*, dominated England after the ninth century Norman invasion (Martin 1983). On August 1, 1086, William the Conqueror held court to acquire the landholders' fealty, which resulted in the recording of their lands and resources in the same year. The subsequent Domesday Book produced an enormous document listing all property and establishing clear tenure (Holt 1997). The feudal system created economic stability and granted political power to the landlords. It was this type of recorded, legal ownership in Western Europe that provided the foundation of capitalist ownership centuries later.

In her classic study of landownership in Persia, Ann Lambton (1953, 2) argues that in early tribal society the village was basically a clan settlement. She infers that the original ownership of land in ancient Persia was possibly communal. When the traditional communal ownership weakened and large landowning emerged, forms of share-keeping according to fixed proportions still remained (Lambton 1953, 5). In ancient times and during the Parthian Empire (250 BCE to circa 230 CE), the nomadic Scythians emerged as the ruling group and created the Persian "feudalism" by creating large properties and connecting them to the council of the king. Under this class was the intermediary class of subfield holders and at the bottom were the peasants (Lambton 1953, 12). Under the Sassanian Empire (224–651 CE), the *dihgan* constituted the landowning class that held large estates (granted by the state or appropriated from others).

Long story short, of this system little remained after the Muslim conquest of the seventh century. Islam liberated Persian peasants from the Sassanid caste system. After the decline of the Abbasid Caliphate in the ninth century, a system of landownership named *iqta'* vastly spread. Although *iqta'* has its origins in the early Islamic period, it was the rise of the Turkic Seljuk dynasty in the eleventh century that *iqta'* gained significance in Persia (Lambton 1953, 23). This system was a response to the economic problem of a declining gold economy and the state's obligation to finance the military in an administratively stable fashion.

In a nutshell, *iqta'* resolved the problem of the state's floundering in military expenditure by assigning land titles to the military so the latter would continuously supply its own revenues. As such, the position of land assignee or *muqta'* was established and routinized. Lambton (1953, 53) warns that "The *iqta'* system is sometimes spoken of as feudalism, but the circumstances in which the *iqta'* system became established and the cause which gave rise to it were different from those which prevailed in Western Europe when feudalism developed." Accordingly, "The results were dissimilar, and it is misleading to talk of feudalism in the lands of the Eastern Caliphate, including Persia, unless it is first made clear that Islamic feudalism does not correspond to any of the various types of feudalism found in Western Europe" (Lambton 1953, 53). Under the Seljuks, a provincial governor acted as a semi-independent prince paying regular *iqta'* instalments to the king and basically controlling the province (Lambton 1953, 107).

As such, Iran did *not* have "feudalism in the classical sense of the term": "Private property in land was weak and tenuous, based as it was on various land assignment systems associated with military/bureaucratic *privileges* rather than with aristocratic *rights*. The state itself directly owned a significant share of the agricultural land, and indirectly controlled the 'ownership' of the remainder" (Katouzian 1983, 309; original emphasis). Calling Iranian landownership "feudalism" is a legacy of the inept application of Marxist theory to Iran (see CPCTP 1985, 18).

The feudal system, as in the case of England, was based on recorded land titles, and thus guaranteed continued property as well as a solid aristocracy. In contrast, *iqta'* was characterized by impermanence, simply because the land title in this system would last as long as the land-assigning dynasty was in power. This particularly Asian system did not escape Karl Marx, who, in his notes on medieval India, explicitly spoke of *iqta'* and rejected the notion that premodern Asia was feudalist (K. Anderson 2010, 210–211). It is well-known that *iqta'* became the most powerful form of economic reward for political allegiance in medieval Persia. As early as the eleventh century CE, Nizam al-Molk (1018–1092) — the Persian vizier of the Seljuk kings Alp Arsalan and Malik Shah — acknowledged this system as ancient (Nizam al-Molk 1968, 43) in his book, *Siyasatnameh* (*Letter on Politics*), advising the kings to frequently substitute *'ommal va moqte'an* (agents and *iqta'* assignees) every "two or three years," so that they treat the subjects/peasants (*ru'aya*) with justice, which ensures that "the country stays prosperous" (Nizam al-Molk 1968, 55). Naturally, the wise vizier's advice would not sit well with the profiteers of *iqta'* as an economic system of rewarding loyalty; a form of ownership unstable by design paradoxically needs stability if the Shah of Persia intends for his rule to enjoy permanence. In other words, "The traditional Iranian village provided the socio-economic foundation for the functionally despotic state" (Katouzian 1983, 310).

Many changes came until the Safavid Empire (1501–1736) transformed military organization by replacing tribal alliances with a standing army under Shah Abbas (1587–1629) who paid his troops by land assignments from state-owned *khaliseh* (*khasseh*) lands that could be inherited by the male heirs as long as they carried arms (Lambton 1953, 107). Land still played a significant role in financing the state under the Qajar dynasty (1789–1925). Abbas Amanat (2017, 224) argues that "Land ownership had been transformed since the rise of the Qajars, although the rules governing the agrarian economy remained essentially unchanged." Amanat (2017, 224) continues: "Most of the land used for agriculture, usually consisting of a village, its orchards, and the surrounding arable land, theoretically was recognized as crown land. Throughout the century, however, more and more land came under private control."

In this period, land ownership by and large fell into three categories: the state-owned or *khaliseh* lands, large landownership or *arbabi*, and religious endowments or *vaqf*. Thus, "The revenue of state-owned lands was at times granted as *tuyul* (fief) allotments to various dignitaries for services performed for the crown and the state" (Afary 1996, 18). Having its roots in *iqta'*, *tuyul* (Turkish) meant assigning a piece of *khaliseh* or state-owned property to an individual so that the latter would acquire income from it, instead of, principally, being salaried by the state. Accordingly, "private ownership (as opposed to individual or communal possession) characterized only a minority of landholdings in Iran before the mid-nineteenth century" (Chaqueri 1995, 16). But in the eighteenth and nineteenth centuries, Iran witnessed a historic shift: a remarkably retrograde and inept dynasty. Persia at the time was besieged by the Ottoman Empire that was undergoing modernization or *tanzimat* in the west; dealing with increasingly aggressive Russian Imperialism in the north; holding off the formidable British Empire eyeing Persian territory; and dealing with various European powers vying to take control of sclerotic infrastructural modernization in Persia. The Qajar dynasty was forced to face its own backwardness by the mid-nineteenth century after they lost major territories in the Caucasus to the Russians (following two wars) and after they lost control of the territory of Herat in the east (western Afghanistan today). Persia had historic claims to Herat and had previously gained control of the territory, but due to the British invasion of southern Persia, the territory was lost to the British Empire. The age of *concession colonialism* began in Persia: Russian and European powers and entrepreneurs took control of developmental projects to create modern infrastructure, and they did this by monopolizing revenue collection and paying a lumpsum to the Qajar monarch. Iran began its marginal entry into the world capitalist market.

At this time, the state needed to increase its land revenue to fund the standing army, to acquire European technology, and to pay for excessive Royal Court expenditures. Consequently, large areas of *khaliseh* lands were sold to the elite. According to Janet Afary (1996, 18), "Much land was sold over a period of ten years. Near the end of Nasir al-Din Shah's rule [1848–1896], he ordered all state-owned lands to be sold except those surrounding the capital." This is where, in my view, private ownership of land as legal and rightful property, transferable through heredity, a type of landownership akin to European feudalism, finally spread in Persia. This process put peasantry under tremendous pressure. Avetis Sultanzadeh (1889–1938), a theoretician of the Iranian Communist Party, rightly recognized the link between capitalism and property relations: "Persia's entry into the world market, the development of external trade, and the introduction of currency and commodity relationships have in the highest degree intensified the exploitation of the peasant masses" (quoted in Afary 1996, 17). In the nineteenth and twentieth centuries, agricultural production was increasingly diverted toward generating cash crops that benefited the big merchants (Afary 1996, 18; Keddie 1968, 70). And this seems to be a universal story in the Third World.

The village has been the basic unit of social organization in Persia since ancient times, but I have only spoken of the process of agricultural production in the abstract. In Persia, the production of crops was customarily based on a particular sharecropping or *muzare'eh*, according to which the annual crop was divided into five shares: land, water, seed, oxen, and labour. The provider of each would take one-fifth of the crop, and it was not uncommon for the landlord to provide irrigated water (in lands where there was a *qanat* or underground water canal), land,

and seeds, thus taking away three-fifths of the crop. Again, it was not uncommon for the peasants to also provide the seed, thus increasing their share. Oxen actually referred to two bulls on a plow, and in case a peasant did not possess two animals, two peasants would pair single oxen each and split the share of crops for oxen (one-tenth each). Abrahamian (2008, 23) shows that "According to custom, village residents enjoyed the right to work on particular strips of land even though that land in theory belonged to the landlord." The proper term was *nasaq*, the right of cultivation given to a specific peasant by the landlord in return for an agreed-upon share of the crop. Holding a *nasaq* was usually a privilege of sorts, as it guaranteed income for the peasant within the perceivable future. This gave a form of security to the peasant, causing them to be dependent on land. Regional differences notwithstanding, other classes of rural residents were present, adding to the complexity of village stratification: the *khordeh malik* were proprietors of small patches of land (which were often not enough to sustain a family); the *gavband* was the peasant who rented a strip of land to cultivate; the *khoshneshin*, the lowest strata in the village, did not possess land or rights and worked as agricultural labourers (Katouzian 1983, 310–311; Keddie 1968, 73).

Iranian agriculture has been historically underproductive in the past two centuries mainly due to significant lack of output-enhancing technology, until the land reform in the 1960s changed the very concept of land (see next section). It was not uncommon to find undernourished peasant families or peasants who would work in villages or cities as wage labourers in the off seasons. Sharecropping indicates that feudalism did not exist in Persia: typically, the Iranian *ra'yat* were not serfs, properly speaking, as they were not bonded to a landowner through indentured servitude, even though they might have been attached to land and lived in chronic poverty.

The Pahlavi Initiative: Modernizing Property Rights

There is a clear consensus that Iranian sociopolitical modernity was launched with the founding of the Pahlavi dynasty in 1925 and through Reza Shah's authoritarian modernization. This is the dominant but formalistic view that regards modernization solely as institution-building and lawmaking, instead of focusing on human development, civil society expansion, and political and civic freedoms. The democratic spirit of the Constitutional Revolution quickly faded with Reza Shah's reign and the state as the exclusive agent of modernization pushed capitalist expansion without notable resistance.

Reza Shah was a product of a specific period. In 1917, a Bolshevik revolution had ended Tzarism in Russia and heralded a new socialist era. A decade earlier, the discovery of oil in Iran circa 1908 by a British entrepreneur, had propelled the British Empire militarily and economically ahead of its European colonizing competitors. Thus, a socialist revolution north of Persia was alarming to the British government. The rise of Reza Shah to power through a coup in 1921 and his founding of the Pahlavi dynasty in 1925 must be contextualized in this transnational, imperialist, and colonial context. In its inceptive years, Iranian economic modernization hinged on land.

Landownership was radically transformed in the twentieth century compared with the way it worked from the medieval times to the nineteenth century. "This tendency was accentuated when the landowner proper was largely superseded, first by the revenue farmer and then, with the spread of the system of land assignment or *iqta'* from the … eleventh century AD onward, by the assignee," states Lambton (1953, 4). "The decisive state in this development was the settlement of the military on the land. Finally, in the twentieth century the assignees were retransformed into land owners" (Lambton 1953, 4). Under Reza Shah, property rights were modernized, as new laws transformed landownership, paving the way for future capitalist expansion in economy. The abolition of *tuyul* by the Constitutional Revolution (Lambton 1953, 178) had already made strides toward a new concept of landownership. Moving away from the traditional rules concerning landownership, the "Constitution recognizes the sanctity of private property. Art. 14 of the Supplementary Fundamental Laws of 7 October 1907 states that no owner can be deprived of his land except by sanction of the *shari'a*, and even then only after the fixing and payment of a just price" (Lambton 1953, 178). Notably, the abolition of *tuyul* reduced the economic and political position of landowners (Lambton 1953, 260).

Naturally, then, the issue of landownership had been the subject of legal revitalization. It is important to note that some of the key functionaries of the state under Reza Shah were influenced by the economist Friedrich List and advanced the idea that a strong state could advance capitalism rapidly (Nomani 2020). As a result, a number of legislations legalized property rights. These included the trademark law of 1925 and the trade laws of 1924 and 1925, the foundation of the National Bank in 1927, and the legislation granting the state the "monopoly of foreign trade" and thus controlling the direction of development (Nomani 2020). At this time, the state ownership of key natural resources (namely, petroleum) allowed the state financial independence from the ruling elite and to impose itself as the exclusive agent of change (Nomani 2020).

A series of land registry laws between 1922 and 1934 changed the essence of property titles (Nomani 2020). A first step was taken in 1922, in the last years of Ahmad Shah Qajar's reign; in order to establish legal process for land registry, the Council of Ministers ruled that villages that were in proven, continuous possession of a person for 30 years or more are legally his own property (Yeganeh 1985, 71). The law ratified in January 1926 "established a uniform land tax throughout the country based on the gross produce, which was to be ascertained by the new survey. Irrigated and unirrigated land was to pay 3 percent on the gross produce before the division of the crop between the landlord and the peasant and the deduction of any changes on the crop" (Lambton 1953, 183). Soon, the Bureau of Land Registry was created under the Ministry of Justice. In early 1928, under Reza Shah, the law of General Land Registry and Time Passage was approved. The Law of Property Registration of 1929 mandated all citizens to register their property within two years; failing that, they would lose any claim and rights and the state would appropriate the land (F. Hashemi 2009, 399). This law placed the onus on those who regarded themselves as landowners, and as we will soon see, in a country where there were no far-reaching mass media and where the majority of the population was illiterate, many small landowners lost their property by missing the deadline to register their land claim. And this constitutes one of the elements of grievance in the long history of the Turkmen council movement.

One reason for moving to organize legal ownership was the unending land disputes: "Many *khaliseh* villages, especially in Mazandaran, had fallen into private hands and the ownership of other villages which had been confiscated by the government was disputed by individuals. Various committees had been formed to decide cases of disputed ownership" (Lambton 1953, 182). The *khaliseh* lands that Reza Shah had received included the confiscated lands of Nader Shah Afshar (reign: 1736–1747), the lands confiscated by Mohammad Shah Qajar (reign: 1834–1848) and Naseraddine Shah Qajar (reign: 1848–1896). In 1931, a legislation mandated the state to sell all *khaliseh* lands (Mirdar, Arabani, and Soltani Ahmadi 2019, 113). The *khaliseh* or state-owned lands constituted very large properties in some of the most fertile and coveted areas in the otherwise arid Iranian plateau. Agriculture was generally underproductive due to backwardness of traditional cultivation and the lack of investment in technology (Nomani 2020). Because in the state sales of the *khaliseh* land there usually was no buyer (who would dare challenge the Shah), Reza Shah would buy them at a cut-rate price. In other occasions when the land that Reza Shah was interested in obtaining already had an owner and was not state-owned, the Ministry of Finance would confiscate the land and transfer it to Reza Shah. In cases where the owners did not intend to sell, local Gendarmerie personnel would force them into selling, at times even by imprisoning them (Gorgani 1979, 22).

While reducing the power of traditional large, landed proprietors, the sales of state lands attracted interest in investing in land, and consequently, "commercial, capitalist and bureaucratic classes began to invest in agriculture" (Yeganeh 1985, 71). But we will soon see that the landed class still exerted significant political influence and its final extraction from power was achieved through the land reform of the 1960s. It is important to note that in the 1930s, to further organize the village under state control, the December 1935 law institutionalized the village headman or *kadkhoda* as the official representative of the landowners and responsible for the application of state laws in the village (Yeganeh 1985, 71): a step toward bureaucratization of village activity.

Reportedly, during Reza Shah's reign, 44,000 land title certificates were issued to his name (Gorgani 1979, 22). The sales of *khaliseh* lands provided Reza Shah with a unique opportunity to become Iran's richest man. Bureaucratic modernization and legal land registry worked immensely in his favour.

Royal Land Appropriation

The legislating of the land registry, the thirty-year proof of ownership law, and the sales of *khaliseh* lands allowed Reza Shah to emerge as Iran's largest landowner. During his reign, 76 percent of the country's population was rural (Nomani 2020). He was uniquely situated to acquire, in his native province of Mazandaran, large holdings of fertile lands that were some of the best in the country. He wielded state power and state regulations to amass personal riches. Amanat (2017, 500) confirms that "The agrarian economy — still the largest economic sector — remained essentially intact and the landowning culture of exploitation was reinforced by Reza Shah's own greed. He built a vast estate through brazen appropriation of the lands belonging to Mazandaran's small and large landowners."

With Reza Shah's land confiscation, a new category of landownership emerged: the Royal properties or Amlak-e Ekhtesasi (Exclusive Estates). Subsequently, Reza Shah created a state office to transfer, oversee, and manage his lands. It was called the Bureau of Exclusive Estates, and Ali Akbar Sha'bani was its first supervisor (Sha'bani 1972). Reza Shah acquired these lands in different ways: recall the 1929 Law of Property Registration that required landowners to claim their right to property within the next two years. Many small landowners, being illiterate, remained unaware of this law, and consequently, the Shah and large landowners exploited it and registered lands to their names upon providing proof (F. Hashemi 2009, 400). Increasingly, the Exclusive States began to resemble the abolished *khaliseh*, and in fact, the sales of state lands (*khaliseh*) served Reza Shah well. Large state lands were transformed into his estates. Lambton (1953, 256) observes that "These [estates] were acquired nominally by purchase, and the title-deeds were handed over under a formal transaction, but in many cases this was merely a cloak for virtual confiscation." But that was not all: "In some cases the holder was forced to exchange his property for property elsewhere, not always of an equivalent value. These estates were kept separate from *khaliseh* and administered by the personal bureau of the ruler. Most of Mazandaran in this way became part of the personal estates of Riza Shah" (Lambton 1953, 256–257). In short, "His estate almost entirely was appropriated by force from large landholders and petty sharecroppers" (Amanat 2017, 464).

The "soldier who had risen through the ranks accumulated enough land during the [16-year] course of his reign to become the wealthiest man in Iran, if not in the whole Middle East. A sympathetic biographer estimates that by the time he died he had accumulated a bank account worth £3 million and farm lands totaling 3 million acres," remarks Ervand Abrahamian (2008, 71). "The lands, concentrated in his ancestral Mazanderan, were mostly plantations for tea, rice, silk, cotton, and tobacco. He also had wheat farms in Hamadan, Asterabad, Gurgan, and Veramin. He accumulated these estates in part by outright confiscation, in part by dubious transfer of state properties, in part by irrigating waste lands, and in part by forcing landlords, both large and small, to sell him property at nominal prices" (Abrahamian 2008, 71).

Right after Reza Shah's exile, a Kerman newspaper reported that he had (US) $360 million deposited in banks outside of the country. He was reported to have said at the time of his departure: "I had accumulated 7,000 million tomans (70 billion rials) and now that I am leaving Iran I have nothing" (quoted in Gorgani 1979, 96). It is estimated that at the end of his rule, Reza Shah owned 10 percent of all agricultural lands in the country, while 70 percent was owned by various landowners and tribal chiefs and 20 percent was endowment estates (Nomani 2020).

Reflecting on the sales of *khaliseh* lands, Lambton observes the reduction of power of the so-called landed aristocracy, calculating that Reza Shah's "policy of land confiscation had … not only direct but also indirect effects upon land ownership. It weakened the position and power of the tribal *khans* and reduced their economic status to such an extent that they were often forced to sell property" (Lambton 1953, 260). Since nomadic tribes were considered a source of nuisance for a centralizing state (as these tribes had always challenged premodern states), the reduction of the power of tribal chiefs would facilitate Reza Shah's next steps toward forcing most tribal peoples into relocation and a sedentary life. At the same time, though, Lambton observes an important transformation of the landed classes: "it is doubtful whether it can be said that the total area owned by the large, landed proprietors has sensibly decreased. In so far as the confiscated lands became *khaliseh* while other areas became the personal estates or *Amlak* of Riza Shah, there was a decrease, but this was offset to some extent by the distribution of certain areas of existing *khaliseh* to those who had been deprived of their property elsewhere" (Lambton 1953, 260). There seems to be a designed and managed displacement of traditional landowners with the new ones, and not simply for garnering political support for the Pahlavis, but perhaps more importantly, for the purpose of capitalist expansion in the country. In short, there was a long-term plan attached to land ownership transformation that indeed made the Pahlavis the country's richest family. "The Pahlavi initiative to pioneer large-scale industrialization was another outgrowth of the state's centralizing mission," states Amanat (2017, 464). "The textile mills, part of any early industrializing project, developed especially in Mazandaran province on or near Reza Shah's vast private estate.... Several state-run textile mills in Shahi, Tabriz, Isfahan, and Tehran produced a variety of consumer and specialized fabrics to meet domestic demands" (Amanat 2017, 464). Reza Shah developed Mazandaran, building roads, seaside luxury hotels as well as textile, sugar, and tobacco factories, and even constructing a railroad that connected Tehran to the newly created port of Bandar Shah on the Caspian Sea. He managed to staff his factories with conscript soldiers and "slave labour" (Abrahamian 2008, 72). Moreover, he used this unique opportunity to forge a new class of landowners from those in service of the state, in a manner reminiscent of *iqta'*, thereby giving them additional reasons for their loyalty to him: "He ... allocated plots of appropriated land to senior army officers and officials whom he favored" (Amanat 2017, 464).

The Anglo-Soviet invasion of Iran in the context of the Second World War came as a shock to Reza Shah: the Allies forced him into abdication on September 16, 1941. His son, 22-year-old crown prince Mohammad Reza, was announced as the new Shah. He inherited a country under occupation, and while he more or less had the support of military and administrative elite, his position among the landed classes — who were now vying for greater power and influence in the absence of the dictator — was rather insecure. On his way out of the country, Reza Shah transferred all his *amlak* to his son. But this transfer, in conjunction with the young Shah's precarious position, evoked the intervention of the parliament and a number of subsequent legislations. The primary reason for this move by Majles was the unending but suppressed grievances around how Reza Shah had obtained the *Royal Amlak*. But we should not overlook the fact that Reza Shah's abdication "made it possible for large landowners to regain much of their economic and political strength" (Katouzian 1983, 312). Even BBC's Persian radio program did not miss the opportunity to broadcast critical reports of Reza Shah's tyranny and greed (Amanat 2017, 496) — an ironic policy for a broadcasting service funded by the British state that had backed his coup.

The young Shah now had to properly respond to growing public outcry as well. In its September 11, 1941, session, Majles passed a law that mandated the Royal Court to return some of the Exclusive Estates to their rightful owners and established a procedure to achieve it (F. Hashemi 2009, 400). After the law was passed, a Royal decree transferred the *Amlak* to the state (Lambton 1953, 257). The Exclusive Estates

(Amlak-e Ekhtesasi) now became the Entrusted Estates (Amlak-e Vagozari) which contained four categories as shown by Lambton (1953, 257): "(1) land bought from its former owners for a price of over 10,000 rs [approximately £59]; (2) land exchanged for estates elsewhere; (3) land taken by usurpation; and (4) land bought from its former owners for a price less than 10,000 rs [approximately £59]." Note how the discursive shift from *ekhtesasi* (exclusive) to *vagozari* (entrusted or ceded) was meant to distance the young Shah from his father in public eyes. Later, on June 2, 1942, Majles passed another law that mandated the government to transfer former Royal *Amlak* to their original owners and set up special courts to receive the claims and rule in cases of dispute (Lambton 1953, 257). At this time, Iran was still under the Allies' occupation. Things changed after the war. The Shah's power rose steadily after he regained control of the country. In June 1949, the Majles passed another law; it legislated that all unclaimed and undisputed estates would return to the Shah under Exclusive Estates (F. Hashemi 2009, 400). Just as small landowners missed the deadline for the 1929 Law of Property Registration, so did many such owners and potential claimants in the September 1941 legislature to dispute the Exclusive Estates. Several letters to the Majles from this time indicate this fact (see F. Hashemi 2009, 405, 407, 409, 411). Land registry and property ownership laws still served as the means of dispossession of land, however.

As we see in Chapter 3, these laws also affected the Turkmens. But before attending to that, we need to address the land reform and its consequences, to which we now turn.

Land Reform and Its Consequences

After the 1953 coup, the Shah reemerged as the uncontested monarch and the ambitious agent of development. Having defeated all shades of opposition, his power was now absolute, and the bequest of the Allies' invasion — the weak state and the semi-open conditions through which civil society and political parties had flourished between 1941 and 1953 — was now behind him. He had already increased his legal powers in the aftermath of the assassination attempt at his life during a Royal visit to the Faculty of Law at the University of Tehran on February 5, 1949. Following the attempt, in which he sustained minor injuries, the Shah convened a Constituent Assembly to pass the necessary amendments that increased his constitutional powers (Abrahamian 2008, 112).

Having acquired full control of the state in the post-1953 era, the Shah's ambition was to turn Iran into an industrial country. But to achieve that he needed to resolve the "land issue" once and for all. His land reform program in the 1960s was a nexus policy that had two simultaneous objectives. First, the Shah would rid himself of the old "landed aristocracy" that still wielded some power. According to Nikki Keddie (1968, 81), the modern state's interest in the land reform had a deep political reason: the political power of the landlords that can be traced back to the reign of Reza Shah. In 1962–1963, the Iranian parliament was still dominated by landlords. The land reform weakened the political position of traditional landowners (Yeganeh 1985, 77) and allowed the Shah to shift his support base from landlords to urban industrialists (Keddie 1968, 82; see also Linklater 2013, 336) as well as the growing salaried middle class that emerged out of the expansion of bureaucracy in the 1960s onward. Second, in a fairly classical transition to capitalism, by freeing peasants from the land, the state was able to supply the inchoating industry with the labour force it needed. In a way, this process had already, if molecularly, started with land registry and through Royal land appropriation as dispossession of the common peasant class. Alongside, the state invested heavily in higher education to train specialists for the growing industry and bureaucracy. To achieve all this, the Shah now enjoyed the Consortium Agreement of 1954 with western oil companies that resulted in secure and continued state revenue, specifically between 1956 and 1960 (Abrahamian 2008, 123–124; Keddie 1981, 140–141).

Still, viewing the land reform in this way reports a developmentalist mindset that ignores the anxieties of the Cold War and Iran's geopolitical position, and thus leaves the false impression of a benevolent state and its progressive reforms. The United States had vested interest in this type of reform because it was fearful of a communist revolution. To initiate Iran's reforms "officials with experience of transforming South Korea were specifically posted to the Tehran embassy to help with its execution. The plan [was] incorporated into a series of reforms that the shah proudly announced as the White Revolution in 1963" (Linklater 2013, 335). A developmentalist approach was promoted ideologically. For example, MIT economics professor Walt W. Rostow's article "The Take-Off into Self-Sustained Growth" (1965) launched him to President Lynden Johnson's administration as an adviser on national security. Rostow argued that "a small industrializing group could quickly achieve what land reform only hoped to do with difficulty over time" (quoted in Linklater 2013, 327). As such, a shock by the industrialists was needed to jolt the old landowning class out of economic and political positions. As a result, "the Shah's rule, however brutal, was judged to be creating the conditions for Rostow's elite group of modernizers to prepare the ground for capitalism and representative government" (Linklater 2013, 336). Rostow's doctrine achieved the status of "economic and social orthodoxy in the 1960s" (Linklater 2013, 328) and became the arch strategy of the United States to counteract communism through fundamental social changes in peripheral countries, offering them a path to industrialization, and supposedly democracy, in the face of the post-Stalin and post–Second World War Soviet Union with its expanding zone of influence.

It is important to acknowledge that the idea of land reform had preceded the Shah's developmentalist plan — an important connection that conventional historiography tendentially ignores. Land reform has always been on the platforms of various Iranian socialists and some nationalists. These included actual analyses and proposed programs for *réforme agraire* (see Hakimi 1952). Aware of the fundamental problems of rural production, Premier Mosaddeq issued the Agricultural Reform decree in early 1953 that included the establishment of village councils, increased share of the yield for peasants, and a 20 percent levy on landowner's revenues to be diverted to a rural development fund.

Prior to the land reform, there was an American survey of 1954 (after the coup) of Iranian agriculture. This research was funded under the auspices of President Harry S. Truman's 1949 Point Four Program: the assistance program to "developing countries" in the context of the emergent Cold War and Soviet Union's alliance with the new, postcolonial states in Africa and Asia. The timing of the study, and the researchers behind it, could not have been incidental. The survey of thirty-seven villages "documented the extremely low living levels, poor resource use, lack of landlord investment, and low yields of Iranian agriculture" (Keddie 1968, 71). Extreme village discrepancies were noted: peasants in the southeast were deemed to be the poorest, with an annual income of $8–14, whereas, in the Caspian Mazandaran region, peasant families had the mean income of $1,037 per year. The average peasant income stood at $516 per annum (Keddie 1968, 72). The survey discovered that sedentary tribes constituted the poorest of all rural dwellers (Keddie

1968: 77). The study also "found appalling conditions; locusts and clover as the main food supply in a few areas; a majority seriously diseased; interest rates at 240–800 percent per annum" (Keddie 1968, 75). Peasants often mortgaged their future crop for half price, and if they defaulted, they would lose their land, which was then appropriated by the landlord (Keddie 1968, 75–76). In the same period, another report noted class inequalities in the country: a 1959–1960 survey showed "that the richest 10 percent accounted for 35.5 percent of the total expenditures, and the richest 20 percent for 51.7 percent. At the other end of the social pyramid, the poorest 10 percent accounted for 1.7 percent of the total expenditures, and the poorest 20 percent for 4.7 percent. Meanwhile, the middle 40 percent accounted for 27.5 percent of total expenditures" (Abrahamian 1982, 448).

Also facilitated by the Iranian state, the extensive Food and Agriculture Organization (FAO) Survey in the 1960s, although performed at the time of greater state revenue (due to petro-income) affirmed the general characteristics of the earlier survey: that agricultural production was in sharp decline. Of the 11.4 million hectares, 39.9 percent was left fallow each year (Keddie 1968, 78). The FAO study, published in fifteen volumes in Persian, found "that 14.4 percent of the employed rural population were wage labourers, and 33.1 percent were 'family workers'" (Keddie 1968, 79). These indicated the decline of a major economic sector. Cyrus Yeganeh (1985, 74) shows that "Agriculture accounted for one-third of the GNP in 1960, as opposed to about four-fifths at the turn of the century; it continued to decrease to about one-fifth by the late 1960s." The increase in oil revenue and the United States Agency for International Development program contributed to decreased reliance on agriculture, and it is in this context that the Kennedy administration pushed for structural reforms in Iran (Yeganeh 1985, 74–75). Political manoeuvrings at this point attested to the Kennedy administration's greater trust in Dr. Ali Amini, a pro-American liberal, veteran politician, and former Iranian ambassador to the United States (1956–1958), than in the Shah. In the aftermath of a disputed parliamentary election, Amini was appointed the Premier in 1961 until he stepped down in 1962. Influenced by the United States administration, Amini was an advocate of land reform, and it was his Minister of Agriculture, Dr. Hassan Arsanjani (an economist), who engineered the land reform (Yeganeh 1985, 76). The land reform law came into effect in January 1962, while

Amini was still the Premier. Arsanjani (b. 1922) died in 1969, just after the second phase of reforms was rolled out; popular belief attributed his death to state conspiracy (Linklater 2013, 336).

With the Shah having taken full control, Arsanjani's plan was incorporated into a series of reforms called the White Revolution. The land reform, introduced in January 1963, was implemented in two major phases. In a nutshell, the reform put a cap of 330 acres on a person's holding and mandated the sale of property beyond that to the state. The land reform also "nationalized common ground, such as forests and rough pasture, amounting to 12 percent of Iran's land surface" (Linklater 2013, 335). This translated into three major rules: no landowner was allowed to hold more than one entire (*shesh-dang*) village (or fractions of villages combined equal to one entire village) but the law excluded "orchards, tea plantations, groves, homesteads, and mechanized areas worked by wage labourers." The property beyond allowable size was to be sold to the state that would compensate the landlords in ten years; the peasant would purchase the land at cost (paid by government) plus 10 percent administration fee through a 15-year payment plan. But only "persons who were members of a village cooperative were eligible for land, and the deeds would remain with the Agricultural Bank as security until all instalments had been paid" (Keddie 1968, 82). The landowning class, however, had sufficient warning as early as 1959, and as such, they had at least a couple of years to conveniently and legally transfer large amounts of land to their family members, even minors, which they then continued to hold notwithstanding the land reform (Keddie 1962, 82). As expected, the landlords retained the most fertile and best located properties to themselves and family members (Nomani 2020), relinquishing the less productive lands. Endowment lands registered to religious institutions (*mowqufat-e amm*) and endowed lands registered to individuals (*mowqufat-e khas*) were exempt from land reform (Nomani 2020). The second phase of the reform in 1968 covered most of the villages excluded from the first phase: "Landlords [were] allowed to retain a maximum of 30 to 150 hectares of non-mechanized land, depending on the region, and [should] dispose of the rest in one of several ways chosen by themselves" (Keddie 1968, 86). These included: renting or selling to peasants, dividing land and receiving an agreed-upon share of the crop, setting up a joint-stock company with peasants, and selling the share to the government (Keddie 1968, 86).

Clearly, land reform changed the age-old relations into capitalist ones. As Nikki Keddie observes (1968, 80), theoretically, the state could have taken the route of instituting cooperative farming but instead pushed for a bourgeois land reform as a way of addressing agricultural unproductivity and diminishing the political power of the old landed class. Keddie is correct, but the land reform pursued multiple objectives. It did weaken the political influence of the old landed class, but this is only half the story; land reform encouraged this class to reinvest in the growing industry, a course of investment encouraged by the state. In practice, the land reform "transformed sharecroppers into family small holders; at the same time, it replaced the traditional landowning class with capitalist entrepreneurs engaged in mechanized commercial agriculture and animal husbandry" (Yeganeh 1985, 74). As such, land reform brought the old landed class, now new industrialists, into the hegemonic orbit of the state as the unrivalled agent of capitalist development. Moreover, the state created a specific form of "land capitalism," a concept that registers my way of understanding the transformation of land in modern Iran. As a case in point, land capitalism is best shown through the dispossession of Turkmens (Chapter 3). In the Iranian case, land capitalism transformed the unproductive tradition of land cultivation into profitable production, and that too not just by mechanizing production. By destroying the unproductive sharecropping, land capitalism intensified the exploitation of peasants either through land dispossession (specifically in the case of Turkmens), or in the case of land reform distribution by increasing the number of rural agricultural workers out of the peasants who had received (and were paying in instalments) unproductive lands, or both. Still, that is not all. Many landlords mechanized agricultural production and employed agricultural workers. Furthermore, city-dwelling capitalists managed to purchase rural lands and turn them into agribusinesses (Nomani 2020). Land capitalism turned fertile lands, like those of the Turkmen region, into highly coveted property whose value was determined by the supply-and-demand rules and marketing efforts of the urban real-estate market. Agricultural land could not be held as investment whose value was expected to increase. Land became capital.

Although the state trumpeted the "abolition of feudalism" in its propaganda that celebrated the distribution of land to peasants, the actual outcome of land reform for changing the fabric of rural Iran has been in dispute. The government spoke of 13,000 to 14,000 out of a total of 49,000 villages where land distribution affected peasants, but according to Hossein Mahdavy, an Iranian economist who participated in studies of the early effects of land reform, the actual number of villages that underwent the land reforms was equal to about 5,000 (quoted in Keddie 1968, 83). Keddie provides an interesting set of figures: "If about 14–16 percent of Iran's villages and villagers were affected by the first phase, and if 40–50 percent of these got no land, it can be seen that about 8 percent of Iran's peasants got land in the first phase," she submits. "In the second phase, relying on official figures we can say that, at most, less than 10 percent of the villagers affected got any land, and that the villagers affected accounted for 60–70 percent of the total, so that another 6–7 percent of the total peasant population received some land; making a grand total of perhaps 14–15 percent of Iran's peasants as new landholders. This is not an insignificant figure, for all its divergence from more extravagant propaganda claims" (Keddie 1968, 87).

In the long term, the land reform resulted in three forms of landownership: the traditional ownership, including family-owned or sharecropping; large-scale capitalist agribusiness that employed wage labour; and state-owned agribusiness, farming companies, and agricultural cooperatives (Yeganeh 1985, 76). The land reform did release labour from land for the purpose of employment in a burgeoning industry. The *khoshneshin* (landless peasant) class grew following the land reform and constituted, according to one source, about one-third of a village (Yeganeh 1985, 78), while Keddie (1968, 79) speaks of 47.5 percent of the rural population that had nothing to sell but their labour, relying on existing landlords or new landowning peasants for work. Since the underproductive agriculture could not absorb the growing rural *khoshneshin*, this class was practically "freed" from land and migrated as unskilled labourers to the cities (Nomani 2020), dwelling in the shantytowns at the outskirts of the cities, unwittingly spurring the Revolution that was to unfold a decade or so later (see Bayat 1997), a consequence of the land reform that neither the Shah nor his American advising think tanks could predict. This is the process that Karl Marx called proletarianization following "primitive accumulation" in England.

The People's Fadai Guerrillas and Land Reform

While the land reform was taking its course, the early nuclei of the People's Fadai Guerrillas (PFG) were in the formation. Speaking of the PFG view of the Shah's reforms may seem irrelevant to this study, but it reveals the PFG's view of the peasants in the 1970s — the view that the Turkmen peasants' movement changed. The 1960s Marxists had rightly realized the significance of the Shah's reforms — the expanding, multi-article White Revolution, which included women's full enfranchisement, and of which the land reform was economically the most substantial article — and had dedicated themselves, as self-didactic researchers, to analyzing them (see Vahabzadeh 2019a, 83–84). The PFG founders, especially the Jazani-Zarifi group, were keen on researching the land reform and its impact on the peasant class because, through the study of national liberation movements in Asia, Africa, and especially Latin America, where in many cases the peasants constituted the bulk of liberation armies, the founders of Fadaiyan needed to probe the revolutionary potential of peasantry. Admittedly, these studies intended to probe whether the objective conditions of revolution were present (OIPFG 1973b). In the early 1970s, revealing its academic and sociological interests, the PFG published a number of studies under the title "Rural Research Series of the OIPFG." To my knowledge, five books were published in the series. After its advent in April 1971, the PFG was entangled in daily combat with security forces, and as the studies suggest, these works must have been done by researchers in the late 1960s, people who were to become future PFG members. Interestingly, one must credit the Social Studies and Research Institute (Mo'asseseh-ye Motale'at va Tahqiqat-e Ejtema'i), attached to the University of Tehran. The Institute was founded in 1958 by Dr. Ehsan Naraghi (1926–2012), a sociologist and former Tudeh supporter who had abandoned Marxism and worked for UNESCO. In the 1960s, the Institute became a hub for dissident intellectuals with interest in social research. The PFG cofounder Puyan was associated with the Institute at some point, and so was Mostafa Sho'aiyan (who briefly joined the PFG in 1973). Interestingly, Sho'aiyan was funded by the Institute to study rural Kerman (Autumn 1966) and rural Shiraz (Summer 1967; Vahabzadeh 2019a, 44, 27). Amazingly, two volumes of the PFG's Rural Studies offer case studies of rural life in Kerman and Fars provinces. There is also a study of Caspian fishermen, the only one not related to land. Logically, while the data appears in the PFG series, it is expected that such data should have existed in the Institute's records as well as in some government office.

The Jazani-Zarifi group, in their 1966 founding treatise, reached the conclusion that the land reform had enfeebled the revolutionary potential of Iranian peasants (Vahabzadeh 2010, 19). If anything, the Siahkal operation in 1971, and the fact that several of the Siahkal guerrillas were captured by frightened peasants, was a practical proof of the conclusion that Zia Zarifi and Jazani had already reached in 1966. I strongly hold the position that although the peasants had occasionally been mobilized, as in the Jangali movement or in particular periods in Kurdistan, Iranian peasants in general have never had a revolutionary potential in the manner perceived by revolutionary Marxism or national liberation movements in Asia (e.g., China, Vietnam), Africa (e.g., Algeria), and Latin America (e.g., Peru and Cuba, among others). This lack of potential may be attributable to the old tradition of sharecropping, which kept the peasants conservatively attached to the land as holders of (projected) interest in cultivation, although most often, this resulted in continued meagre existence for them, in the depths of illiteracy and superstitious worldviews, often living on the verge of losing everything and becoming *khushneshin* — a curious reality that several novels of Gholam Hossein Sa'edi brilliantly capture as surreal. The Iranian peasant could not be farther from the Latin American peasant and its revolutionary potential. Several Iranian Maoist groups (of intellectuals) erred by ineptly following Mao Zedong's path (peasant army) or copying the Latin American experiments and trying to organize rural, even tribal, peoples, and they tragically failed in the 1960s. Iranian peasants therefore had generally no historical agency. Land reform, in part informed by the United States doctrine of "obstacles to [peasant] revolution," removed the traditional dependency on land by rendering the upper echelons of the peasants into small landowning farmers and turning the rest into migrant wage workers. If the peasants were indeed organized in revolutionary action in one unique experience — the Jangali movement — it was because of the specific historical context and the indigenous revolutionary leadership of Mirza Kuchek Khan. The Turkmen peasants also marked another historic exception to this tendency.

The most important text in the series was *On the Land Reform and Its Direct Consequences* (published circa winter 1973). The study provides a detailed account of the two stages of land reform and offers an analysis by using specific jargon to connect the study to the treatise of Ahmadzadeh, which, in turn, was the founding theory of PFG. The study characterizes Iran as a semi-feudal semi-colony, and submits, rather surprisingly, that the land reform did not change this character, although it has dismantled the class alliance of aging feudal and rising comprador bourgeoisie in favour of the hegemony of the latter (OIPFG 1973a, 5–6, 8) — note the use of a Marxist lexicon. Based on case studies of eighty villages in three distinct regions (OIPFG 1973a, 21), the PFG analysis rightly points out the rising role of Iranian economy in the periphery of world capitalism and its concomitant requirements of releasing labour from land and increasing consumer commodities (OIPFG 1973a, 11–14). Peculiarly, though, the PFG analysis attributes women's suffrage (a component of the White Revolution) to imperialist interest in the cheap labour of women — a clear testament to the group's schoolish ideology and lack of understanding of women's political rights (OIPFG 1973a, 16). Contrary to the analyses of PFG cofounders, the treatise still insists that "the revolutionary force of the village comprises of the large layer of semi-proletariat and middle-class peasants" with revolutionary potential that the vanguard should mobilize (OIPFG 1973a, 19, 124–125).

Another study by the Organization of Iranian People's Fadai Guerrillas (OIPFG), published in the summer of 1972, speaks of field research of forty-four villages in Fars province. Having collected data (population, acreage, income, produce, existing modes of landownership), the study submits that the land reform, first, retained large landownership and put peasant land recipients in debt, and second, that the land reform caused the proletarianization of peasants. The village was thus encroached by the comprador bourgeoisie. Informed by formulaic ideology, the study prematurely regards the proletarianization of peasants as a positive factor in the future of a revolutionary movement that contributes to its potential socialist character, a testament to how imperialism intensifies class antagonisms. This, of course, indicates the implicit admission of the peasantry's lack of revolutionary potential. In Fars villages, *nasaq*-holding (land assigned through rent) and *khushneshin* (landless) peasants were increasingly polarized following the land reform. The entrance of the tractor also contributed to the proletarianization of landless peasants, forcing them to migrate to the city in search of work (OIPFG 1973b).

A parallel but less analytical study of twenty-nine villages across Kerman Province also offers detailed data and similar conclusions. It speaks of four types of villages: those where "feudal" relations are still dominant; those with primitive capitalist relations; the ones with capitalist economy; and those that are rug-weaving (OIPFG 1974, 4). In the first type, declining agriculture and rampant poverty were evident, while in the second, peasants who received small pieces of land through the land reform were being crushed by the costs of production, and emerging class polarization was evident. In the third, joint-stock agricultural companies and mechanized agribusiness had changed the village, and in the last category, the village economy was largely based on nonagricultural products such as rugs and handicrafts (OIPFG 1974, 4–10). The program of joint-stock agricultural corporation was ratified in February 1968 in the second phase of land reform and clearly aimed at commercializing large-scale agriculture. In designated areas, the government created large agricultural corporations in a village or several villages by incorporating all small-sized lands and instead giving peasants shares of the corporation relative to the size of their original holding. Then the government ran the corporation through mechanization and the hiring of wage workers (OIPFG 1973a, 77; OIPFG 1973c, 1–2, 6–7). The peasants become shareholders of the company and partner with the government. These units hire rural men but also women and children at half the wages paid to men (OIPFG 1973c, 12). The research published in October 1973 included four case studies, and primarily speaks of such issues of implementation as share discrepancy and corruption or destruction of the traditional socioeconomic fabric of the village (OIPFG 1973c, 14–18, 21). The lengthy appraisal of PFG speaks of the neocolonial nature of such plans aimed at impeding a peasant revolt (OIPFG 1973c, 32–38, 40).

These studies reveal the scholarly interest of Iranian Marxist revolutionaries in the land reform, though the conclusions were slanted by ideological assumptions. While some of the original PFG founders had correctly admitted that the land reform had weakened the revolutionary potential of peasants — a "potential" that I contend did not exist in the first place — based on the studies conducted in the late 1960s, the PFG (in the early 1970s) still wished that land reform would strengthen peasant agency. It did not. The shantytown dwellers in the city outskirts, estranged from their rural origins, became alienated foot soldiers of the

1979 Revolution, mobilized by abject poverty, conditioned by religious beliefs, and without any agency.

In contrast to the latter group and to the erroneous appraisals of the PFG in the early 1970s, the Turkmen peasants' council movement emerged under impossible conditions with vision, agency, and resilience. Chapter 3 discusses the region, its history, and the way the Pahlavis dispossessed the Turkmens of their ancestral lands.

Conclusions

Iranian legal and bureaucratic modernization fundamentally transformed landownership in the country by detaching land from its traditional and largely unproductive forms of ownership and management. Land registry, therefore, realigned land with capitalist production in the decades to come. As elsewhere in the modernizing world, land registry laws and subsequent amendments legalized the above processes. Several key land registry laws and decrees in the 1920s and 1930s aimed at ending the traditional forms of landownership, while in actuality they functioned as means of land dispossession of mostly Iranian farmers and peasants and expropriation by the Pahlavi monarch and other large landowners. As the exclusive and unrivalled agent of modernization, the autocratic state championed this process. Not surprisingly, the entire process rendered Reza Shah — who was previously a salaried officer of the Cossack Brigade from the countryside — the largest landowner and the wealthiest man in the country. Royal land accumulation was such an enormous feat that it needed an entire bureaucratic office (Exclusive Estates) to handle its affairs. In the decades to come, land dispossession became equally a source of riches for the Royal Family and the ruling elite and a source of endless grievances of the rural populace. This is why one cannot simply view this process through the neutral and confounding language of "modernization": what we witness was clearly land dispossession for the purpose of capitalist expansion in the Iranian economy.

The land reform of the 1960s ended the country's "land issue" by reassigning land to capitalist and increasingly large-scale production, thereby releasing rural labour from land and relocating them to the marginal squatters of industrial cities and towns as cheap labourers of boomtown construction or unskilled hands for industrial factories. In other words, the land reform unleashed the process of proletarianization of rural labour, to be employed as unskilled workers in ongoing and future infrastructural or urban expansion plans under capitalist modernization. This process escaped the gaze of neither scholars nor the emerging Marxist guerrillas whose struggle characterized Iranian politics in the 1970s. Despite their analytical errors, the Fadai Guerrillas rightly recognized the capitalist nature of the land reform as a means of bringing Iran into alliance within the capitalist world system.

Chapter 3

Land Is Life

The Prolonged Dispossession of Turkmens

The plateaux and meadows [of Yamut region in Plains of Turkmen] sometimes offer such vistas that leave painters and poets with awe and wonder.

...

The lands of Yamut are indescribably fertile. And the work of peasants entails no great toil. Every clan residing in an area, in the surrounding meadow, has a plot as their personal or clan yurt. They identify the size of plots and lightly plow it using a horse before sowing the seed. At the harvest, men and women cooperate, collecting the produce of obeh.

...

The grass of the valley of Gorgan River or on the banks of Qarasu River grow so tall and thick that they are used to fatten horses and animals.

— Mohammad Ali Qorkhanchi, *Elite Swordsmen*

IN ORDER TO FULLY UNDERSTAND THE Turkmen Council Movement of 1979, we needed to attend the long history of Turkmen dispossession within the process of authoritarian state foundation and its land appropriation and land reform. The Chapter 2 offered the relevant aspects of this process in due detail. This chapter ushers in long history to the short history of Turkmen land dispossession, as well as language and cultural repression and assimilation of non-Persians including Turkmens by the Pahlavi state. I demonstrate how, since the 1930s, Royal dispossession sine qua non prefigured the grievances that led to the Turkmen council movement under the revolutionary conditions of 1979. I begin by offering brief notes that intend to situate the Turkmen people geographically and historically in Iran, before attending to the highlights from the involvement of Turkmen people in the movements of the early twentieth century. Next, I will discuss the dispossession and repression of Turkmens during the late Pahlavi era. I end the chapter with remarks on cultural domination.

Situating Iranian Turkmens

Originating in Central Asia, the Turkic-speaking people that gradually branched off and became today's Turkmens are spread across a vast area that includes parts of today's western China to regions in Russia, Afghanistan, Uzbekistan, Tajikistan, Iran, Turkey, and northern Syria, in addition to the Republic of Turkmenistan. Turkmens are descendants of Oghuz Turks (originally western Turks, occupying the vast region to the east of the Caspian Sea and encompassing the Aral Sea) and the names of their tribes and clans have Oghuz origins (CPCTP 1985, 14). After the Islamic conquest, the Turkmens converted to Islam, and a majority are Sunnis of the Hanafi school of jurisprudence. The Seljuks of Central Asia were also Oghuz Turks, which, at the time, were called Turkmens (CPCTP 1985, 10). They occupied a vast area and created the Turko-Persian Great Seljuk Empire (1037–1194) in a territory that stretched from Central Asia to Anatolia. The time when Turkmens first settled in the Caspian region that includes today's Iran is unknown; however, they were reported to have lived in these areas at least since the Seljuk Empire, for longer than a millennium (Gorgani 1979, 4, 6, 10). Turkmen migrations are attributed to tribal wars. The Mongolian onslaught in the thirteenth and fourteenth centuries pushed the Turkmens farther to the west. Consequently, the Turkmen language is one of the many Turkic languages and dialects that spread from the Uyghurs in China to the Turks of Turkey. Specifically, Turkmen language is from Oghuz group of Turkic languages, and in Iran it consists of several dialects (Knüppel 2000). By the fourteenth century, the Turkmens finally settled in their current region (CPCTP 1985, 18). Turkmens were originally nomadic peoples. They perpetually sought pastural lands for their herds and engaged in raids of villages and agrarian settlements throughout the centuries.

Political developments in recent centuries had an impact on Turkmens of Iran. The Safavid Empire (1501–1736) was the direct successor of the Turkmen dynasties of Aq Qoyunlu and Qara Qoyunlu, but later, Safavid Shah Tahmasp disbanded these tribes because of their nomadic culture and in the interests of strengthening the authority of the central government (Lambton 1953, 106). Turkmens of the current location suffered through the Safavid imposition of the Shi'i religion on Sunni Turkmens (Salaman 1980, 57). According to Lambton (1953, 141), in return for the Turkmen support for Aqa Mohammad Khan (1742–1797; reign: 1789–1797), the founder of the Qajar dynasty (1789–1925), Mohammad Khan allowed Turkmens "to move from the banks of the Atrak [River] into the Plains of Gorgan and gave them as *tuyul* the villages on the banks of the Qara Su." The raiding custom of Turkmen tribes had caused havoc for the region's villagers and continued until the early twentieth century and caused great trouble for the authorities (Lambton 1953, 141), including Qajar governments. Turkmen raiders often disappeared across the unguarded borders to the north (Lambton 1953, 385), until Reza Shah conclusively ended such raids by forced settlement, militarization of the region, and later land dispossession.

It must be noted that the warrior spirit and raiding custom of Turkmens entailed also kidnapping Persians, especially women, taking them across the borderland between Persia and the Russian Empire, and selling them in central Asian towns. Because these continuous raids during the late nineteenth century took place in the *borderland* between the two countries, the raids, conversely, urged Iran and Russia to agree on fixed borders. Moreover, one particular raid in November 1905 and the kidnapping of Quchan girls for slave trade across the border caused national uproar in Qajar Iran and pushed forward the cause of constitutionalism (Najmabadi 1995).

Today's Turkmens live in culturally diverse regions and have often mixed with other peoples, as they are one of the oldest cultural groups from Central Asia with diverse tribal branches and with expansive migratory routes over the centuries. The northern part of the Turkmen territory was annexed to the Russian Empire between 1868 and 1885 (CPCTP 1985, 20), now the Republic of Turkmenistan. As a result of this annexation, the Turkmens of Iran were set upon an entirely different historical trajectory in comparison with the Turkmens of the north who, as an agrarian people, experienced the Bolshevik revolution and the subsequent state-forced collectivization of land, the collapse of the Soviet Union, independence, the post-Soviet authoritarian state, and cultural revival. The exact number of Turkmens in Iran within a decade or so before and after the 1979 revolution remains undetermined; scholars report different figures, including 800,000 circa 1980 (Salaman 1980, 56), approximately 400,000 in the late 1990s (Knüppel 2000), or between half-a-million and one million (Arakelova 2015, 279). The unexplainable discrepancy is partly due to internal migration to the Turkmen region and the lack of an accurate census.

Geographically, the Plains of Turkmen or Turkman Sahra in Iran is located between 54.15–56.30 longitude and 36–38 latitude, stretching within the current provinces of Golestan (created in 1997) and North Khorasan (created in 2004). In 1979, Turkman Sahra was located within Mazandaran and Khorasan provinces. The Plains has an area of 16,375 square kilometres or 1,637,500 hectares. To the north, it stretches to Atrak River and the border with Turkmenistan, while to the south, it reaches Shah Marz, a stretched mound of earth that, in the nineteenth century, separated the Turkmen and Persian regions. In the east it reaches the town of Bojnord and in the west to the Caspian Sea (see Maps 1 and 2). In previous geological ages, this region was under the sea. The elevation of the Plains of Turkmen is below the Caspian Sea level, but it progressively rises as one moves to the east, toward the town of Gonbad Kavus, reaching 38 metres above sea level. At some point in previous geographic ages, the Plains of Turkmen were filled with wetlands and ponds that gradually dried out, leaving behind a soil rich with minerals and nitrogen, ideal for agriculture. Continued annual precipitation and the subsequent deluge caused rivers like Gorgan, Atrak, and Qarasu to be formed (Gorgani 1979, 1–3; LSTP, 9; Salaman 1980, 56).

The term "Turkman Sahra" is an intentionally politically loaded term, as it is a term used by Turkmen activists and no state has officially recognized it. With the founding of modern Iran, all regions of historical dwelling of national minorities have been divided into provinces by the state, and interregional migrations have complicated the issue of identification with land. Consequently, today's Turkmen region has become demographically diverse, and while Turkmen language remains the main language of the region, Mazandarani, Persian, Azeri Turkish, and Baluchi are also spoken in particular districts in the region. Modern Iranian states have always had deep anxieties about protecting the constructed nationalist narrative and the propagated identification of the nation with the centralized state. To achieve that, the state has been suppressing claims of peoplehood. This is why the Turkmen region is divided across the provinces, and the recognition of the Plains of Turkmen as a political unit with Gonbad Kavus as its centre was one of the demands of the Turkmen council movement (LSTP, 9). To complicate matters, in the twentieth century (until 1991), the Iranian state — both under monarchy and the Islamic Republic — has always regarded the Turkmen region, and thereby the Turkmen movements, in terms of state security because of it being situated along the borders of the Soviet Republic of Turkmenistan at the time. The Islamic regime exploited the border issue to crack down on the Turkmens' movement after the Revolution (as we see in Chapter 4).

Gonbad Kavus stands at the heart of the Turkmen regions. The modern town was built over the small town of Gonbad Qabus in 1926 with Reza Shah's ascent to power. It was designed by German experts. This was the site of the ancient city of Hirkan, later renamed Jorjan. Jorjan was the capital city of the regional Caspian dynasty of Ziyarian (or Ziyarid; 928–1043 CE). Gonbad Kavus (Gonbad Qabus) was named after the tallest brick tower in the world (53 metres), built by Ziyarian and called the Qabus Ibn Voshmgir Historical Tower. The ancient town was destroyed during the Mongol onslaught in the Khwarazmian Empire (1219–1221). The modern town was cleverly designed to embrace the tower that stands atop an elevated, grass-covered rectangular knoll within the National Garden (Bagh-e Melli) so that the tower shines at the heart of the town like an amber signet pointing at the sky. According to one source, the town's first public library (the birthplace of the Turkmen council movement; see Chapter 4) was founded in 1965 on the efforts of Barkley Moore, a volunteer with the USA Peace Corps (founded by President John F. Kennedy in 1961) in collaboration with the educated citizens of Gonbad Kavus on the second floor of the Mohammadi shopping centre. It later moved to what was then Pahlavi Street near the famous tower. For his efforts, Moore was awarded the Honorary Citizen of Gonbad Kavus (Khazaineh 2020). Unbeknownst to Dr. Moore, some of his pupils would turn out to be Turkmen activists more than a decade later (see DCM2, 395).

Traditionally, before the twentieth century, Iran's Turkmens were able to produce grains (wheat, barley, sesame seeds) prolifically due to fertile land, and they sold the extras in Astarabad (called Gorgan today) whence their product would be taken to Mazandaran and to the Caucasus. The tribes' other source of revenue was the sale of sheep and goats. Turkmens were (and are) internationally renowned pedigree horse breeders (and horse racers); they sold horses to regions as far as Europe. In addition, they sold Turkmen-style rugs and handicrafts known for their geometric motifs and vivid red colours. The cash returned to the Turkmens as gold and silver and was often kept in the form of women's elaborate ornaments (Gorgani 1979, 16, 19).

Turkmens of Iran belong to one of two major groups: Yamut and Goklan (Gorgani 1979, 15; Qorkhanchi 1981, 34; Lambton 1953, 160; Salaman 1980, 56;). Lambton (1953, 160) shows that "Each tribe was composed of several *oubeh* [*obeh*], each of which had its leader, who held a private or hereditary *yurt*." The Yamuts consist of two large clans: Sharaf Jafarbay (about 8,000 families living around Bandar Turkmen) and Aqabay or Chuni (about 7,000 families living around Gorgan and Gonbad Kavus) circa 1980s. The Goklans consist of six groups: Qa`i, Bayandor, Qoroq, Aydarvish, Chefer Bigdeli, and Yanfaq. They live on the eastern heights around Gorgan and Atrak rivers (Salaman 1980, 56–57). Turkmen society is patrilineal and patriarchal, with an elderly man as the head of the extended family. There has existed, as does still, gendered division of labour, with the women assigned domestic tasks related to the *oy* (a decorated and movable family house made with lightweight interwoven wooden strips and straws, covered with felt), food preparation, rug-weaving, and the care of domestic animals, and of course, rearing children, while men attend to farming, herding, and trading. The domains of activity and socialization are also strictly gendered. The *oy* constitutes the basic unit of social organization, and a Turkmen family lives in an *oy* (or *alachiq*), and the complex of several *oys* constitutes an *obeh* (village), which, with the transformation of traditional ownership, has now become a village with sedentary residence (Kamali and Arfa 1992, 4, 9; see also LSTP, 12).

It is important to note that, according to Lambton (1953: 160), "There was no leader over the whole tribe; when necessary, the elders of the *oubeh, shaykhs*, and old men assembled for consultation and decided upon action in accordance with the views of the prominent members, elders and even of the ordinary members of the tribe." This traditional lack of hereditary khans and hierarchies, as we see in the next section, provided the culturally sanctioned foundation of modern councils in the Turkmen peasant movement.

Turkmens Between the Constitutional Revolution and the Rise of Reza Shah

I have reviewed the importance and impact of the Constitutional Revolution (1906–1911) in Chapter 1. During the Constitutional Revolution, the Turkmens of Iran were politically split. Sources about Turkmen activities at this time are scarce. Certain Turkmen tribes supported Mohammad Ali Shah Qajar who had staged a coup and his troops had shelled the constitutionalist Majles. When constitutional forces fought back and finally defeated the Shah, he found asylum in Russia. Later, the Shah who still dreamt of returning to power relied on certain Turkmen tribal forces for military support, but these were eventually defeated by constitutionalist forces. On the other hand, urban and educated Turkmens sent tribal warriors to support the constitutionalist forces (PSRI nd; see THD, 68, 75, 76, 78). Existing evidence, albeit scattered, registers Turkmen support: a telegram (dated December 7, 1908) confirms that 2,000 Turkmen volunteers from Astarabad prepared to move to Tehran to help the constitutional forces (THD, 68). A report (dated June 27 1910) also registers a telegram by Yamut and Goklan tribal leaders stating, "We, 40,000 strong Turkmen families, with our strong arms and drawn swords, have held our lives (heads) in our hands to reinforce the edifice of constitutionalism and support its foundations" (THD, 73).

Janet Afary (1996) rightly characterizes the Constitutional Revolution (Chapter 1) as an anti-colonial revolution. It brought a glimmer of hope for the masses, the peasants included. No wonder, then, that with the Constitutional Revolution's failure to usher rapid and meaningful change — epitomized by the ascent of Reza Khan to power and then to the throne — Iran experienced intermittent autonomous movements in Gilan, Azerbaijan, and Khuzestan, as well as a Kurdish revolt. The Turkmen region also witnessed an uprising. In Gilan, a short-lived, autonomous Soviet Republic was founded (1920–1921) through the precarious alliance of the Jangali movement and Iran's communists. The movement directly addressed decolonization and moved toward the distribution of land (see Chaqueri 1995) but was defeated by government forces supported by the British. This movement — the most extensive and sophisticated of uprisings between the Constitutional Revolution and the ascent of Reza Shah to the throne — clearly indicates that constitutionalism, a prominently urban revolution, did not properly address the question of land. In fact, the Jangali movement was a direct response to the lack of revolution of agrarian classes in the nineteenth century. Bizhan Jazani (2009, 138) observes that the lack of participation of peasants in the Constitutional Revolution meant that the "land issue" continued to persist.

In Tabriz, the heart of Azerbaijan, the short-lived city-republic of Azadistan (1921) directly addressed the failure of the Constitutional Revolution and aimed to restore its democratic and participatory aspects and maintain security. This experiment, too, was crushed by government troops within a couple of months. In 1924, after a long career in political manoeuvres and collusions with the British, the Qajars, and neighbouring Arab states, influential Sheikh Khaz'al, the separatist grand chief of Bani Ka'b tribe in today's Khuzestan Province, declared autonomy in major parts of the province, now renamed Arabestan, but was eventually captured by Reza Khan. Unlike the first two movements, this uprising was not a response to the constitutional movement and was about power and control over the region where, just over a decade previously, the British had drilled for and discovered Persian oil (Amanat 2017, 441–444). Lastly, backed by an army of tribal warriors, Kurdish tribal chief Isma'il Aqa Shikak, better known as Simko Shikak, also took control of the Kurdish region in northwestern Iran bordering the Ottoman Empire and around Lake Urmia from 1918 to 1922. His tribal revolt was crushed by Reza Khan as well, though it had elements of Kurdish nationalism that later developed into the Kurdish nationalist movement after the Second World War (Jahani Asl 2017, 170–212).

At this historic junction, a short-lived Turkmen revolt also challenged the authority of the nascent, central government. Iranian Turkmens, living in the region that bordered the then Bolshevik state, were not only impacted by the revolution to the north, but also by the aforementioned Jangali movement (1915–1921) led by Mirza Kuchek Khan (1880–1921) and the subsequent Soviet Socialist Republic of Iran (1920–1921; Chaqueri 1995). But the impact was limited due to the socioeconomic underdevelopment of the Turkmen region. Sources diverge on the relations between the Jangalis and Turkmens: one source denies any solid evidence indicating contacts between the two (Atayev 1987, 40). Yet, according to a historical report, the Turkmens sent a two-person delegation via the sea to Kuchek Khan, and in return, Jangali representatives were received warmly by Yamut, Jafarbay, and Atabay leaders. Reportedly, the Turkmens sent arms to the Jangalis. Mirza's representative had purportedly declared to his Russian (Soviet) interlocutor that the Turkmens had supported Kuchek Khan and would stay with the Jangali movement (THD, 155–156). In any case, in 1920 Turkmen peoples were largely organized around tribal alliances, and their revolt was against the central government's attempt to disarm the Turkmens and impose taxes (as per the government's policy of forcing nomadic peoples into sedentary residence). These tribes allegedly asked for assistance from Soviet Turkmens (Atayev 1987, 39) to no avail. Calling this revolt a fight for "liberation" (Atayev 1987) is far-fetched and ideologically propelled. Without any long-term objectives, these revolts were chiefly tribal raids and uprisings against local lords, governors, and authorities. The revolt was led by a cleric named Osman Akhund from the Jafarbay tribe (THD, 173–174). The Turkmen tribal elders convened, resolved their own conflicts, and organized themselves in 1922. The unification of Turkmen tribes worried Reza Shah, given that a Soviet Republic had been established north of the border. Agents of the state succeeded in part to create schisms among revolting tribes. The Turkmens demanded the right to keep their guns and patrol the area themselves instead of Gendarmerie forces. When the negotiations failed, the government deployed four columns to the region to face about 4,500 Turkmen warriors. The army took the town of Gonbad Qabus in 1925 and several leaders of the revolt escaped to the Soviet Republic of Turkmenistan (Mofidi 2011). The army disarmed the Turkmens, collecting 6,000 weapons (PSRI nd; see THD, 204–213), and the revolt faded away.

The diversity of the movements at this time notwithstanding, their common denominator was the weakness of the post-constitutional state, a phenomenon that the founding of the Pahlavi dynasty intended to overcome. The Constitutional Revolution, in retrospect, left a paradoxical legacy: its democratic spirit only produced an authoritarian state.

The Appropriation of Turkmen Lands

The roots of Turkmen land dispossessions in modern Iran must be traced back to Reza Shah's reign and the enactment of multiple property registry laws aimed at destroying traditional landownerships — state- or individual-owned as well as communally owned — to ensure capitalist relations over land, turning land into a commodity.

Beginning in the 1930s, the encroachment of Iran's neocolonial state on Turkmen ancestral lands was launched by Reza Shah who especially eyed the fertile lands of his native region of Mazandaran. Through systematic land dispossession, the traditional socioeconomic structure of Turkmen society began to change rapidly. The land reform in the 1960s, a requirement for the state's transformation of the sclerotic, traditional agriculture into capitalist enterprises and the freeing of labour from land, intensified land grab in the Turkmen region. In researching this subject, however, we inevitably rely on fragmentary data, most likely because of little interest in the subject of Iranian modernization through so-called legalized land appropriation. What is known, however, is that land reform prepared Turkmen land for large-scale, mass-produced agricultural production. The state also significantly damaged the livelihood of Turkmen fishermen by instituting the state's own, centralized fishing corporation known as Shilat (LSTP, 21–22). What is more, with large-scale agriculture firmly in place, beginning in the early 1960s, the state encouraged the migration of workers from Sistan and Baluchistan Province, known as the Zabolis and also Baluchis (LSTP, 31–32). These migrants constituted lower class rural workers in the region and remained isolated from the Turkmens due to their cultural, religious, and linguistic differences.

Fortunately, we have access to the singular but forgotten work of legal research and advocacy by Dr. Mansour Gorgani (1928–1993). He was born in Tehran to a family originally from Gorgan, the capital city of today's Golestan Province, the province in which the majority of Turkmens live and where the Plains of Turkmen is partially located. He was a lawyer who also held a PhD in Economics. Gorgani returned to his parental city of Gorgan and the Plains of Turkmen in the 1960s to work as a lawyer-advocate and to represent Turkmen peasants whose lands were taken by the Pahlavi *Amlak* bureau. Gorgani was also a farmer and helped create peasants' cooperatives in the region. Unpublishable under the monarchy, Gorgani's 1979 book, *The Land Issue in the Plains of Turkmen*, registers the process of land dispossession and the peasants' fighting back based on selected legal documents, land registry records, and court cases to which Gorgani had access as the Turkmen plaintiffs' lawyer.

Let us look at the early twentieth-century landownership among the Turkmens. Until the mid-1930s, the Turkmen lands were communally and tribally owned, and shared ownership was also common. In other words, "feudal" relations had not extended into the Plains of Turkmen. Turkmen clans (*tavayef*) owned specific lands whose boundaries — often marked by natural landmarks like rivers, creeks, and hills — were known and mutually respected by the clans-peoples. This specific piece of land was called a *yurt*. Within a *yurt*, ownership was common and shared (*moshtarak va mosha'*). In terms of production, Turkmens were traditionally divided into two groups: *chamur* and *charva*. The *chamur* were sedentary farmers while engaging in limited sheep and goat herding; the *charva* were nomadic herds-people, while they also had limited land cultivation. The objective of this economic system was to obtain subsistence through self-sufficient households of an *obeh* (village) and sell the extra produce or animal products on local markets or to city merchants. While the Turkmens did not pay land-use or pasture-use fees among themselves, they did charge fees to non-Turkmens, and the Persian herds owners often paid to use Turkmen fertile lands (Gorgani 1979, 11–12; Qorkhanchi 1981, 34; Salaman 1980, 57).

As mentioned earlier (Chapter 2), the first land registry law that legalized capitalist property ownership happened in 1922, only to be expanded by the law of 1926 (Mirdar, Arabani, and Soltani Ahmadi 2019, 117), as well as the subsequent amendments to the law. The law of January 7, 1934 required the state to liquidate all *khaliseh* (state-owned) lands. This is when in the vicinities of the city of Astarbad (Gorgan today), there were 130 *khaliseh* villages, none of them located in the Turkmen lands. They were sold through state auctions, but since the only buyer of these lands was the intimidating agent of Reza Shah, these lands were sold to the (Shah's agent's) lowest bid (Gorgani 1979, 24–25). To show how the state auction benefited Reza Shah, let us refer to a (different) study that mentions the number of the aforementioned *khaliseh* villages to be 125. These lands were bought for Reza Shah at the price of 750,000 rials while its real value at the time was 2.5 million rials (Mirdar, Arabani, and Soltani Ahmadi 2019, 114). As regards the land grab in the Gorgan area, I found a historical document in the personal archives of the late historian Cosroe Chaqueri: a letter from British Legation in Tehran to Great Britain Foreign Affairs (dated November 28, 1935) that reports Reza Shah's "land-devouring greed" and land takeover "without paying a dinar" ("A Document" 1979, 127–131; see also Gorgani 1979, 22–23). To register the Shah's greed, let us foreground the amazing case where, according to the registry record of Land Registry

Office of Gonbad Kavus, the entire town of Gonbad Kavus (*shesh-dang arseh-ye qasabeh-ye Gonbad Kavus*), the heart of Turkmen peoples, was "assigned in peace" (*solh*), on September 19, 1941, to "His Majesty Mohammad Reza Shah Pahlavi for the price of 2.5 ounces of crystalized sugar (*yek sir nabat*)!... (Registry No. 6538, Office No. 7, Isfahan)" ("Gonbad Kavus" 1979, 149–150). This happened when Reza Shah was on his way out of the country and (forced) into exile, so this "property" was "transferred" (*solh*) for that nominal value (2.5 ounces of crystalized sugar) to His Majesty Mohammad Reza Shah Pahlavi. The town was immediately thereafter transferred to the Iranian state on the Shah's decree (*farman*) on September 21, 1941 (note the dates; "Gonbad Kavus" 1979, 150), but the detail of the transfer remains unknown. Interestingly, a Majles ratification (*maddeh-ye vahedeh*) dated 10 May 1954 (after the 1953 coup) the entire (*sheh-dang*) of Gonbad Kavus is transferred to Mohammad Reza Shah! ("Gonbad Kavus" 1979, 150) Clearly, no distinction between public lands and Royal Estates existed under monarchy.

According to the land registry law of February 10, 1933, the Shah was entitled to register land to his name. This is when the Bureau of Exclusive Estates was established. In the Turkmen lands, Reza Shah also bought four *khaliseh* villages (Mirdar, Arabani, and Soltani Ahmadi 2019, 114). But Gorgani (1979, 108), being a lawyer, attests that legally none of the villages and lands in Turkman Sahra were within or overlapped the 130 *khaliseh* pieces registered in Gorgan. In any case, the encroachment of Reza Shah soon led to his takeover of Turkmen lands in Aqqala, Gomesh Tapeh, Qajaq, and Goklan. This was not simply a case of a "new owner" but in fact a "new mode of ownership" altogether that disturbed the Turkmens' traditional relation to land and labour. This transformation forced Turkmen farmers into becoming agricultural labourers, often with low or no pay, as well as construction workers in nearby towns. Herdsmen would now have to pay user fees for pastures to the Pahlavi Estates office (Gorgani 1979, 25–28). According to Gorgani (1979, 28), this system (1) destroyed communal ownership, (2) created a "free" labour force, and (3) forced Turkmens to expend their savings (in the form of ornamental gold) to bribe or pay rents to the authorities. Capitalist land ownership in fact impoverished the Turkmens who had previously lived off these lands in a sustainable way. In the years to come, the now landless Turkmens, deprived of their agricultural and pastural revenue, increasingly engaged in carpet weaving and handicraft production to generate household income. This labour was exclusively that of women — child, adult, elderly — of the *obeh* (Gorgani 1979, 6). One can safely assume that carpet weaving must have intensified the patriarchal relations within the family. Accordingly, land dispossession has a gendered component that a fresh study can reveal and register, but it is important to note that while the Iranian state moved toward greater implementation of women's rights in the 1960s — for instance, women's suffrage, family protection law, and increased women's education — modernization and capitalism, being gendered practices, only strengthened the patriarchal and androcentric power over working and rural women in various ways.

It must be mentioned that by dispossessing the Turkmens, Reza Shah also intended to forcefully settle the Turkmens and transform their semi-nomadic existence into a completely sedentary one (Salaman 1980, 58). The forced sedentary life damaged the Turkmens' traditional pastural activity and paved the way for takeover of agricultural land by non-Turkmens, beginning in the reign of Reza Shah (LSTP, 16). Although land dispossession destroyed the traditional governance of Turkmens, as we see in Chapter 4, the spirit of the tradition returned through the modern vision of the Turkmen council system of production and self-governance. Moreover, when Reza Shah forced the sedentarization of Turkmens as a part of his authoritarian government of regions, he and his advisers could not have imagined that this process would reinforce solidarity among the Turkmens that decades later provided the foundation for the Turkmen council movement. The dialectics of history work in uncanny ways.

Transference and Aggressive Privatization

The Allies invaded Iran and forced Reza Shah into abdication on September 16, 1941. The next day, on September 17, 1941, the Majles held a closed session to discuss Reza Shah's estates and wealth. On the afternoon session of Majles on the same day, 22-year-old Mohammad Reza Shah was sworn in as the new Shah. Two days later, all political prisoners were released. Reza Shah had already cashed out a lot of the land he possessed while still owning numerous estates. Because of the rushed nature of his removal from the throne, on his way out of Iran and into exile, Reza Shah issued a transference memo (*hebeh-nameh*; literally, "gift-letter") in Isfahan. He stated that because the country's development was his primary concern, his estates served as models of management and growth for others, and now he wished to transfer them all to his son at the price of "10 grams [actually, 2.5 ounces, as shown above] of crystalized sugar"! In turn, young Mohammad Reza Shah issued a statement declaring that those who might have claims over these estates were entitled to file proper complaints with the authorities (Gorgani 1979, 32–33). After Reza Shah's departure, the Turkmens began to speak out publicly about the way they had been robbed of their lands. They did not hesitate to rally to government offices to voice their grievances (see THD, 334, 358–359).

Mohammad Reza was a young Shah with precarious power reigning over an occupied country. It is not surprising that he wished to distance himself from his father's image as an autocratic ruler and propagate the public image of a modern, just ruler. On May 22, 1942, the Majles ratified a new law called Remittance of Entrusted Estates (Esterdad-e Amlak-e Vagozari) that gave claimants 6 months to file complaints with a special commissioner endowed with the power to issue a decision. As a result, the former Bureau of Exclusive Estates (Edareh-ye Amlak Ekhtesasi) was transferred to the government and renamed the Bureau of Entrusted/Remittance of Estates (Edareh-ye Amlak-e Vagozari). The legislation of 1942 held that the commissioner's decision was final, and it could not be appealed, although the decision could be revisited within ten days of issuance (Gorgani 1979, 34–35). The fact that this law did not allow any appeals indicates that the process was meant to be rushed by design, so the issue of disputed estates could be settled quickly. More interestingly, though, was the fact that this new legislation was announced in the newspapers in a country in which most people were illiterate or had little access, in the age of print media, to such information (see Gorgani 1979, 97). Consequently, the whole legislation had a class bias: most of the claimants ended up being from the educated landed class, and the average peasant or farmer simply missed out on the six-month deadline, as the news hardly reached the countryside.

However, while some Turkmens missed the deadline, the majority of Turkmen *yashulis* (elders) filed claims. But the problem was also a colonial one: communal ownership was not eligible to file landownership claims because the law recognized owners only as persons. This forced the Turkmens to nominate a few *yashulis* to claim ownership on behalf of the *obeh*. As a result, after many years of legal battles, the villages of Qajaq area were won back. After victory, the *yashulis* went to a land registry office and signed a document affirming that the land belonged to every member of the Qajaq tribe. This is how Turkmens tried to revive their ancestral ways under colonial-legal conditions. Most other Turkmen tribes also succeeded in taking their lands back (Gorgani 1979, 37–39).

Let us pause here and return to 1941: with the Soviet invasion of northern Iran during the Second World War, the Red Army occupied the Turkmen lands. During the occupation, the Shah's agents had vacated the region and their estates, and this gave an opportunity for Turkmens to take over their ancestral land. For a short time, collective ownership returned, and Turkmen farmers sold their crops to the Red Army (Gorgani 1979, 28–29). History is not without irony: Turkmens gained the right to their lands only under occupation!

At this time, while the northern regions of Iran were under the Red Army occupation, in Khorasan Province twenty pro-Tudeh Party and left-leaning army officers staged a mutiny on 15 August 1945. Two members of the Officers' Organization of the Tudeh Party of Iran led this mutiny. The officers and their units left Mashhad where they were stationed, drove north to Quchan, and then east to the Turkmen towns of Bojnord and Gonbad Kavus. On the way, they disarmed Gendarmerie posts and acquired weapons. In Gonbad Kavus, they were met with the fierce force of the Gendarmerie under orders from Tehran that the mutineers must be crushed at any and all costs. Many of the renegade officers were killed and the mutiny was conclusively suppressed on August 20, 1945. The fleeing and wanted officers hid for several weeks in Turkmen villages (arranged by Turkmen officers) until they managed to leave the area (Shafai 1986, 67–132; Tafreshian 1988, 63–91). The surviving officers mostly joined the Azerbaijan Democrat Party (Ferqeh-ye Demokrat-e Azerbaijan), founded in Tabriz on September 3, 1945, under Red Army occupation. These officers were active with the autonomous National Government of Azerbaijan (Azerbaijan Milli Hekumati) until its defeat by the Iranian army on December 13, 1946.

Although the objective of the mutineers was to connect with Turkmens and stage an uprising by distributing arms among Turkmen tribesmen (Abrahamian 1982, 336; Shafai 1986, 66), they had no organic connection with the Turkmen people. As a commander of the mutiny reflects, "It was only later that I was convinced that what we did on those days was rushed, unthought, and opportunistic" (Tafreshian 1988, 64). Ervand Abrahamanian (1982, 336–337) shows that "Although in later years the Tudeh lauded the rebels as 'national heroes,' at the time it refused to be associated with the rebellion" (see also THD, 370–374). This adventurist mutiny had no impact on Turkmen society and did not contribute to the struggles of Turkmens or improve their conditions. The Tudeh Party was active in the Turkmen region during this time and published the periodical *Gorgan* and the biweekly *Turkmen Sesi* (Turkmen's Voice; THD, 342–345, 350–352; 365, 375–377, 381–387; 396–397, 404–408, 420–423). Tudeh activists staged a rally celebrating May Day in Gonbad Kavus in 1946 (THD, 403). One historic incident that became a part of the collective memory of the Iranian literati is when the armed forces raided the Tudeh Party club in Gomesh Tepeh on August 16, 1946. They shot pro-Tudeh Turkmen teacher Aba Aba`i who died later due to his injuries (THD, 383–386). Aba`i was immortalized in a celebrated and widely read poem by the great Iranian poet Ahmad Shamlu entitled "Of the Wound of Aba`i's Heart" (1951): "Among you / tell me / among you who / is honing / Aba`i's blade / for the day of vengeance?"

On February 4, 1949, an assassination attempt at the Shah's life on the University of Tehran campus provided him with a unique opportunity to grab significant power. The occupying Allied forces had left the country, and now the Shah had a chance to not only defeat the landed aristocracy, outlaw the Tudeh Party, and crush civil society associations and labour unions, but also increase his constitutional powers. The latter he achieved by having Majles ratify amendments to the Iranian Constitution (see Chaqueri nd). Later, on June 22, 1949, Majles ratified the return of all of the deceased Shah's properties to Mohammad Reza Shah (*madeh-ye vahedeh mosavab-e*; 20 Tir 1328), a gross contradiction of the young Shah's previous pledge that he would return his fathers' estates to their rightful owners. At that time, many Turkmen lands had been returned to them legally, but at this time, agents of the government appeared in the Turkmen region again, demanding interests and land-use fees for the previous years. Turkmen farmers resisted. At this time, the Bureau of Pahlavi Estates was managed by Asadollah Alam (Gorgani 1979, 40–42), the future Minister of Interior, Minister of Royal Court, and the Shah's confidant.

What is more, having the state machinery at his disposal, the Shah pushed for acquiring quick cash for his lands. According to Gorgani (1979, 59), the decree of 1950 ruled that 2,000 villages in possession of the Shah be distributed among the peasants. I must note that the word "distribution" (*taqsim-e arazi*) is a misnomer: the Shah in fact *sold* the lands he distributed (see "Gonbad Kavus" 1979) — in many cases, not surprisingly, to the lands' rightful owners! This meant that the Shah could now cash out a part of his estates. This process lasted until 1958, and according to one source, about 25,000 peasants received land (OIPFG 1973a, 33).

But we need to take a closer look. In Turkmen lands, the so-called distribution was done through lottery: pieces of land 4 to 15 hectares in size were *sold* to Turkmens, but often such patches of land had no access to water and the buyer did not have the finances to develop the land. In contrast, seized lands, 50 to 1,000 hectares in size, were sold to the generals and officers of the armed forces who had proven their loyalty to the regime in the 1953 coup (Gorgani 1979, 97–98). As a case in point, some villages in the Qara Qaniqmaz area were distributed by lottery, but the "surplus" land was auctioned and bought by members of the Royal Court. The pastures were totally taken over by non-Turkmens, resulting in major setbacks for their herding life and revenue (Gorgani 1979, 99). The Turkmens all had *dastarmi* ownership, which is a time-honoured tradition in the Gorgan, Gonbad Kavus, and Plains of Turkmen region that regarded ownership in terms of custom that, in Turkmen view, superseded land registry. But in these cases, the Pahlavi *Amlak* agents, backed by Gendarmerie personnel, forcefully occupied these lands and ousted the Turkmens.

The Shah could have chosen to simply sell the Turkmen's own lands back to them at this time; Turkmen farmers were willing to accept this gross injustice and purchase their own traditional lands for good. But the objective of distribution was twofold: Turkmen dispossession and reallocation of these lands as a form of reward to the monarch's cronies. Many of the regime's favourites and generals gained huge patches of fertile land. Reportedly, these included Generals Oveisi (1,400 hectares), Badrehe`i (1,500 hectares), and Qarabaghi (1,200 hectares; LSTP: 25; for landowners around Voshmgir Dam alone seventy-five out of ninety-four or 79.8 percent of registered owners were military officers; see also "Plains of Turkmen" 1979). The Pahlavi Estates sold the lands that were still under the Shah's title by instalments. But because the Shah wanted quick cash, he had Bank Omran (Bank of Development) pay him cash in full by borrowing from the country's Central Bank and take over the instalments of the peasants (Gorgani 1979, 59–61). No component of this process was transparent. In fact, it was often the case that the Turkmens suddenly realized that they no longer were the owners of their land. To counteract *dastarmi* ownership, the Ministry of Justice and Land Registry personnel would forge depositions that confirmed the new owners. This is how the Jafarbay, Atabay, Goklan, and Qajaq peoples lost their lands (Gorgani 1979, 62). As expected, this process had a clear impact on Turkmen traditional self-governance and landownership.

A Glance at Turkmen's Traditional Life

Recall Lambton (1953, 160) who stated that the Turkmens did not have khans or tribal chiefs, and that they traditionally managed their affairs through councils of respected elders. Because of that, the Turkmens had no hereditary authority. Instead, the men who had earned the respect of others would become prominent members of the clan, usually elderly men (*aq saqal* or *ak sakgal*; literally, white-bearded man). Turkmen tribes were governed by *yashuli* or *rishsefid* (elderly or white-bearded men), but there were no universal rules of authority and the *yashulis* would convene only when the necessity arose. Decision-making was by consensus (Qorkhanchi 1981, 34). The council would also settle disputes among members of the clan. In cases of natural disaster, the council would organize work parties to assist the victims and would ask the *obehs* to collectively pay for the losses of those affected. People would also volunteer to work to help others, a custom called *yavar* (Gorgani 1979, 13–15; LSTP, 12; Salaman 1980, 57–58;). It must be noted that the patriarchal *yashulis* were not "councils" in the modern sense, but they were not hierarchical authorities either (Salaman 1980, 58). These councils usually convened on need-to-meet bases, which suggests the self-regulating nature of *obeh*. In his 1903 treatise on the Turkmens, the then Governor of Astarabad (today's Gorgan) Mohammad Ali Qorkhanchi (Sowlat Nezem; 1981, 34) writes: "Each *obeh* obeys its leaders (*bozorgan*) to some extent. When there happens an incident or a change for the clan, the leaders, the sheikhs, and elders convene and deliberate; however, whatever the leaders and elders but also the subordinates (*zirdastan*) of the clan find appropriate, [the clan] will do. At that time, [they] are solidly united."

It is also important to recall that traditional Turkmen society did not recognize private ownership of land, and land was always collectively owned by the tribe. Likewise, there was no class inequality in the modern sense. Of course, there were those who garnered significant wealth, mostly through trade. But all Turkmens were generally able to live on or even above subsistence. As such, there was no poverty within Turkmen society (Gorgani 1979, 16; LSTP, 12). Achieved through land registry laws and land reform, the destruction of traditional Turkmen communal land ownership and lack of governing hierarchy was the necessary step for installing land capitalism in the Plains of Turkmen.

Although short-lived, the premiership of Dr. Mohammad Mosaddeq had some positive impact on Turkmens. When in 1950 the Shah decided to sell his lands, Turkmen lands were surveyed. Alerted, the Turkmens complained to Mosaddeq who ordered the survey to stop (Gorgani 1979, 45). During this time, Turkmens took the initial steps to mechanize cultivation and invested in land by purchasing combines and tractors. They also created cooperatives. In a successful case, the Chin Seblidaz village cooperative allowed the maximum of six shares to be purchased by any individual (Gorgani 1979, 46–47), thus preventing potential inequalities and hierarchy.

The Impact of Land Reform

Things changed dramatically after the 1953 coup. The Shah was now the uncontested ruler. The Pahlavi Estates tried to take back all the land it had distributed. As mentioned earlier, distribution meant giving the rightful owners of dispossessed lands a chance to purchase their property back ("Gonbad Kavus" 1979). Re-dispossessing land was done by several legal manoeuvres; for example, all previous decisions on land remittance by the Ministry of Justice were suspended, the Gorgan Land Registry Office was placed under the authority of Pahlavi Estates, and land redistributions were reversed. This shows that previous Royal decrees or Majles rules were political tactics meant to protect the Shah at a time when his grasp on power was not sufficiently solid. Consequently, the Royal Family found its way to Turkman Sahra and started seizing lands. The Gendarmerie acted as the enforcer. Those resisting would be imprisoned; even the lawyers of Turkmen claimants went to jail (Gorgani 1979, 49, 51–53). Existing Turkmen cooperatives were destroyed by the Royal Guards.

After the land reform of the 1960s, the process of dispossession only accelerated. With the traditional landed families in total retreat politically after the land reform and having to shift their investments into other sectors (namely construction, industrial, or trade), members of the Royal Family now owned vast stretches of land; members included Shams Pahlavi, the elder sister of the Shah and the source of many grievances in the region, particularly in Qajaq lands. Ashraf Pahlavi, the Shah's twin sister, took over Qaleh. The Royals often appointed retired army or police officers as their local agents (Gorgani 1979, 76–80). General Mansour Mozayan was one of the key oppressive agents of the Royal Family in the region, selling Turkmen lands by using force for sixteen years (Gorgani 1979, 93). In a process that took several years, according to Gorgani (1979, 6), about 75 to 80 percent of Turkmen lands and pastures were appropriated by the Shah and his family, who also diverted the Gorgan River water to their own lands and the farms of the Royal Family and generals. Mohammad Hossein Rahbar was appointed by Alam to manage the Pahlavi Estates in Gorgan. Rahbar sold Turkmen lands by selling (ownership) bonds. The sales were so hot that the elite in Tehran bought these bonds without troubling themselves to take the trip and see the property listed in the title (Gorgani 1979, 55; Salaman 1980, 58). It must be noted that the occupied lands were among the best in the Plains of Turkmen, and the rest of the lands were distributed among 800 Turkmen villages (Salaman 1980, 58). The village of Qezeljeh (Marjanabad) stands out as a microcosm of all the injustices committed by the Pahlavis against Turkmen peasants: it involved illegal land transfer, deploying armed forces to supress and even torture the peasants, bringing in Baluchi workers to weaken the natives' position — in short, a tearful story of impoverishing a once thriving village by greed and by power over a few generations (DCM2: 240–244; Taimaz 1979). To add insult to injury, the managers of Pahlavi *Amlak* required free labour (*bigari*) from Turkmen peasants on the Royal lands on regular, scheduled bases (see Khajehnejad 2020, 48; LSTP, 17–18).

According to an unconfirmed account, the total of area of lands registered to the Royal Family in the Turkmen region exceeds 30,000 hectares (Atabay 2023). The vast majority of Turkmen lands were distributed/sold by Pahlavi Estates, and, based on Gorgani's research (1979, 68), 13 billion rials were transferred to the Shah's accounts. If this figure is correct (I have no way of confirming it), with the exchange rate of 90 rials (9 toman) per US dollar after 1953 (Shamdanihagh 2022), this amount would equal US$ 145 million. The figure makes sense when we consider that, depending on location, top property could be sold by

Pahlavi Estates for as much as 5,000 rials per square metre ("Gonbad Kavus" 1979). Similar to Reza Shah's practice, at this time, Bank Keshavarzi (Bank of Agriculture) granted loans to individuals for purchasing Pahlavi lands and paid lumpsums to Pahlavi Estates (Gorgani 1979, 67). This would be the quickest way for the Shah to turn his estates into cash, exploiting the country's banks as his own private financial institution. These are all instances of transforming Turkmen lands into capitalist property.

As mentioned earlier, after the 1953 coup, loyal top generals of the Iranian army received lands as their reward (Gorgani 1979, 57). Undoubtedly, this was a modern version of medieval *iqta'*, and it was not a one-time phenomenon: in 1961, the Shah allocated large stretches of land in the Plains of Turkmen to the Royal Guard Corps, an elite, special regiment, thereby allowing the Royal Guard generals to engage in a lucrative business to generate income for the regiment and themselves. Let us not forget that this is exactly how the Islamic Republic of Iran has been partially funding its armed wing: the IRGC (Islamic Revolutionary Guards Corps) is the largest capitalist conglomerate in the country, involved in urban and rural construction, dam building, massive production of steel for export, financial institutions and banks, import and export (including illegal merchandise such as drugs and alcoholic beverages and sex trafficking), even printing (illegally) the country's currency.

The Turkmens often resisted these incursions by appealing in the courts to their right to "ancestral lands," but they were met with pugnacity (Gorgani 1979, 83). Gorgani offers a glimpse of the legal cases he was involved with as the lawyer for Turkmens. He speaks of the legal battle of the Daz tribe that took nineteen years. In the end, the seventh court proceeding ordered the Gorgan Land Registry Office to register Daz lands to the Daz people, but instead of implementing the court's order, the head of Gorgan Land Registry issued fourteen land titles in Daz lands in the Shah's name (Gorgani 1979, 62–66). Many Turkmens soon lost their faith in the judicial system. In Ataabad village, the people met the Gorgan Land Registry and Gendarmes, who had come to enforce evacuation, with clubs, forcing them out of their village. Two days later the local officials, protected by thirty-five Gendarmerie personnel, returned with a vengeance, killing a 5-year-old, injuring four women, and stealing women's jewellery. The prosecutor ordered the arrest of more than one hundred peasants in Ataabad and nearby villages. The villagers filed a complaint. After investigation, a report was submitted to the Minister of Justice of the time, Nuraddin Alamuti, who relayed the report to the Shah, who, in turn, ordered investigation and the arrest of the Head of Pahlavi Estates in the region named Rahbar. A crony of Alam, however, Rahbar was rewarded by becoming a Majles Deputy from the town of Birjand (Gorgani 1979, 87–94)!

We have already reviewed the national and international conditions that cultivated the drive for land reform in the 1960s (Chapter 2). One observer erroneously holds that the Shah "was less interested in creating property than in the intimidation of the country's powerful landed families" (Linklater 2013, 336). This observation is partial and incorrect. The land reform killed two proverbial birds with one stone: it diminished the power of the landed elite, pushing them in the direction of investing in emerging industries or industrial agriculture, although the extent of this shift needs further research. However, the Shah did gain from land reform, and not just significant wealth — a modern form of *iqta'* returned, and much of "the land was usually awarded not to the peasant but to the shah's cronies and his adherents in the army as a reward for their loyalty" (Linklater 2013, 336). The Plains of Turkmen continued to experience the sheer force of land dispossession after the land reform.

To understand land dispossession properly, we also need to attend to cultural assimilation and the state's colonizing project of Persianization of Iran in order to offer a glimpse of its impact on Turkmens and to speak of the cultural and political dimensions of land dispossession.

Cultural Hegemony

It is well-known that the Pahlavi modernization was accompanied by a propagated state ideology that celebrated the rebirth of a nation. This ideology identified the new, refashioned Iran with the (perceived) ancient glory of the Persian Empire. The search for pre-Islamic roots of Iran was influenced by secular Europeans' own search, in the Enlightenment era, for discovering their ancient (pagan, pre-Christian) roots in ancient Greece and the Roman Empire, as well as European Orientalism, and in particular, the German and British archaeological excavations in Persia. The idea of a unified and rejuvenated Iran, of course, preceded the Pahlavis and was present in the intellectual debates and cultural components of the Constitutional Revolution. The literati who acquired governmental positions under Reza Shah and advised him on various developmental plans advocated a patriotic identity for the new nation-state and advocated Persianized nationalism as the pillar of national unity in this otherwise nationally, culturally, and linguistically diverse country. Gradually, in Iran, "bureaucratic middle classes" (Anderson 1983, 76), many of whom from national minorities and speaking non-Persian mother tongues, rose as the salaried and technocratic protagonists of not only state ideology but also as officials of its culturally and linguistically assimilative policies and projects. By mid-1930s, influential patriotic efforts were amplified by the rising Aryanism (under the cultural stimulus of the Nazis) as expressed by certain intellectuals in the elegantly published weekly, *Iran-e Bastan* (est. 1933).

Iran is irreducibly a historically and culturally diverse country. According to Amanat (2017, 473), "In the early twentieth century speakers of Azerbaijani Turkish, about 20 percent of the total population, and Kurdish (the three languages of Kormanji, Sorani, and Gorani), about 10 percent of the population, accounted for nearly one-third of the people of Iran." Moreover, "Speakers of Gilaki and Mazandarani dialects, Luri dialects of Western Iran, Baluchi of the southeast, the Arabic dialect of Khuzestan, Turkic of eastern Iran, and other dialects together accounted for another 20 percent of the population" (Amanat 2017, 473). In 1956, according to Abrahamian (1982, 12), out of the population of 18.945 million, 8.2 million were Persians, while 5.130 million were Turkic peoples (4 million of them Azeris), and 2 million Kurds; Arabs stood at 567,000; Baluchis, Mazandaranis, and Gilakis each stood at half-a-million; Bakhtiaris and Lurs at 400,000, followed by Talleshis, Hazars, Afghans, and others. Armenians, Assyrians, Jews, Zoroastrians, and Baha'is together accounted for 478,000 of the total population.

In premodern Iran, Persian had almost invariably been the official language of various administrations of mostly non-Persian rulers; Persian was the lingua franca across the region. Now with the modern state that had print media and then national radio and television at its disposal, Persian grew at the expense of the country's other precious languages and local dialects, or in short, language became a means of assimilation into Iranian identity. According to Benedict Anderson (1983, 44–45), print language "laid the basis for national consciousness" by creating "unified fields of exchange and communication," just as "print-capitalism gave a new fixity to language" and "created languages of power." These conditions apply to Iran, except that Iranian print capitalism, while a private enterprise, was deeply connected to the state and its policies, to the extent that "free" press did not exist under monarchy. State-funded modern education also played a key role in this respect, as the state only allowed Persian as the language of curriculum; other languages were banned. The imposition of a Persian high culture "came at the cost of ignoring, or actively suppressing, a plethora of languages and dialects throughout Iran, along with their associated regional cultures and folklores. Equally prevalent was an obsession with 'purifying' Persian of its foreign words — from Arabic, Turkish, and Mongolian — as relics of what was considered an alien and embarrassing past" (Amanat 2017, 473). In the nineteenth century, every newly formed modern nation-state officiated a "national" language, just as older empires that had transitioned into nation-states preferred and sanctioned a shared language or a selected number of them. In the Iranian case, officiating Persian was achieved at the expense of marginalizing other languages (so was the case with modern Turkey and several other newly formed nations). In the state's view, promoting non-Persian cultures and languages would potentially be tantamount to feeding separatist views (Amanat 2017, 473). The Pahlavi state's irremediable anxieties about Iran's northern neighbour partially compounded the urge for assimilation into state-sanctioned language and culture, including the myth of Persia's ancient glory as the roots of modern Iran. The ban on non-Persian languages often became aggressive, to the extent that the state prohibited publications in Turkish, Kurdish, and so on. A scanned document found on the internet clearly establishes this point. It is an order, marked "confidential," issued by the Intelligence Bureau of Ministry of War and dated February 20, 1935. It is received by the Ministry of Science and Endowments (later Ministry of Education). I invite the reader to pay close attention to this directive of the Ministry. It speaks for itself and is quoted here in full.

> Turkish and Kurdish teachers who teach in the provinces where the population is Turkish- or Kurdish-speaking must be banned from teaching, and in principle, the speaking of Turkish and Kurdish languages in Iran must be abandoned as soon as possible, and if a fundamental decision is not made regarding their [minority teachers'] different opinions, their training the children in this system may one day grow into the enemy's hands, because it has not yet been seen that

Turkish, Kurdish, and Assyrian bunch (*jama'at*) offer any decent services to the very homeland that has cultivated them in her bosom.

The racist and assimilative language of this order is compounded by a deep anxiety. The parlance is hostile and humiliating. To complete this picture, we should also note the forced internal exile of "undesirable" Turkmens under Reza Shah (THD, 313–314) — a common practice at the time.

Furthermore, to force Iran into a superficial homogeneity presentable to the world as a "modern" nation, the self-orientalizing masterminds of Reza Shah's policies ended up forcing state-sanctioned clothing on the nation as well. In December 1928, the state decreed a dress code on males of school age and older, mandating men to wear "European-style jacket and trousers and a short, cylindrical rimmed hat, known as the Pahlavi hat, similar to the French kepi" (Amanat 2017, 487). Traditional attires — in their many shapes and colours, a reflection of Iran's cultural diversity — were banned. Assimilating the nation into a uniform mass, the dress code became the sign of status and singled out the clerics, nomads, peasants, and so on (Amanat 2017, 488–489). The 1934 unveiling decree, as well, expressed the state's deep anxieties about the nation's modern appearance in the eyes of the "West" that the self-orientalizing Reza Shah and his advisers tried to mimic, not knowing that every mimicry produces only a distorted and cheap double. With the forced unveiling, as feminist scholars have already mentioned, the woman's European public appearance was displayed as the sign of state authority over Iranian modernization, just as forced veiling under the Islamic Republic served as the return to the "authentic" (male-defined) Muslim woman and the signifier of an Islamic state. It should be noted that if the policies of Reza Shah ultimately failed, it was not for lack of trying.

What happened under Reza Shah represents a classic colonial approach: by virtue of identifying the modern state with ancient Persia and thereby (somehow) with the Persians and Persian language, he politicized cultural-national minorities as fixed and unchangeable identities belonging to a premodern past (presumably as opposed to Persians). Then by fixating these attributed identities, the state rendered the ethnicized others the objects of the state's nationwide policy of assimilation. Of course, such a mode of confronting the cultural-national-linguistic minorities could not be blamed on the Persian majority. The state's Persianism, in fact, forced Persians into a privileged hierarchy fabricated by the orientalist and colonizing gaze of the state. Universal citizenship under Iran's modern state could then only embrace the (acculturated) persons who would identify, and in fact emulate, the (idealized) Persianized citizen of the state.

Following the 1979 Revolution, the bitter legacy of internal colonialism that was born with the founding of Iran's nation-state and manifested through the cultural and linguistic repression of non-Persians grew into a major source of grievance on the part of Iran's national minorities. The Turkmens were no exception: in the Turkmen region, modern schools did not teach Turkmen language, and speaking or corresponding in Turkmen language was banned in government offices (LSTP, 18). As such, language revival of cultural groups shaped up within intellectuals from Azeri Turks, Kurds, Baluchis, Arabs, Gilaki, and other origins, publishing in these languages.

Antonio Gramsci (1971) teaches us that the state's hegemony, as the process of propagation of the worldviews of the ruling class upon the subaltern, is primarily achieved once those worldviews are disseminated through cultural products and educational curricula. Hegemony is therefore achieved through intellectual and cultural *leadership* that gradually braids the ruling class's initial *domination* with the life activity of the subaltern, and accordingly the latter's worldview is gradually aligned with that of the ruling class. Today's successful liberal hegemony within stable parliamentary democracies is a case in point. Under Reza Shah, the attempt at state-sanctioned cultural reconstruction of modern Iran did not grow into a hegemonic process of realigning the people's worldviews with those of the rising ruling elite. What remained vividly was mere domination and dictatorship. The process of building hegemony was launched later by Mohammad Reza Shah in the 1960s and 1970s, and it was mostly successful within the demographic category of urban salaried technocrats and intelligentsia. However, the Shah's dictatorship and intolerance for dissent only sowed the seeds of his demise. This is why, in the absence of hegemony, the choking force of assimilation has been profoundly felt by Iran's cultural, national, and linguistic minorities.

Dispossession has many dimensions, and it is never about land alone. In Turkman Sahra, the state policy meant to scatter Turkmen peoples. Gorgani (1979, 54) astutely observes that "On the one hand, the lands of Plains of Turkmen were transferred to the country's elite, particularly associates of the Royal Court and their relatives, so that the land would be vacated of Turkmens, or at least their racial, ethnic, linguistic, and cultural characteristics would diminish as others would settle in their lands." Gorgani (1979, 54) continues: "On the other hand, the government apportioned the Plains of Turkmen into divisions that would be annexed to the neighbouring Persian-dominating regions so that the Turkmens would be deprived of political expression."

Aside from linguistic assimilation through media and curriculum that developed throughout the Pahlavi dynasty, Reza Shah took it upon himself to rename and Persianize the historical names of cities and towns throughout the country. Key cities in today's Iran still bear these names: for instance, Dozdab became Zahdan, Naseri was changed to Ahwaz, Barforush was renamed Babol. Turkmen towns were largely renamed: Astarabad became Gorgan, Bandar Turkmen was renamed Bandar Shah, Aqqala (Aq Qal'eh) became Pahlavi Dezh, and Jorjan was renamed Gonbad Kavus. This was meant to not only de-ethnicize these places, thus subsuming them under a nominally homogenized geographical designation, but also to de-historicize the significance of these places that aided the new Persianized Iran in constructing a nationalist narrative.

Political boundaries were redrawn to increase the power of the state. This process led to official jerrymandering: the parliamentary ridings changed so that the nominal power of electors in the Turkmen areas would shrink, although no genuine parliamentary election was ever held after 1953. Bandar Shah (Bandar Turkmen) was attached to Kardkoy; Bandar Gaz, Pahlavi Dezh (Aqqala), and Gomesh Tapeh were annexed to Gorgan; and Jargalan remained under Bojnord (Gorgani 1979, 54). The designation Sahra-ye Turkman was changed to Dasht-e Gorgan (Abrahamian 2008, 88).

The demographics of the regions also began to shift dramatically. The most visible case was the early 1970s expedited migration of landless peasants, now agricultural workers, from the southeastern city of Zabol and its adjacent areas in Sistan and Baluchestan Province. This process continued after the Revolution. As lands in the Turkmen region were concentrated in the hands of the urban elite associated with the monarchy who wanted to increase profit, agricultural workers were needed in ever greater numbers for mechanized farms. By 1979, the Zabolis (the colloquial name given to these migrant workers and their families) constituted a visible minority in the Turkmen region. The demographic diversity of the Turkmen region also includes long-time Turk and Persian residents.

The complex processes of land takeover, cultural assimilation, language suppression, riding redesign, and population intermixing all aided the dispossession of Turkmens of their ancestral lands.

Conclusions

The founding of the Pahlavi dynasty unleashed extensive land dispossession in the Turkmen region that contributed to the creation and expansion of land capitalism in Iran. It adversely affected the ancestral structure of Turkmen society, in particular the communal landownership and non-hierarchical social order. The fertile lands of the Plains of Turkmen attracted the Royal Family's attention, and with the various institutions under the state at his disposal, Mohammad Reza Shah was able to find ways to take over great parts of Turkmen lands. As Iran went through political upheavals such as the invasion by the Allies, the short-lived semi-open civil society, the 1953 coup, and the years of land reform, the Turkmens experienced hardship and impoverishment. Their legal challenges against legalized but also arbitrary dispossession of their ancestral lands were overall long, exhausting, and eventually unsuccessful, even though they won those cases. The process of depriving Turkmens of their lands was accompanied by the state's colonizing approach toward national minorities through cultural assimilation and a publication ban on Turkmen language (and other non-Persian languages).

The 1979 Turkmen council movement was a direct response to the processes that had started several decades earlier and had remained unresolved. This chapter's short history indicates that the movement was a cry for justice in reaction to the policies of the Shah. In launching the council movement, Turkmen activists had rightly understood that their struggle was about both land and culture as a people. The next chapter registers the advent and challenges of this unstudied world-historical movement.

Chapter 4

The Turkmen Council Movement
Advent, Challenges, and Thriving

It is the natural and undeniable right of every nation to write and read in its own mother tongue and have schools and centres through which it can revive its ethnic (qowmi) culture.
— Cultural-Political Centre of Turkmen People

BY TERMINATING THE MONARCHY, THE 1979 Revolution concomitantly imposed a conclusive setback on the Iranian bourgeoisie that had thrived under the Pahlavis and in tandem with the Royal and ruling elite, severely damaging its economic base. Promptly, the revolutionary government confiscated assets and properties of large landowners, factory owners, bankers, large-scale investors, and the top-ranking administrators and generals of the ancien régime — with most of them having already fled the country. The confiscated assets — often occupied by the peoples, workers, students, and peasants, among others — included those of the Royal Family. The clerical rulers used this momentum as a political manoeuvre of the new regime: by associating Iranian bourgeoisie with the bygone monarchy, the emerging Islamist state legitimized the seizing of huge wealth and funnelled it to the newly formed state foundations — above all the Mostaz'afan Foundation — while pretending that the now nationalized wealth of the overthrown regime's associates was to be diverted to the poor people of Iran in a revolution identified by its cunning clerical leader as that of the downtrodden. In the revolutionary months of 1979, little did the poor realize that this was the beginning of the formation of a new ruling oligarchy, arising from the clerical and bazaar classes and their cronies, forming around the now Islamicized rentier state, eyeing to "extort" the hopeful disenfranchised masses that yearned for social justice, while diverting these foundations' wealth into their bottomless pockets in the name of privatization in the decades to come (Vahabzadeh 2017b). The working class and working poor were the first classes to be hit hard by this devilish manoeuvre during and especially after the war (1980–1988; see Maljoo 2017), followed by the Iranian middle class in recent decades. Having risen mostly from humble backgrounds in traditional families and loaded with a power complex, the expanding nouveau riche around the state soon appropriated wealth beyond their wildest imagination through preferential licences and privileged positions in state auctions of national resources and contracts, often without even having to pay for them. Neoliberal policies of privatization in Iran only fed a gluttonous kleptocratic oligarchy around Iran's military-security-trade complex, leading to the formation of a new capitalist class that benefits from state monopoly and insider connections. In post-Revolutionary Iran, therefore, the state became the agent of a new capitalist class formation. This process took some decades to evolve but it was launched full-fledged after the war. The initial and partial glimpses into what was about to come was not lost on secular opposition (leftist groups in particular), working class leaders, and several minority groups.

Given the historic process of land dispossession (Chapter 3), the Turkmen council movement organized the peasants and launched an attempt to take control of their ancestral land in order to rectify past injustices. Moreover, intuitively, this movement was a reaction to the very early stages of the process of reallocation of their dispossessed lands to the new claimants gathering around the Islamist state.

Turkmen Activism in the 1970s

I have already alluded to the legal battles of dispossessed Turkmens in the two decades prior to the 1979 Revolution. In addition to such efforts, there was political activism among educated Turkmens, a process that gradually shaped up in the late 1960s and 1970s, as young Turkmens entered university programs across the country. This historic junction is crucial: first, the late 1960s was also the time when the state embarked upon investing massively in the higher education institutions and universities, thanks to the oil revenue, for the purpose of manning the state's ambitious industrialization and modernization plans. Second, by the late-1960s, Iranian intellectuals, weary of continued state repression and censorship, had gathered around cultural activities and literary journals, producing a widening stream of literati that defied the regime's cultural symbolisms and political vision. When, by the mid- to late-1960s, left-leaning intellectuals reached the conclusion that armed struggle was the only way to dismantle the hegemonic image of the regime in the minds of the masses, the literati supported the emergent guerrillas through their arts and literature (Vahabzadeh 2022b). It was in this context that Turkmen university student circles were formed and accumulated the experience that was needed for many of them to take on the leadership of the 1979 Turkmen council movement. According to one source, between 1969 and 1972, Dr. Bardi Ahangari and Beik Moradgari created a circle to promote Turkmen culture and attracted several young Turkmens. Some of them utilized their positions as employees of the Ministry of Culture and Arts or Radio Gorgan to promote Turkmen culture. In 1972, this circle was raided by SAVAK (Iranian intelligence) and twenty people were arrested (Naderi 2011, 23–24; PSRI nd). Ay Mohammadi, Qelich Tagheni, Akhun Bar, Tavaq Bardi Sowqi, Safar Azad, Kaka Onsori, and Badakhshan were among other members of this group (Khajehnejad 2020, 37). Many Turkmen intellectuals and university student activists gradually leaned toward armed struggle and supported the People's Fadai Guerrillas (PFG).

A native of Gonbad Kavus, Bardi Ahangari (1943–2012) graduated as a Doctor of Pharmacy from the University of Tehran in the 1960s. He was a student representative during his university years. After returning to Gonbad Kavus, he was hired as the head of pharmacy and laboratory of Gonbad Kavus hospital in 1969, while he also became the unpaid director of the town's Culture and Arts Bureau which allowed him to promote Turkmen culture by sponsoring the music, plays, and poetry readings of Turkmen artists. He created a circle of dissident intellectuals. He was arrested in 1972 along with his comrades and spent the next thirteen months in Gorgan prison. After his release, he created a drama group, staging plays in Tehran and Yazd. In 1978, he was the head of the postsecondary institute in Gonbad Kavus (that later became an Azad University branch). After fleeing Iran with his family in 1983, during the height of the Islamic regime's repression, Ahangari died in exile in Cologne, Germany (DCM2, 427–429). Cultural activities such as his provided the groundwork for the Cultural-Political Centre of Turkmen People that Ahangari had an influence in founding. In addition to participating in cultural activities, several activists of Turkmen origins were left-leaning university students in the 1970s, some of whom also served time as political prisoners.

One cannot speak of Iranian Turkmens and ignore Nader Ebrahimi's seven-volume historical-realist novel, *Fire Without Smoke* (1992) that won him several awards, including Iran's Book of the Year and a UNESCO recognition. The novel was written over a long span of time, starting in early 1973 with the first three volumes; the next four volumes were finally completed over the next 20 years, as the later volumes of the novel could not have been published due to Pahlavi censorship. This novel's narratives unfold over the span of a century, beginning with the time of the Qajars to that of the Shah, encompassing three generations. Its zenith is the love story that takes place in the 1850s; the novel traces the generations following this heroic love story in the decades to come. The first three volumes of the novel had the fortune of being adapted for a popular, thirty-two-episode (sixty minutes each) TV series, under the same title and directed by Ebrahimi himself, that was aired in 1974–1975 on national television. Without a doubt, the TV series had a significant and positive impact on the collective imagination of Iranians and depicted Turkmens as free-spirited tribes-peoples driven by warrior codes, communal fidelity, and devotion to their land and people. The novel begins with the conflict between the two great Turkmen tribes, Yamut and Goklan. Yamut warrior Galan Oja falls in love with Solmaz Ochi of Goklan. As legend has it, this turns out to be the greatest love of Turkman Sahra. Galan Oja enters the alachiq of Solmaz Ochi alone and abducts her in full view of her family. This unleashes a tribal war, as Solmaz's brothers try to take her back but fail, losing their lives in the attempt. Solmaz's love for Galan complicates the whole affair. What follows is an absorbing odyssey of an impossible love that ends in tragedy as Galan is finally killed by Yetmish, Solmaz's older brother. Solmaz and her two sons return to Goklan land, where Solmaz dies after vengefully killing Yetmish. The black-and-white TV series offered a beautiful depiction of Turkmen everyday life and rituals. Most captivating were the traditional Turkmen outfits with their vivid motifs combined with depictions of the Turkmen warriors on nimble horses holding rifles and Turkmen women's assertive power in decision-making. This TV series gave Turkmens admirable visibility in the Iranian collective imagination.

Following the historic 10 Nights of Poetry event held at the Goethe Institute in Tehran in October 1977, Turkmen intellectuals and activists were inspired to rekindle their focused activism. The Goethe Poetry Nights had ushered together dissident artists, intellectuals, writers, and poets who presented fiery works in defence of freedom and in support of dissidents. Attended by tens of thousands, these ten nights launched the initial process that led to the revolution of 1979. The return of educated Turkmens to their home had a vivid impact on the events leading up to the Turkmen council movement. In the months to come the Turkmen Teachers' Association was founded in secret. Key leaders of the teachers association were high school teachers, including Begmorad Gari, Mohammad Qoli Azizi, Ashir Mohammad Shirmohammadi, and Sarabi (DCM1, 18). In 1978, some Turkmen university students and intellectuals in Tehran, notably Qorban Shafiqi (Arqa) and Haj Rahim Ajami, founded the secret group news of which spread among Turkmen activists. Gorkan Behlekeh was also involved in this group's formation. Shafiqi was a student activist and graduate of the Tehran School of Commerce. His life was cut short when he was wounded by friendly fire and died in hospital on April 4, 1979 (a school was named after him later). This group joined other Turkmen activists, including Ane Galdi Goklani, and named their group Savaluni, after Fadai martyr, Mehdi Savaluni (d. 1972). Later, this group renamed itself Fadaiyan-e Turkmen (Atabay 2023; DCM2, 336, 359–364, 379–380). While clearly this group was inspired by and supported the Fadai Guerrillas, Fadaiyan-e Turkmen were intent upon promoting the cause of Turkmen people, instead of regarding themselves as a regional branch of the Fadaiyan (DCM1, 14). At this time, the leftist Turkmen activists mainly studied the works of Bizhan Jazani (Atabay 2023).

This group was later joined by other Turkmen and non-Turkmen activists and focused on organizing their activities in Gonbad Kavus. Organized by Turkmen and Persian students, a book festival in October 1978 in Gonbad Kavus, Aqqala, and Bandar Turkmen was enthusiastically received, registering unprecedented sales — reportedly, sales equalled 170,000 tomans (US$ 24,285) according to one account or 200,000 tomans ($US 28,500) according to a Turkmen leader as reported in an interview with *Peygham-e Emrooz* (April 9, 1979) — and it is regarded as one of the first open activities of Fadaiyan-e Turkmen (DCM2, 55, 336–338; LSTP, 39). Fadaiyan-e Turkmen also distributed the Organization of Iranian People's Fadai Guerrillas (OIPFG) tracts in town by adding their signature to them (Khajehnejad 2020, 39). The success of the book fair indicates the insatiable craving for political and cultural self-education in the region. This was followed by film screenings of a couple of Soviet-made movies, held on the premises of the (future) Azad University, including the film based on Maxim Gorky's 1906 novel, *Mother*. Reportedly, pro-Khomeini students also participated in these activities (Khajehnejad 2020, 71).

After school reopening in September 1978, Gonbad Teachers' Association in Gonbad Kavus would often cancel classes and encourage students to rally in the streets, although such demonstrations were sporadic and at times were met with resistance by the locals led by Turkmen clerics and their supporters who would occasionally attack the rallying students and teachers. Like any other parts of Iran, the Turkmen region was also divided between the supporters and opponents of the regime. As the revolutionary process soared, the activists began distributing tracts and wrote pro-OIPFG graffiti. On October 30, 1978, Fadaiyan-e Turkman staged the first anti-Shah rally in Gonbad Kavus. It was attended by 500 protesters. Aside from anti-Shah slogans, they shouted, "We want Turkmen language and writing taught at school" and "Down with exploitation, long live the toilers." These demands show that in the Revolution the Turkmens sought not just the overthrow of monarchy but equally an end to discrimination against their cultural rights as well as a fair distribution of land. In short, both culture and land informed their vision of a free Turkman Sahra. At this time, supporters of other dissident groups — the Tudeh Party, People's Mojahedin, and Peykar — also began activities in the region (DCM1, 11–16; LSTP, 40). The next protest in January brought out some 5,000 protesters (LSTP, 41).

Despite these activities in the weeks leading up to the Revolution of February 1979, the Turkmen masses did not generally engage in anti-Shah protests, in contrast to much of the rest of the country, and it was the non-Turkmens who largely manned the anti-Shah rallies. The Islamic regime's security, in producing its partial and ignorant "history" of the events, disregards the long-term activisms of Turkmen intellectuals, claiming with racist disdain, "As a result of such [Turkmens'] cultural and political poverty, not only did the Turkmens join the revolution late, they even stood up to it until the last moment, in contrast to the non-Turkmens of the region" (Naderi 2011, 24). In contrast, Turkmen researcher Arne (Amin) Goli provides a convincing observation. Pointing out the aforementioned aversion of some Turkmen clerics to the anti-Shah protests, Goli argues, "The other reason for the delay in protest movement against the Shah was diverting the [anti-Shah] slogans to those in favour of Shi'ism, and the Turkmens [being Sunni Muslims] did not want to submit to this." There are further reasons: "On the other hand, the main slogans were anti-Shah; there was no mention of Iran's future politics, nor of any idea about the future of oppressed nations. That is why the Turkmens viewed the protests with doubt and hesitation. The third reason was fear of heavy reprisal in case the revolution was defeated" (DCM1, 15).

Two important events in Gonbad Kavus preceded the February 10, 1979, uprising that overthrew the monarchy. The first was the poster and book exhibition held in Bagh-e Melli, the town's park, in January and February 1979. The theme of the exhibition was clearly in favour of the OIPFG. The other event was the February 10 pro-monarchy rally organized by SAVAK, large landowners, and pro-regime and conservative Turkmen clerics led by Anaqelich Naqshbandi who delivered a speech to that rally alongside Colonel Didevar, Commander of Police (Khajehnejad 2020, 39–40). Reportedly 20,000 Turkmens were bused

Poster and book exhibit of Fadaiyan-e Turkmen, Bagh-e Melli, Gonbad Kavus, circa March 1979. The emblem of the Organization of Iranian People's Fadai Guerrillas (OIPFG), images of Fadaiyan's deceased founders and that of revolutionary poet Khosrow Golesorkhi (executed by the Shah) clearly indicate the organizers' affiliation. (Source: DCM2; image courtesy of Arne Goli)

to Gonbad Kavus and rallied there, threatening non-Turkmen residents, and they clashed with a few activists who tried to dissuade the protesters. Many people were injured by club-wielding pro-monarchy protesters (Hamidian 2004, 243). Newspapers reported that the protesters were armed and caused extensive property damage, killing two people and injuring fourteen (DCM2, 93–94).

This rally clearly came too late: in the next couple of days, monarchy in Iran became history. With popular armed uprisings in the rest of the country, the supporters of Khomeini raided Gonbad Kavus central police station and disarmed it. On the same day, Turkmens approached the station, asking to be armed (Khajehnejad 2020, 109), which the former refused. Meanwhile, Turkmens in Gonbad Kavus, Aqqala, and Bandar Turkmen regions raided and disarmed police and Gendarmerie posts, although in the last location reportedly the post had already removed their weapons (Khajehnejad 2020, 114). The pro-Khomeini residents created the Imam's Committee (later Islamic Revolution Committee) or simply Komiteh, and took over the occupied posts and the army bases by excluding the Turkmens (LSTP, 41; see below). This was the beginning of a rapid pace of events in the weeks to come.

The Advent of Councils and Leading Turkmen Organizations

Four days after the armed uprising that ended the monarchy, on February 15, 1979, a number of Turkmen activists associated with Fadaiyan-e Turkmen and Gonbad Teachers' Association held a meeting in the Gonbad Kavus library located in Bagh-e Melli and founded Kanun-e Farhangi va Siyasi-ye Khalq-e Turkmen (Cultural-Political Centre [Association] of Turkmen People or CPCTP; DCM1, 18). At that time, they could not have imagined, not even in their wildest dreams, what an enormous task of leadership was required of them within just a few weeks from the peasants' grassroots movement that was at this time only in its embryonic stage. Begmorad Gari, Mohammad Qoli Azizi, Ashir Mohammad Shirmohammadi, and Sarabi of the Gonbad Teachers' Association, and Anin Goklani, Taji Talebi, Ajami, Ghaffur Goklani, Amir Ahangari, Yarali, Hakim Makhtoom, Onsori, Makhtumi, and Ghaffur Emadi of Fadaiyan-e Turkmen were the founding members of CPCTP (DCM1, 18). For the next little while, the library became the CPCTP headquarters until CPCTP moved to the Governor's building

(Farmandari; Hamidian 2004, 243).

The CPCTP issued its first announcement: it spoke of the people's cultural rights and condemned discrimination against minorities. Culturally, the CPCTP's objectives entailed (1) reviving Turkmen literature through publication, (2) reviving Turkmen music and folklore with the assistance of elders and experts, and (3) holding cultural events and exhibits. Politically, its objective entailed (1) democratic education of Turkmen people by holding public events, and (2) encouraging people to create councils, which included (a) workers' factory councils, (b) farmers' and herders' (*aq saqal*) councils and occupation of stolen lands, (c) rug-weavers' union, (d) students' and teachers' committees, and (e) government employee councils (LSTP, 161–162). The demands were ambitious, and soon a different body to attend to the needs of the envisioned council system was created (below). The CPCTP expanded on the above by including greater constituencies (e.g., fishermen), demanding a popular defence force, declaring solidarity with the Kurds, demanding the abolishment of Komiteh, free education, and creating health care centres (*Kar* 1979a: 2). This was the first statement of the CPCTP published in OIPFG's weekly, *Kar*. The position of the OIPFG was now clear: to defend popular movements of national minorities, especially in Kurdistan and Turkman Sahra.

The CPCTP designation caused some initial disagreements that were later settled in practice. There were objections to the word "political" in its designation, and the reminisces of Turkmen activists at the time show diverging accounts about the role of OIPFG in creating CPCTP. Naturally, any memory of historic events is prone to distortion with passage of time. Yousef Kor was a Marxist student activist in Ahvaz University in the early 1970s who had spent six months in prison for his connection to the clandestine group, Red Star (Setareh-ye Sorkh; Hamidian 2004, 240). The first OIPFG delegation to the region included Heshmat Ra'isi and Mahmoud Hassanpour (Atabay 2023; Naderi 2011, 25). This happened a couple of days after the Revolution (Atabay 2023), when the OIPFG was just emerging in the open political scene without any clearly articulated strategy and still trying to connect with the local and regional organizations that Fadaiyan's supporters had created at their own initiatives. In Kor's account of his talk with Fadaiyan in Tehran, "it was agreed that cultural and artistic activities be separated from political-activist organizations, and [the two bodies] keep their independence, and the OIPFG would support them through its support network that would be created *after* the establishment" of CPCTP (in DCM1, 20; my emphasis). Ra'isi contacted the Turkmen supporters of OIPFG in three towns and informed them of "creating the Turkmen People's Cultural Association as the OIPFG's first directives." Kor recalls that the CPCTP did not submit to the OIPFG's vision of the Turkmen organization: "because of [Fadaiyan's] unstudied recommendations, the decision that was made in the Organization [of Fadaiyan's] headquarters (in Meykadeh Street) pertaining to both Cultural Centre [CPCTP] and creation of [OIPFG] support network was never realized" (DCM1, 20; see also Hamidian 2004, 240). Bandar Turkmen activist Juma Budesh holds that the OIPFG did not agree with creating an independent Turkmen body, and he attributes the word "political" in the CPCTP designation to the OIPFG attempt to attach CPCTP to itself. He and his comrades envisioned a future Turkmen party; however, he asserts, pro-Fadai Turkmens could not perceive a movement without the OIPFG support and involvement (in DCM1, 19).

The foundational rift is clear: one view, held by several Turkmen activists, perceives the movement as autochthonous and authentic, which the OIPFG gladly supported and tried to contribute to organizationally, while another view, offered by some Fadai and (former) pro-Fadai Turkmen activists attributes the movement (entirely) to the OIPFG initiative. The point is, however, *not* to conflate the Turkmen council movement with the OIPFG, despite their camaraderie and convergence. According to Kor (2013), "The people of Turkman Sahra's connecting with the Fadai Organization was only expected and likely (*addi va tabi'i*). The fact is that the supporters of the People's Fadaiyan were far greater in numbers than those of other political organizations." But this does not negate that some activists and supporters of Fadaiyan insisted on the movement's independence and inclined toward greater Turkmen nationalism. Juma Budesh's perception probably explains why two weeks after the foundation of CPCTP, Bandar Turkmen activists created their own (short-lived) Kanun Farhangi-ye Khalq-e Turkmen (Cultural Centre [Association] of Turkmen People; DCM1, 21). The rift in these recollections indicates that both accounts are somewhat angled. Mehdi Fatapour's account annuls the fundamental assumption of both views that give readers the impression that the OIPFG actually had any kind of policy regarding the national minorities. A leader of the OIPFG at the time, Fatapour (2023) confirms that "after the Revolution in most of the major cities, headquarters of [our Fadaiyan] Organization were set up. These headquarters were created *without a central plan* and with the initiative of the Organization's local forces" (my emphasis). Specifically, Fatapour reminisces, in Gonbad Kavus a group of Turkmen intellectuals had created the CPCTP within a few days after the Revolution. Accordingly, "This association [CPCTP] planned to promote and defend the national and cultural demands of the people of Turkman Sahra, and considering the conditions of Turkman Sahra where most people were distrustful of the new regime, [the CPCTP] ... quickly grew into the most influential political force in the region" (Fatapour 2023).

In fact, the OIPFG did not have the theoretical capacity or sufficient personnel to respond to every event and crisis in the turbulent post-Revolutionary times. As it happened in Kurdistan, the Turkmen region, and other places, the OIPFG basically followed the flow of events, insofar as its general Marxist ideas allowed, and any council movement would certainly qualify. At least in the first few weeks after the Revolution, Fadaiyan found it to be their unwitting and unplanned policy to generally support popular movements of the subaltern, but they were also cautious about radicalism. Note that the general context of Turkmen councils was the workers' strike committees and the factory councils that flourished with astonishing rapidity across the country (see Chapter 1). These were progressive initiatives, which a Marxist party would only celebrate and support.

Arne Goli rightly points out that the accounts that attribute the Turkmen grassroots movement to the OIPFG initiatives are "illogical" precisely because they do not match the realities of the time (in DCM1, 22). OIPFG's first official delegate to the region, Naqi Hamidian (2004), speaks of Turkmen supporters of OIPFG contacting the group's headquarters in Tehran, but he does not suggest any organizational connection. He confirms that Ra'isi had met with some Turkmen activists, but what was discussed in these meetings remains unknown (Hamidian 2004, 239, 241). Ra'isi's visit was clearly not an organizational decision, and it was a common practice among the Fadaiyan to take individual initiatives first and discuss them with the group only later (Vahabzadeh 2010, 59, 149). The OIPFG's official delegation consisting of Hamidian, Nahid Qajar, and Abbas Hashemi entered the city of Sari in "early Esfand" (February 20 and later) to establish the Fadaiyan's chapter in

Mazandaran province. Clearly, by this time the CPCTP had been established for about two weeks already and spreading fast in the region. The point is that the Turkmen activists took the initiative in creating their own organizations, as did Turkmen peasants in occupying their ancestral lands. One cannot attribute these achievements to OIPFG policies, which at this time were nonexistent. It is true that most Turkmens, according to Hashemi (2001, 44), who was in charge of the Turkmen region, "regarded themselves as supporters of Fadai" (see also Fereidoun 2001, 45). But the Turkmens "had already started to confiscate the landowners' lands, and a part of [Fadaiyan's] job was really 'to correct' the confiscations in the sense that [Fadai representatives] discouraged them from confiscating small lands (*khordehmaleki*)" (Hashemi 2001, 44). Such advice, however, came only later. The connection between Turkmen organizations and the OIPFG was oblique and complicated, although the two converged in the turbulent months ahead through an "elective affinity": the Turkmen organizations needed Fadaiyan's support while the newly emerging regime grew increasingly hostile toward their movement; Fadaiyan had found in the Turkmen council movement a concrete embodiment of the group's socialist visions and popular values. After the initial visit to Gonbad Kavus, Hamidian and Qajar returned to Sari to manage the OIPFG affairs, leaving Hashemi and Hassanpour in charge of Gonbad Kavus and Bandar Turkmen (Atabay 2023).

It is true that the founding and supporting intellectuals and activists around CPCTP and the Turkmen council movement were supporters of the OIPFG before having any contact with the group. Mehdi Fatapour (2003) makes the vague statement that the leaders of CPCTP "were mostly (*omdatan*) of [Fadai] Organization forces," suggesting that Turkmen leaders were actually "supporters" (implicit meaning of "*niruha*," literally, "forces," as opposed to members) of the OIPFG. But this association should not leave the impression that these activists either acted on Fadaiyan's initiative or were detached from Turkmen masses. On the contrary, the founding of the CPCTP was supported by Turkmen people. Turkmen clerics generally sided with the movement, often issuing statements that condemned warmongering, petitioning the government to take peaceful approaches to the just demands of Turkmens, and asserting the rights of the Turkmen minority (see DCM1, 113). Vali Mohammad Arzanesh was a highly regarded Sunni cleric and high school teacher who later negotiated with the government on behalf of Turkmens. He affirms that the Turkmen council movement was rooted in both "national oppression" and the "land issue" (in LSTP, 127–130). Interestingly, Sunni clerics of Baluchistan and Kurdistan also defended the people's movements in their region. Kurdish cleric Sheik Ezeddin Hosseini stood out as an outspoken defender of Kurdish rights to culture and self-governance within a federated Iran. Baluchi clerics also supported the Turkmen cause (LSTP, 125). That said, there have been exceptional cases of clerics who had old ties with landowners: for instance, Anaqelich Naqshbandi and his short-lived "Cultural-Islamic Centre of Turkmen People" (LSTP, 54; DCM1, 26). It is interesting that although Naqshbandi had received many recognitions by the Royal Court and the Ministry of Interior in the previous regime, including a medal for his role in the 1953 coup (LSTP, 44–45), he nonetheless became a supporter of the Islamic regime in the region.

Meanwhile, the supporters of the new regime, mainly from the Shi'i and non-Turkmen communities within the region, quickly tried to get the upper hand in controlling the main towns, above all Gonbad Kavus. In the months prior to the Revolution, they were organized by the Qa'emiyeh mosque that had organized anti-Shah rallies in town (PSRI nd). In the days of the uprising, they had taken over government buildings and bureaus, establishing in Gonbad Kavus and elsewhere the armed Islamic Revolution Committees or Komiteh (in Gonbad Kavus it was called Imam's Committee, as mentioned earlier), consisting of men loyal to Khomeini. They tried to assert the new regime's authority by openly expressing hostility toward the new Turkmen groups and trying to confiscate the weapons Turkmens had taken from police and Gendarmerie posts during the February uprising. Komiteh's policy was to exclude Turkmens from participating in any decision-making process and exploit religious or "ethnic" divides to achieve its objective (Hamidian 2004, 243; Khajehnejad 2020, 137–138; LSTP, 42, 46). We can already see that Komiteh drove a policy of segregation and discrimination by trying to drive a wedge between Shi'is and Sunnis, non-Turkmens and Turkmens (see Khajehnejad 2020, 11). Turkmen activists, in contrast, advocated a policy of integration and solidarity among all residents regardless of their cultural origins. As the Turkmen land occupation spread fast in the region, the unholy alliance of religion and wealth surfaced as armed Islamists, unpopular among Turkmens and educated residents, collaborated with the landowners and their Turkmen supporters, causing conflicts and clashes.

We have seen the process of dispossession of ancestral Turkmen lands in Chapter 3. It should not, therefore, be surprising that within days after the collapse of monarchy, the Turkmen villagers, witnessing many former landowners having escaped the country, took over their lands. The pioneers of the land occupation movement were villagers who had made sacrifices under the former regime (like Khojeh Logarkaz, taken by Gholam Reza Pahlavi) or had legal documents pertaining to their entitlement to land (LSTP, 46–47). According to one account, the first lands occupied by the peasants were occupied a few weeks before the Revolution and were actually in the villages of Peshmak and Yelgay (Salaman 1980, 55, 59). The CPCTP names Marjanabad (Qezeljeh) as the first village to confiscate land (of Mohammad Faryabi Hamedani), create a five-man council, decide to farm collectively, and create a rural union made up of eight of its neighbouring villages (LSTP, 97–98). The CPCTP press release (March 6, 1979) states that the first peasant council (*showra*) was founded in the village of Khojeh Logarkaz in Esfand 1979 (February 20 and later) after taking back 1,500 hectares of land (LSTP, 164–165), and theirs was actually a *yashuli* and *aq saqal* council — one of trusted elders.

These cases clearly indicate that the Turkmen peasant's council movement was a grassroots one, and its advent precedes the arrival of any political party (including the OIPFG) in the region. Soon, fifty peasant councils emerged in the region and collective farming was established. To emphasize: *only then* was a central organization for coordinating the councils established. Expectedly, the idea of councils spread from the villages to factories and rug-weaving shops, and the *showras* became self-governing (Salaman 1980, 59–60). According to one account, within two months of the Revolution (by late March) there were councils in place in fifty districts. From the beginning, the CPCTP steadfastly supported land occupations (LSTP, 48). On March 6, a statement by Turkmen mandatory military servicemen was released: it demanded the abolition of the standing army and the institution of a people's army, announced the refusal to submit to existing commanders, supported revolutionary army personnel, and proposed the formation of a Turkmen regiment as the protective force of Turkman Sahra (*Kar* 1979a, 5).

One cannot help but invoke Hannah Arendt's astute observation (1963; Chapter 1) that when left to themselves people are willing and able to create power from below and converge on making a participatory body politic to govern themselves democratically. The grassroots nature of Turkmen councils and their spread affirms Arendt's point by reminding us that the "social issue" (which she flagged in her work) can indeed become the foundation of council self-governance if properly articulated. In other words, the "social question" cannot be reduced (in Arendtian abstraction) to "need" or "want." In the Turkmen case, it actually became the foundation of a Turkmen-wide grievance that was inevitably political in nature. Land was life for the Turkmens and taking control of land — and thus the means of collective subsistence and thriving — was indeed the foundation for a new, egalitarian, and participatory body politic.

The CPCTP was rather engaged in promoting cultural revival and dealt with the issue of land from a political and legal standpoint. With their incredible popularity and rapid spread, the councils needed a dedicated body for coordination and professional advice. According to a CPCTP activist in an interview with *Peygham-e Emrooz* (April 9, 1979; in DCM2, 55–56), the CPCTP had created a "Rural Research Committee" tasked with studying the conditions of Turkman Sahra villages. The activist asserts that "In its investigations, the committee reached the conclusion that the villagers were ready to occupy their dispossessed lands. So much so that the villagers had already taken action to occupy land in a couple of villages. We began organizing councils in the villages." What is important in this activist's statements is the fact that the councils of villages "did not divide the lands but confiscated them for the whole village, which means that all residents of the village co-owned the lands, taking a share of the harvest. The pace of this process was so quick that we could not keep up with the details and respond to the needs of the villagers."

Consequently, Setad-e Markazi-ye Showraha-ye Turkman Sahra (Central Headquarters of Councils of Plains of Turkmen; CHCPT) was founded on March 16, 1979. It was housed in the canteen of Gonbad Kavus Governor's building (DCM1, 24).

In his memoir, Hamidian (2004, 245) suggests that the OIPFG played a role in the CHCPT formation. Stating that the "creation and expansion of villagers and agricultural workers' councils was a golden and unique

The first office of the Central Headquarters of Councils of Plains of Turkmen (CHCPT), Gonbad Kavus, March 1979 (Source: DCM2; image courtesy of Arne Goli)

opportunity" (Hamidian 2004, 244–245), he frames the entire move as Fadaiyan's brainchild. But "opportunity" for whom? For the OIPFG? As mentioned, the first councils had already emerged by the time the first "official" Fadai delegates arrived in the region and councils were spreading fast by the time these delegates had an opportunity to understand what was going on. This is a distorted view of the past. That said, Fadaiyan representatives were indeed active within the CHCPT.

The CHCPT oversaw the issue of land, land occupation, and the processes of peasant councils (LSTP, 48). In its first press release dated April 4, 1979, the CHCPT demanded the following: (1) creating councils "based on Turkmen people's free vote"; (2) distributing lands that were stolen by Pahlavis and other large landowners under the councils' auspices; (3) forgiving all debts of peasants, workers, craftsmen, and state employees; (4) cancelling all cultural and national restrictions; (5) establishing a new province that encloses the Turkmen region with Gonbad Kavus as its capital under a "unified and shared" authority; (6) creating a popular army; (7) setting up revolutionary tribunals to prosecute the agents of the toppled regime; and (8) unseating appointed officials (LSTP, 159–160).

These demands, reflecting the political imagination of Turkmen leaders, were indeed refreshingly radical. The fifth demand clearly reports a vision of a semi-autonomous Turkmen province within a federal system ("unified and shared," popular and official authority) — an idea neither Pahlavi nor the Islamic state would tolerate. This demand did not escape the gaze of officials, and Abdolali Moshef, Governor of Mazandaran province, called it "unacceptable" (Khajehnejad 2020, 85). The popular foundation for this demand was the councils. Also, recall the CPCTP demand for elders' councils (*aq saqal*) — that may have been the original idea to initially operationalize the councils through tradition. Notably, however, the rural councils were soon aided by enthusiastic, young (urban) activists who participated in the villages as organizers (DCM2, 56). It was through CHCPT's work that the early *yashuli*-style councils, a timely return of tradition, evolved into elected councils revitalized by young activist presence. Members of these councils often signed petitions, affirming their collective decision to work with the CHCPT (see LSTP, 51–53).

Due to the importance of the council movement, and given that both CPCTP and CHCPT had common roots in Turkmen activities, as mentioned, it was decided that the CPCTP — the cultural and political centre — should be organizationally placed under CHCPT — the headquarters taking charge of the land issue (DCM2, 56; LSTP, 151). With this arrangement, cultural activities were diverted toward supporting the council movement. In reaction, the Ministry of Interior released two statements promising a judicious solution to peasants' issues, insisting that the lands with disputed ownership would be under the government's auspices until a special commission determined their legal ownership. It also decreed that the harvest would be done under the government supervision (Khajehnejad 2020, 142–143). Registering a legalistic approach that upheld private property as sacred, the Ministry's rules could not have been farther from the realities of the region, and report the extent of estrangement of Tehran-based politicians from the lived realities of Turkmen.

With the founding of the CHCPT, two prominent leaders — truly organic intellectuals — of the Turkmen council movement also emerged immediately: Shirmohammad Derakhshandeh Toomaj (aka Shirli Toomaj; 1947–1980) and Hakim Makhtoom (1950–1980). They were destined to rise to the national spotlight in the months to come. Toomaj was born in the Turkmen village of Yalmeh Salian in the vicinity of the town of Aqqala. He was a geography student at Isfahan University when he was arrested in 1971 for political activism and spent 6 months in prison. Upon release, he served his mandatory military service after which he was once again arrested in 1975 and sentenced to 3 years. When he was released in 1977, he returned to farming in his native village. He was an organizer of land occupations in February and March 1979, and after the CHCPT foundation he became its spokesperson (DCM2, 370–371). Makhtoom was born in Gonbad Kavus to a poor family, and after earning his high school diploma and completing the mandatory military service, he became a rural teacher. He was active during the revolutionary months leading to the overthrow of the monarchy and joined CHCPT leadership, playing a key role in organizing the peasant councils (DCM2, 373–374). The OIPFG claimed that Toomaj was its member and in charge of the Turkmen region (*Kar* 1980f, 8). Such a claim, however, brings into question why the OIPFG would assign a representative (Esfandiar Karimi) to the region from Tehran, if Toomaj was the OIPFG member already.

One of the immediate issues with peasant-occupied lands was how to deal with the farms that had already been cultivated before land takeover, and it was ruled that the (now) previous landowners should be levied 20 percent of produce (Salaman 1980, 60–61). Within the next few months, the number of peasant councils reached 300 while eighteen peasant unions (of five to eleven villages) had also been established (Salaman 1980, 61).

Enjoying popular support, the CPCTP and CHCPT soon became de facto governing bodies of semi-autonomous Plains of Turkmen, while Komiteh, the armed forces, and former landowners and their Turkmen supporters constantly tried to assert the central government's authority and delegitimize land occupation and the councils by confronting Turkmen organizations and bodies. To challenge these popular organs, a number of conservative Turkmen clerics around Naqshbandi created the Cultural and Islamic Centre of Turkmen People, but it was unpopular and soon dissolved (LSTP, 54). Other such short-lived, parallel, and unpopular groups were the Islamic Movement of Turkmen Youth and the Turkmen Islamic-Cultural Centre (in DCM1, 89, 98).

Fadaiyan's Dilemma

Because of the impressive cultural and organizational activities of Fadaiyan-e Turkmen, more precisely due to their success in their activities just within weeks after the Revolution, the OIPFG was literally drawn into the already in-progress developments of Turkman Sahra. A quick glance at Fadaiyan's weekly, *Kar*, reveals that at this time the OIP-FG's (newly created) Central Committee, aside from engaging with the newly installed Provisional Government, attended mainly to issues that had gained nationwide significance. These included workers' issues and councils as well as the popular movements in Kurdistan and the Turkmen region. Thus, it is clear that the OIPFG's involvement in Turkman Sahra was an effect of its supporters' tremendous field activism, and not a planned entry into the region. However, this last claim rhetorically dominates the "research" publications of the Islamic Republic's official "history": in trying to attribute Turkmen council movement to the conspiracy of Fadaiyan, Iranian intelligence insists that the CHCPT "was continuously in contact with the [OIPFG], inquiring about its directive regarding their activities" in wishing to control the region (Khajehnejad 2020, 113, 121). This claim is far from the truth.

Therefore, it is useful to clarify the OIPFG's connection with the movement, as well as the perceived differences between CPCTP and CHCPT. When Hamidian was deployed by the OIPFG Central Committee to take the helm of Fadaiyan's Mazandaran chapter, as an outsider he observed two "groups" of Turkmen activists; for him the differences between the two are more than differences of focus and function. Trying to organize OIPFG supporters in the region, he and his comrades made first contact with Turkmen activists through Hassan Ja'fari, who, in Shiraz prison, had been acquainted with a Turkmen comrade named Yousef Kor, a student of Ahvaz University and a member of the short-lived group, Red Star. After introductions, Kor, Haminidan, and Ja'fari travelled to Gonbad Kavus (Hamidian 2004, 240). Hamidian observed that the CPCTP immediately grew popular among the Turkmens who gathered in city parks or CPCTP headquarters to support it. Of the two "groups" of activists he mentions, the first group, having observed the "objective and subjective conditions and contexts" at the time, diverted their attention to CPCTP. The CPCTP activists, intended to "organize and advocate for the Turkmen people's (*khalqi*) (ethnic [*qowmi*]) rights. Although these friends more or less emphasized on the activities pertaining to creating the councils and participating in the occupation of dispossessed lands by absentee landowners ... they attended cultural efforts" (Hamidian 2004, 244). Hamidian (2004, 241) suggests that both in terms of self-organization and numbers, this group stood higher than the other group, as "the quality of their engagements and political and revolutionary positions was generally 'softer' (*narmtar*)" compared with the second group, and that "they were more inclined toward cultural and political activity." Hamidian (2004, 244) then refers to the second group, the "radical" field activists who had participated in the formation of the councils "through the involvement of the local white-bearded men and the assistants of the supporters [of OIPFG]." He refers to the "spontaneous" character of some Turkmen initiatives. Accordingly, "Depending on their own vision and zeal, the supporters of ... [the OIPFG] *spontaneously* [*khodangikhteh*] and based on their own decisions and responsibility dedicated all they had to the organization and expansion of [the councils]." Clearly, by taking initiatives these pro-Fadaiyan field activists expected support from the OIPFG. "Simultaneously, they were waiting to connect and establish contacts with ... [Fadaiyan] in order to discuss their issues and activities and receive support, directives, and political guidance and national organization of ... [Fadaiyan]," as Hamidian (2004, 244) reminisces. "Such reports [about the councils] contained new and surprising potentials and prospects and therefore invoked our theoretical and ideological temptations and ambitions within us" (Hamidian 2004, 244).

There are several points that need unpacking in this outsider's observation. Upon arrival in Gonbad Kavus, Hamidian was hosted by Dr. Ahangari and thus associated with the first "group" (Hamidian 2004, 240). Therefore, he observed the events through this particular position. While he admits that the cultural activists (of CPCTP) and the field activists (around CHCPT) overlapped, he still insists on the difference between the two (alleged) tendencies, calling the activists involved with the councils "radical" (a word which is vague but suggestive), implying that they were driven by "ideological temptations and ambitions" from which he clearly distances himself in his memoir. In other words, his views are not only influenced by his being an outsider, but also coloured by his new, liberal-left values twenty years later when he wrote his memoir in exile in Europe. Moreover, he attributes the flourishing of the councils to the Turkmen supporters of the OIPFG. This may be true, but it homogenizes the efforts of Turkmen activists. Hamidian's observations are therefore informed by a misunderstanding and an omission.

It is important to remember that right after the Revolution, the pro-Fadai activists in the region, mostly non-Turkmen residents and especially in the towns such as Gonbad Kavus, Bandar Turkmen, and Aqqala had organized themselves into Javanan-e Pishgam-e Turkman Sahra or

Pishgam Youth of Plains of Turkmen in March-April 1979 and occupied the Scouts Organization building for their headquarters. Reaching hundreds in membership, Pishgam high school students participated actively in the councils and urban activities, organizing rallies and distributing OIPFG literature (Atabay 2023). Throughout the country, the OIPFG enjoyed a huge support base among high school and university students. Once the monarchy was toppled, pro-OIPFG student activists, under Fadaiyan's directives, created Pishgam (Vanguard) Organization in schools and universities. This is how the Pishgam Youth grew into the native activist body of the OIPFG supports in the Turkmen region. That said, the OIPFG clearly lacked sufficient knowledge of Turkmen culture and life. This is why in the aftermath of the first armed conflict, surprisingly, Fadaiyan distributed a long questionnaire among Turkmen council activists — a curious document ignored by activist memoirs or documents — to gauge their worldviews. Strange questions appear in it: questions about what the council (which?) thinks of the OIPFG; how it relates to CHCPT and with what expectations; what it thinks of the government; how much influence clerics have; and who was responsible for the war and how to win the next war (in Khajehnejad 2020, 101–103).

First, I need to reiterate that the Turkmen council movement was for both land and culture and these two could not be regarded as distinct or parallel efforts. Land occupation and councils were inseparable from cultural revival. Thus, the aforesaid division between two "groups" of activists is simply false, the effect of the observer's gaze and preferences. The activists certainly had different fields to attend to, but regarding them as "softer" and (more) "radical" sounds judgmental, not objective. Second, Hamidian (2004) rightly points out the "spontaneous" character of the councils but disregards it as he is more interested in linking this spontaneous movement to his Fadaiyan organization. Here we need to invoke Arendt and her ageless observation again that once the authority of the state is suspended, informed people spontaneously and quickly build the bodies of self-governance and self-management. Such bodies — as in (workers') councils and townhall meetings (of the American revolution) — are egalitarian and participatory, in short, the highest form of democratic life.

The OIPFG was therefore drawn into the grassroots movement of Turkmens, and it is still important to register that certain council activism would resonate with the OIPFG's ideological inclinations and their vying for popular authority, although such tendencies were not yet theorized by the Fadaiyan. As such, the relationship between the Turkmen council movement and Fadaiyan, as mentioned earlier, was one of "elective affinity." This also happened to lesser extent in Kurdistan and mixed-Kurdish-Azerbaijani provinces. Chapter 5 shows that it was actually the experience of Turkmen councils and certain councils in Kurdistan in the early months of 1979 that radicalized the OIPFG program of February 1980. To reiterate, the OIPFG mainly followed, without any clear prior plan, the course of action already taken by Turkmens that included Fadai supporters.

The Provisional Government and Complications

It is utterly curious to witness that following a revolution whose leader had rhetorically trumpeted their advocacy for the poor and freedom, a provisional government was installed by the very same leader (Ayatollah Khomeini) that adversely reacted to the initiatives of popular self-control in Turkman Sahra, Kurdistan, and in the factories, positioning itself to repress them by unleashing the new state's newly propped armed wing, Komiteh, and in the interest of upholding a strong, domineering state. In the Turkmen region, the Provisional Government, and the Islamic Republic, thereafter, supported not the peasants but landowners; in the case of émigré landowners associated with the fallen monarchy, the regime moved in to confiscate their lands in a process that eventually led to the creation of a new oligarchy in the next decades.

It is important to note that Iranian Kurds emerged from the Revolution as a formidable force demanding recognition of national-cultural rights as well as a federalist arrangement with the new government. Led by the Democratic Party of Iranian Kurdistan (DPIK) and the Party of Kurdistan's Toilers (Komala), armed Kurdish *peshmergas* clashed with the government troops between March 18 and 21. Subsequently, Kurdish regions were heavily militarized, and grassroots, civil society associations were attacked. Critical and volatile conditions ruled the region before a civil war ensued. In the course of a civil war, the Islamic Revolutionary Guards Corps (IRGC) and the military eventually pushed Kurdish militants to the Iraqi side of the border in the early 1980s. The Kurds, both the civilians and the militants, suffered heavy casualties. The year 1979 witnessed continuous Islamist mob attacks on unveiled women, secular and leftist political parties, and various unions and associations, leaving behind significant human casualties and property damage. Although condemned in the official statements of the government, these pressure groups served the new regime immensely by weakening the foundations of the rising civil society in the country.

With the foundation of CPCTP and CHCPT, the new regime's worst fear was realized. The Turkmen region was now under a dual authority: the popular Turkmen authority led by its two robust grassroots organizations and the official authority of a weak state. In every respect, Turkman Sahra frightened the regime as potentially a new Kurdistan. Abdolali Moshef, the Governor of Mazandaran, speaking on the TV debate pertaining to the "second war" in the Plains of Turkmen (aired on National Television on March 1, 1980), stated that from the early days after the Revolution he felt that "Gonbad [Kavus] is where the government has no influence [and] cannot assert its decisions; we had installed a Governor [in the town] but … the one who made decisions in this region was a different force … named the Turkmen People's Headquarters [CHCPT] in connection with the People's Fadaiyan" (quoted in Khajehnejad 2020, 41). Within a couple of weeks after the Revolution, cleric Mohammad Baqer Shari'ati was deployed to the region to provide an assessment. He met with prominent Turkmens and left the region with a realistic appraisal, writing two reports to Ayatollah Khomeini, advising him to prevent armed conflict with the Turkmens and insisting on land distribution. But as he reminisced, "neither Imam [Khomeini] nor [Premier] Bazargan responded to me" (quoted in Khajehnejad 2020, 43). To some extent the Kurdish resistance, especially the armed conflict in the Kurdish city of Sanandaj, had overdetermined the Turkmen situation at this time.

As mentioned, following the fall of the monarchy through an armed uprising, the armed followers of Ayatollah Khomeini were asked to gather in mosques and form local security bands usually known as Komiteh (Komiteh-ye Enqelab-e Eslami). These constituted the new state's provisional protective armed force. Let us not forget that the Revolution had brought freedom to diverse political tendencies and given hope to peoples from all walks of life for a new, participatory order. Despite the clerics' spreading their dark robe of reactionary values over the country, the people had found "Iran" to be the expanse of novel experiments in self-assertion. The Turkmen council movement represents one of the most vivid and inspiring experiments of this short-lived era (the other being that of the Kurds, which requires an independent study). It is important to note this context. Untrained, ideological, and often highly agitated and aggressive young Komiteh personnel in the early days of the Spring of Freedom of 1979 usually took the law into their own hands.

In Gonbad Kavus, the Shi'i, non-Turkmen supporters of the new regime created Komiteh-ye Imam, as mentioned earlier, that played a significant role in stirring up conflicts with the supporters of the two Turkmen organizations, Pishgam Youth, and the grassroots councils. What infuriated Komiteh in Gonbad Kavus was the uninhibited and relentless tract campaigns of Pishgam Youth that had covered the Turkmen districts and towns with pro-OIPFG posters and graffiti, leaving the visual impression of a huge support base for OIPFG among the Turkmens (see DCM1, 29). Just as the new regime that was about to solidify into the Islamic Republic, the Komiteh based its policies on discrimination — the regional governorship and Komiteh systematically excluded the Turkmens from participating in any process relating to management of needs of Gonbad Kavus. Komiteh consistently agitated non-Turkmen residents against Turkmens (LSTP, 46). The IRGC was initially formed on Khomeini's orders on 28 February 1979 and placed under the Provisional Government's authority. Soon, though, Khomeini ordered its restructuring and placed it under the clerical-ruled Revolutionary Council's auspices, and the IRGC was formally founded on April 22, 1979. It gradually incorporated the Komiteh personnel and became the unwavering protective armed force of the new regime that played a key role in the suppression of opposition in the post-Revolutionary years.

The Provisional Government's approach toward the Turkmens was dismissive. The new regime recognized neither the cultural grievances nor the land issue in the Plains of Turkmen. The grassroots council movement was a huge headache for the new regime, and as such, the government let Gonbad Kavus Komiteh take care of the issues in their own manner. The Provisional Government–appointed Gonbad Governor, Madarshahi, encouraged Imam's Komiteh to distribute arms among Persian-speakers of the town (LSTP, 142), further alienating the Turkmens. In the eyes of the people, Madarshahi was unfit for this position, as he was a landowner with large plots that he had previously purchased from the Royal Court (Khajehnejad 2020, 139).

Meanwhile, hundreds of petitions and letters of Turkmen peasants were sent to the Premier's Office and other government ministries, and they were completely ignored. Many of these letters have survived as they were published in newspapers at this time. In contrast, the large landowners successfully lobbied the government with the Red Scare and filed complaints against the councils with the Premier, the Ministry of Interior, and Imam Khomeini's office. Their lobbying was made from the particular angle of land title, and therefore, they diverted the land issue to a legal issue. Of particular significance in this context was the sit-in protest of some landowners or their agents in the Gonbad Kavus office of the Ministry of Justice on March 11, 1979. Calling themselves "some farmers of the Gonbad region," they posed the occupation of their lands by peasant councils as injustice and unlawful. The protest of landowners found keen ears in the Provisional Government, which sent a special taskforce to resolve the land issues in the region. Abbas Radinia represented the government and a cleric named Omid Najafabadi the Imam's Committee in Tehran. They met with the landowners in closed sessions, reportedly promising them to retrieve their lands. Turkmen activists discovered that the government's taskforce had carried a stash of weapons in their Chevrolet Blazer SUV and questioned the motives of this taskforce. They confiscated the weapons. This taskforce returned to Tehran with negative and provocative comments about the Turkmens. In response to Turkmen demands, Omid Najafabadi reportedly stated, "How many casualties did the Turkmens sustain for the cause of Revolution to deserve so many rights?" When the government delegates returned to Tehran, they accused Turkmens of theft and rape and of making the region insecure (DCM1, 26–27; DCM2, 57–58). One wonders why the government delegation would go to the negotiation table while, admittedly and according to Omid Najafabadi's own statement, they had in their vehicle "ten assault rifles, thousands of rounds of ammo, and a few grenades" (Khajehnejad 2020, 116).

A report on "assaulting" government representatives published in Tehran newspapers caused dozens of Turkmen clerics, including Arzanesh, to write a letter to Khomeini (published in *Kayhan* [no. 10666; 20 March 1979]: 7) and caution him about the allegations against Turkmen people (in Khajehnejad 2020, 117–118). On return to Tehran, Omid Najafabadi did his best in his interview with newspapers to frame the situation as an ethnic conflict and implicate the Turkmens in vile deeds. He said, among other things: "Some [Turkmens] attack the farms.

At night, they raid the houses of migrant Zabolis and rape women and girls" (quoted in Khajehnejad 2020, 116).

To be sure, the region's situation was volatile. A tragic incident eerily anticipated the armed conflict that descended on the region in less than a month. On March 10, 1979, some residents of Bandar Shah, who were trying to change the name of their town to Bandar Turkmen on signposts, were fired upon, and thirteen of them were injured (DCM1, 28; DCM2, 56; LSTP: 170). In response, the CPCTP announced rallies, attended by 50,000, in Bandar Turkmen and Gonbad Kavus. Another rally was held in Aqqala the next day. In reaction, the state ordered the air force to fly F-4 Phantom supersonic fighter-bombers in low altitude above the protesters, break the sound barrier, and cause mayhem (DCM2, 96–97, 98; LSTP, 169). Had this incident not been caught on camera, it would have been unbelievable. Two days after the Bandar Turkmen shooting, newspapers declared that the very same designation for the town — Bandar Turkmen — had been ratified by the Revolutionary Committee (the Provisional Government's authority; DCM2, 100).

An Iranian Airforce F-4 Phantom flies at low altitude and breaks the sound barrier on March 11, 1979, to intimidate Turkmen protesters who marched to condemn Komiteh's indiscriminate firing on Bandar Turkmen residents the day before. Photo credit: T. Seyyedi. (Source: DCM2; image courtesy of Arne Goli)

Another view of the rally of March 11, 1979. The presence of Turkmen women in traditional apparel is significant. (Source: DCM2; image courtesy of Arne Goli)

The Spring of Councils: The "First War" of Turkman Sahra

It was in this turbulent context that an armed conflict, known as the "nine-day war" or the "first war," broke out during the Iranian New Year (Nawruz) holidays of 1979. In trying to install his envisioned new regime at the height of his popularity, Ayatollah Khomeini ordered the Provisional Government to rush into an undemocratic referendum in which the people were asked to respond yay or nay to the "Islamic Republic," without knowing its proposed constitution or even what it meant. Any democratic mind would object to such a referendum.

Given their brief but bitter experience with the new regime already, Kurdish parties and Turkmen organizations, as well as the OIPFG, the National Democratic Front, the National Union of Women, and the Union for Freedom boycotted the referendum. So did many secular, educated individuals, and some members of religious minorities. Contrary to the groups outside of the state that advocated (however reluctantly) in favour of voting for the proposed Islamic Republic as an attempt to ingratiate themselves with the country's new rulers, as announced in the March 29, 1979, issue of *Kar* (no. 4), the OIPFG took the principled position that boycotting the referendum was the right decision, thus exposing the opportunism of those "opposition" groups that advised to the contrary. Obviously influenced by the struggles of Kurds and Turkmens (with the armed conflict in the Kurdish town of Sanandaj coming to an end and the one in Gonbad Kavus continuing at this time), Fadaiyan declared: "We endorse any form and content that strongly supports the interests of the oppressed peoples of Iran." Since nobody knew what an "Islamic Republic" really was, the OIPFG continued: "The foundation of any republic is its constitution, not its designation. Can one judge a republic without having its constitution written and its content clarified?" The article then suggested the proper procedure — that first the people's representatives to the constituent assembly must be elected, and then they must draft a new constitution and put it to popular vote; it would be only then that people could legitimately vote on the new political system (Kar 1979b, 1–2). The Turkmen organizations' boycott dwelled on this principled approach, which is evidence of the growing convergence between Turkmens and the OIPFG on matters of nationwide interest. No reasonable human would vote for an unknown political system while the advocates of this system have deployed armed forces to crush their movement. In other words, marginalized groups boycotted the referendum, a testament to their critical stance.

The armed conflict between Turkmens and Komiteh started following reports of an incident that occurred in Gonbad Kavus on March 25, 1979. When Komiteh militias tried to arrest a cigarette vendor and he resisted arrest, Turkmens passing by gathered and objected to his arrest. The Komiteh men fired, killing 22-year-old Araz Mohammad Dardipour and injuring another person. Araz's body was taken to hospital where thousands of Turkmens converged the next day (March 26), took Araz's body, and drove it to his hometown of Bandar Turkmen for burial. On the same day (March 26) the CPCTP invited a protest held in front of its headquarters at 2:00 p.m. It was attended by 15,000 to 20,000 people. Prior to the demonstration, the OIPFG representative in town, Abbas Hashemi, called the commander of Gonbad Kavus Komiteh, named Nowruzi, and warned him about the simmering unrest, asking him to scale down Komiteh activity, but Nowruzi hung up on him. About half-an-hour into the peaceful protest, the crowd was suddenly attacked by armed, masked men wearing armbands with the words "Islamic Revolution Guards." They opened fire, killing six and injuring twenty-six on the spot, and the protesters responded by throwing rocks at them.

Masked men also attacked the headquarters of CHCPT, and arrested many including Hashemi who had surrendered to avoid conflict. The number of all arrestees summed up to about 100 at this time; they were taken to army barracks in Nodeh. The Turkmen organizations decided to resist, and the people armed themselves. Komiteh militiamen closed off the town on March 27 by setting up roadblocks on all major roads leading to the town. The town was practically divided into Turkmen and non-Turkmen neighbourhoods, and barricades in the streets and above the roofs were manned by each side. Turkmens from other towns who could find a way into Gonbad Kavus joined to assist their comrades. On this day, Turkmen forces succeeded in taking back the headquarters of CPCTP and CHCPT. In exchanges of fire, twenty-six people were killed and seventy-seven people were injured belonging to both sides.

On March 28, Turkmens in Aqqala and Bandar Turkmen staged a protest against repression, while Turkmen clerics sent telegrams to offices of the Premier and Imam. On March 30, Komiteh forces received reinforcements from Qom and Mashhad. Prominent and progressive cleric Ayatollah Seyyed Mahmoud Taleqani (1911–1979) intervened and encouraged the government to deploy a peace delegation to the region. His appeal to the Turkmens, published in daily papers, invited calm (DCM2, 109). This delegation included Khalil Reza'i (SAVAK had killed four of his children; he was close to Mojahedin-e Khalq and a revered national figure), Dr. Ali Rasuli (Ministry of Interior representative), Malihi (from the National Front of Iran or Jebheh-ye Melli), Dr. Gorgani, and Dr. Seyed Ahmad Tabataba'i (Governor of Mazandaran; Gorgani 1979, 7). The OIPFG sent Fatapour, Amir Mombeini, Mastureh Ahmadzadeh, Ashraf Dehqani, Mehdi Same', and Mohsen Modir Shanehchi to Gonbad Kavus. Finally, the Turkmens were represented by clerics Arzanesh, Makhtoom, Toomaj, Bahman Jabal Ameli, and Mohammad Talebi (DCM2, 137). The negotiations of the three parties took place in Sina Pharmacy, owned by Dr. Ayisha Makhdumi (DCM1, 31; DCM2, 130). They decided on an immediate ceasefire for 72 hours to reach an agreement. The ceasefire began on 7:00 a.m. of Sunday April 1, which was also the first day of the previously mentioned referendum. But the ceasefire was violated several times. The government had threatened to deploy the army to the town should an agreement fail. On April 2, a national holiday and the second and last day of the referendum, the following agreement was reached: (1) taking the injured to hospital; (2)

releasing all who had been arrested; (3) evacuating and removing the barricades; and (4) agreeing to have the army in charge of order in town (Atabay 2023; Khajehnejad 2020, 123, 145–154; LSTP, 58–73).

These events need unpacking. According to CPCTP (1980, 58), in the days prior to the conflict, the Gonbad Kavus Komiteh had been reinforced by volunteers from surrounding towns and cities but also from towns as far as Tehran and Quchan. According to Fatapour (2023), an OIPFG peace delegate, the Komiteh militias who were brought in from other cities insisted on dispersing the CPCTP protest as a show of force, and eventually, the Komiteh troops from Mashhad attacked the demonstration on March 26. The conflict immediately escalated, as protesting Turkmens, now escaping the wrath of the Komiteh, rushed to CHCPT headquarters to seek refuge, demanding also to be armed to defend themselves. A published eyewitness account of the events by *Tehran Mosavvar* reporter Davud Zavareh`i (1979) clearly registered the questionable moves of Komiteh personnel prior to the conflict, the celebratory demeanour and peaceful turnout of Turkmens in the CHCPT rally, the rabid assault and atrocities of Komiteh forces, and the conspiratorial role of large landowners in stirring up confrontation.

It is clear who caused the conflict. Amazingly, though, Hamidian, the head of the Fadaiyan chapter in Mazandaran province, implicates Abbas Hashemi in causing the conflict. Based on his (two) reported conversations with Qorban Ali Abdulrahimpour (aka Majid) who had warned him about Hashemi's being "maverick and/or extremist" (*takravi va ya tondravi*; Hamidian 2004, 239). The question is, if Hashemi was such a character, why would the OIPFG select him for this mission? Why would Hamidian leave him in charge of Gonbad Kavus (Hamidian 2004, 255) and return with his future wife (Qajar) to his hometown of Sari? When the news of the conflict reached Tehran, Abdolrahimpour called Hamidian, objecting that he had "left Hashem alone" (2004, 261). Hamidian secretly left for Gonbad Kavus but could not reach the town because of roadblocks and instead went to Gorgan, only to reach Gonbad Kavus the day after and find out that Hashemi was arrested (Hamidian 2004, 261). Hamidian's vilifying of Hashemi did not escape the gaze of Iranian intelligence "historiography" that echoed his memory to intentionally displace the reproach for instigating the conflict on Fadaiyan (Khajehnejad 2020, 154). This view of Hashemi is also reported in T. Atabay's memoir: "Abbas Hashemi who proudly did not separate himself from his weapons believed in spreading revolutionary zeal and excitement in the region.... Abbas believed in robbing [military] posts and seizing weapons.... Before the first conflict, he had sent some activists to disarm Incheh Borun and Maraveh Tapeh posts" (Atabay 2023).

On the same day, sometime after Komiteh personnel opened fire on peaceful Turkmen demonstrators, another band of the Komiteh attacked the CHCPT headquarters with heavy fire. An eyewitness to this attack, Hashemi called the OIPFG headquarters in Tehran (Fatapour 2023) and spoke to Farrokh Negahdar, a member of Fadaiyan's Central Committee. A quick detour is in order to clarify who had the authority to issue directives: the new ten-member Central Committee of OIPFG (soon to change) was formed on February 10 and included Abdolrahimpour, Fatapour, and Negahdar among others (see Vahabzadeh 2010, 58). When Hashemi phoned to report that they were under attack, Negahdar reportedly replied: "You respond in kind (*shoma ham javab bedin*)." However, Hashemi did not. He moved some weapons and a few people to the building next door before surrendering without resistance, along with 102 other persons in the headquarters whose ages ranged from eight to eighty-two years old (A. Hashemi 2001, 44; 2016). They were taken to Nodeh army barracks.

The nature of the conflict — Komiteh's surprise attack — leaves no doubt that, contrary to the claims of Iranian intelligence or of Hamidian, this "war" did not really involve the OIPFG. In a post-conflict interview with *Peygham-e Emrooz* (April 9, 1979), and in response to the claims made by state media that the conflicts were instigated by Fadaiyan and supported by the Soviet Union, a CPCTP representative denied both allegations, stating that while some armed Turkmen militants were pro-OIPFG (probably referring to the Pishgam Organization), but with emphasis, this was a grassroots Turkmen resistance (Mahfuzi 1984, 4). The OIPFG was not ready for it, nor did Fadaiyan have any concrete plans for supporting the Turkmen councils. The OIPFG's only contribution to Turkmen resistance in those days was sending a medical team to treat the wounded (DCM2, 57); this medical team set up a temporary hospital in Bizhan Jazani school (renamed by Pishgam student; Khajehnejad 2020, 197). Of notable mention also is the deployment of a medical team of nine doctors, nurses, and medics — followers of Komala — to the Turkmen region. This was a vivid show of solidarity across movements. Unfortunately, the entire team was killed in a motor vehicle accident on the way to Turkman Sahra on March 29, 1979. When their bodies were returned to Kurdistan, in a remarkable show of honouring their activists, 100,000 residents of Sanandaj attended their funeral.

The fictional Soviet Union involvement in the conflict had a background. When the Turkmens were under attack, they raided a few of Gendarmerie's border posts and seized their weapons. The exact number of these raids remains unknown. State-run *Ettela'at* (no. 15819; April 1, 1979) reported that eighteen Gendarmerie posts on the Iran–USSR border had been disarmed "by Turkmens and with the assistance of the People's Fadai Guerrillas" (Khajehnejad 2020, 176). Independent newspaper, *Ayandegan* (vol. 12, no. 3321; April 10, 1979) also reported that Turkmens had occupied all the Gendarmerie border posts except for two ("Plains of Turkmen" 1979, 1, 3). Hamidian (2004, 258) reports a failed attempt at disarming the Maraveh Tapeh post, encouraged by Hashemi, prior to the conflict. Note that we do not know how many border posts there were in the region at the time or how large they had been. One imagines that some border observation posts probably had only a small platoon while others (like Maraveh Tapeh) were larger and more significant. The point is that reports about seizing posts falls into a rhetorical game best played by the government's obsession with border security. In the context of the Cold War, the Turkmens' actions were deemed to be weakening the country's defences, a claim aggrandized on state-run newspapers and national radio and television. Clearly, at this particular time, the Soviet Union had no interest in occupying or manipulating a part of revolutionary Iran, given that the Shah, the key US ally in the Middle East, had been toppled. In fact, on several Radio Moscow broadcasts transcripts which were published in Iranian dailies, the USSR denied having any involvement in the conflict (see DCM2, 51–53). Thus, in retrospect, such an allegation was meant to justify the regime's heavy hand. It is surprising that the regime's propaganda reverberates in Hamidian's memoirs some two decades later (2004, 258–259). Dr. Gorgani who had come to the region alongside the government delegation rejected the USSR influence; instead, he asked the government to distribute all Pahlavi lands among the peasants (Khajehnejad 2020, 196).

Fatapour's recollection provides a different angle. When the news reached Tehran, on March 27, Negahdar had a telephone conversation with Ayatollah Taleqani, expressing Fadaiyan's view that the conflict should cease immediately. A while later Taleqani informed him that the government delegation was already in Mazandaran waiting for the OIPFG delegation to act as an intermediary between the government and Turkmens. It is important to note that being an influential cleric, Ayatollah Taleqani issued a statement promoting peace and truce on March 27 (in Khajehnejad 2020, 162–164; see Mahfuzi 1984, 4–6). This was a clever move: Taleqani wanted the Turkmens to avoid another civil war like that of Sanandaj in the previous days. There is another version of these contacts: Alireza Mahfuzi claims that the OIPFG did not wish to confront the Provisional Government that had the support of Ayatollah Khomeini. This sounds reasonable. So, the Fadaiyan leadership reportedly debated if they should blame the conflict on Hashemi and expel him from the OIPFG as a gesture of good will in negotiating with the government. This did not happen. The Fadaiyan Central Committee (namely, Negahdar) also wanted to contact the government and promise to negotiate peace with the government on behalf of Turkmens, which they did. But after the peace, the OIPFG leader Ali Keshtgar announced in an interview that Fadaiyan steadfastly supported the Turkmen council movement (Mahfuzi 1984, 5–6). It seems that Mahfuzi's version is informed by future events — namely the May 1980 split. The story is coloured by the view that Negahdar and his comrades in the Central Committee already meant to abandon the Turkmens to get closer to the regime, which certainly was not the case at this time. Without a doubt, the seeds of the 1980 split were being sown at this time; however, future events in Turkman Sahra and the OIPFG policy in 1979 do not support this conspiracy theory.

Following conversations with Taleqani, Central Committee member Fatapour headed the aforementioned OIPFG delegation, and they reached Mazandaran Governorship in Sari by 8:00 p.m. on March 30, expecting to meet Governor Dr. Tabataba`i, who had already been in Gonbad Kavus. It is noteworthy that Tabataba`i was (secretly) a member of Mojahedin-e Khalq and was executed in 1981 by the regime. Because of the Mojahedin's sympathy for the struggles of Turkmen people while criticizing the approaches of Fadaiyan and Turkmen organizations, Tabataba`i was instrumental in reaching peace. The next day (March 31), Fatapour, Same', and Modir Shanehchi reached Gonbad Kavus and met the government delegates there. Fatapour reminisces that the approach of the Turkmen delegation, Toomaj and Tavaq Mohammad Vahedi among them, was delicate and measured. They argued that the Turkmens did not want any conflict. They demanded security for Turkmens, the release of prisoners, and the guarantee that the CPCTP and CHCPT would be allowed to continue with their activities (Fatapour 2023). It took two days to reach an agreement, and according to Fatapour, the difficult part was to convince Komiteh to agree and commit to the ceasefire. After the ceasefire, the prisoners from both sides were freed. Turkmen and Fadaiyan delegates proposed that the air force technicians or *homafaran* take charge of the city's security after truce, but because *homafaran* had a reputation for being pro-Fadai, the three parties finally agreed on the infantry division of the air force or *havaniruz*, and they arrived in the region the next day (Fatapour 2023). Soon after, the CPCTP released the names and biographies of forty-nine Turkmens killed in the conflict. Interestingly, these casualties were categorized in terms of their implicit affiliations: "Turkmen People's Fadai," "martyred comrade," and "martyr" (LSTP, 216–255).

On March 31, while the conflict was continuing, a three-person delegation of the Iranian Human Rights Society, headed by Kourosh Kakwan, travelled to the region. In an interview with *Peygham-e Emrooz* (vol. 20, no. 26, 8 April 1979, pp. 1, 7), Kakwan spoke of his observations: there were hundreds of refugees, mostly women and children, who were fleeing their town for fear of Komiteh reprisals; there was collaboration of former SAVAK agents with Komiteh (he actually identified Fathollah Dara`i, assistant to notorious SAVAK interrogator Azodi); and they were being detained for four hours by Azadshahr Komiteh. He stated that the OIPFG did not start the war and their only involvement was to send a medical team ("Why Did They" 1979, 1, 7; LSTP, 132–135).

It is appropriate at this point to note that as the events unfolded in Turkman Sahra, the Tehran daily *Peygham-e Emrooz* (Editor-in-Chief, Reza Marzban) offered daily updates of the conflict, negotiations, and peace, enriching its reports with its correspondents' field observations and views of Turkmens, as opposed to state-run dailies *Kayhan* and *Ettela'at* whose reports demonized the OIPFG and Turkmen activists for positioning themselves against the Islamic Revolution. While the role of *Peygham-e Emrooz* as a democratic-secular medium at this stage needs independent research, suffice it to say that it played a key role in bringing the Turkmens grievances about land and culture to public view. It also offered independent reportages from Kurdistan, promoted workers' councils, and held forums on the future of democracy.

Curiously, a certain discursive element permeated the analyses of all involved. Almost invariably, the OIPFG, Turkmens, and the government blamed the conflict partially on the conspiracy of the secret cronies of the old regime, members of SAVAK on the loose, and "agents of imperialism" (LSTP, 74). These ghostly instigators appeared in almost every printed report published in *Kar*. On the other side, in response to the journalists' question about who attacked the demonstration on that fateful day, Governor Tabataba'i replied: "The causes of this incident are not yet clear. But we believe that SAVAK agents and some influencers (*motenafezzan*) and possibly large landowners promoted these incidents" (quoted in Khajehnejad 2020, 152; LSTP, 124). In his interview in Reza Allamehzadeh's documentary, Toomaj also spoke of these invisible, omnipresent agitators. Discursively, referencing these clandestine agents served as the elephant in the room. In this sensitive situation, this reference allowed the opposing parties to speak about unease and volatility without pointing fingers at each other, while in their hearts the Turkmens knew that the regime was the instigator, just as the government completely believed that the whole affair was a handiwork of the OIPFG and their Turkmen followers.

In a way, the Turkmen council movement emerged from this first war with remarkable poise. Most Turkmens had boycotted the referendum, and in Gonbad Kavus the conflict had practically indicated that the Turkmens were not fond of the new regime. Interestingly, an Iranian regime's analyst attributes the boycott to the people's not being able to attend the polling stations because of the shootings (Khajehnejad 2020, 173). After the conflict, Madarshahi, whom Turkmens never trusted, was replaced with Khoshru'i as the Interim Governor of Gonbad Kavus.

Still, the armed conflict was the most unfortunate turn of events for the innovative council movement of Turkmens. The conflict sealed the future relations between the council movement and the central government: in Turkman Sahra the state found only a threat against its sovereignty, control, and respect for private property. At the same time, the conflict accelerated the process of council and union building as the Turkmens now clearly understood that without popular bodies of self-governance, they would have no chance against the regime's encroachments. The conflict also overshadowed the Turkmen experiment, and the state-run media used it to objectify the Turkmen attempts at egalitarian self-management as an attempt at undermining the sacred rule of the Islamists. The conflict also solidified the relationship between the OIPFG and the Turkmen council movement: for the next year, Fadaiyan stood by the movement as its unwavering advocate on the nationwide level.

Khalil Reza`i, Khomeini's delegate to the region (before he parted ways with the regime), was uniquely respected by all political tendencies in Iran. Some years later, he gave an interview about his observations. Stated Reza`i: "I think the whole affair was about poverty, misery, and deprivation. The Turkmens were very good people.... They were hardworking and poor, had little possessions, and when I saw their homes and living and subsistence, I was astonished [to see] how in the north of our country with all of its resources these people were deprived of everything" (DCM2, 307).

Dr. Gorgani (1979, 7) observed that the real cause of the conflict was land. This was the most matter-of-fact truth of the time.

Expansion of the Councils

A curious paradox of history unfolded in Turkman Sahra. By giving confidence to activists and the people alike, the "first war" contributed to the expansion of the councils and boosted grassroots self-organization. Once the armed clash was over, the Turkmen council movement emerged in the Iranian political vista as dignified, proud, undefeated, and steadfast. Despite having arisen from one of the most impoverished regions in the country — due to capitalist onslaught and cultural repression — the Turkmen experiment captured the imagination of poor and disenfranchised people in the country. The regime's only weapon against it was to exploit religion, mobilize repression, and smear the movement. In just a couple of months into the Spring of Freedom, the movement had offered a model of popular, participatory, social justice–oriented self-governance, alongside, but also notwithstanding, the state's institutions within a country where, as future turn of events proved, a closed-minded, retrograde Islamist regime was intent upon destroying the democratic elements and achievements of the irreducibly diverse social and political forces in the country. This was the moment of rebirth for Turkmens: "On the social field, close relations were established among Turkmen tribes and clans that stretched from the eastern shores of the Caspian Sea to Maraveh Tapeh and Jargalan [in the northeast near the border with the Republic of Turkmenistan], which had been kept disjointed. Turkmen clerics and elders (*rishsefidan*) had become so close to one another and defended the popular institutions [councils in ways] that had never been recorded in recent Turkmen history" (Atabay 2023).

The Turkmen activists' literature generally offered celebratory views of the council movement that were somewhat wrapped in ideological self-righteousness. This literature also heavily entailed criticisms of the government and the regime's armed forces; it also exposed the region's conspirators. The downside of this discourse is clear: there is little to no reference to the concrete challenges and setbacks that the CHCPT and the movement faced. Land occupation often involves serious conflicts between landowners and their salaried thugs on one side, and the landless peasants and their advocates on the other. In the Plains of Turkmen, most of the largest of farming properties legally belonged to the now absentee monarchists who were largely fugitives at the time, that is, if they had not already fled the country, while other large landowners stayed away from the region, using their lawyers to pursue the land issue. This situation contributed to the rapid expansion of the councils, as the dispossessed peasants initially saw little to no resistance to land occupation.

The CHCPT and OIPFG literature remains steadfastly oblivious to the complications of colonial dispossession. In their harmonized discourse, anyone challenging the councils was vilified as agents of SAVAK, the previous regime, and large landowners. This discursive dismissive tone obscured the complex realities of land occupation. Earlier, I noted that some landowners had already taken legal action against the councils as early as February–March 1979. These should be small landowners or the ones who had purchased their lands from the Royals or generals and thus regarded their ownership to be legal and legitimate. It is difficult to find actual documents (not narratives) that show grievances against the council movement, unless one has access to the records of the Ministry of Justice at that time (which I do not). However, scattered documents provide a glimpse into the complications: for instance, in a complaint filed to the Gorgan Komiteh (April 11, 1971), the Zaboli peasants of the lands of Dr. Pezeshkan near Kalaleh reported that the Turkmens had forcefully taken over the land and threatened the Zaboli farm workers and their families, ordering them to leave the area or their homes would be destroyed (Khajehnejad 2020, 337).

At times, intercouncil conflicts also existed. Another letter, signed by "members of council of Okhlibala" and addressed to the

Revolutionary Council of Gonbad Kavus complained about the arbitrary confiscation of 20 percent of the crop of this village by the council of Qorchai (Khajehnejad 2020, 351; on the 20 percent issue, see next section). Moreover, general security was also a concern. A letter to the Ministry of Interior delegation complains about the theft of fifteen cows by armed men, although it is not clear who the perpetrators were (Khajehnejad 2020, 340). Another letter signed by the locals to the Governor of Mazandaran reports repeated harassment of residents of Kalehfar village in Minoodasht by *pasdaran* (Revolutionary Guards) and *ma'murin* (roughly, Gendarmerie or police agents) at night. They frightened and threatened the Turkmen villagers to the extent that some residents, especially women and children, fled and found refuge in nearby jungles (Khajehnejad 2020, 348). These reports are published by Iranian security with the intention of denigrating the movement, and they are few. One expects that if there were more of such damning reports the regime would have generously published them. Still, these reports point out the obscure corners of a popular movement whose leading organizations should have been forthcoming with all aspects of running an *exemplary* but also *precarious* movement beyond capitalist and state domination.

The Spring Wheat Harvest Festival

After the imposed, armed conflict, the regime's forces, above all Komiteh and newly founded IRGC, remained in the region but the CHCPT and CPCTP clearly had the upper hand. While peace prevailed, throughout the spring, periodical news of violence made the headlines in state-run newspapers and local sources. For instance, the state news agency alleged, rather pointedly, the theft of sheep, flock, and household items of non-Turkmens and their distribution among Turkmens in the aftermath of conflict (Khajehnejad 2020, 209–210). The newsletter of CHCPT reported that on the morning of May 30, 1979, the residents of the small village, Kuchek Nazarkhani, stopped a combine from harvesting their lands. In the afternoon, the landowner reportedly came to the village in the company of armed Komiteh men, who opened fire, killing three teenagers and injuring two residents (DCM1, 136–137). Furthermore, *Kayhan* reported an explosion on June 10 in Gonbad Kavus that left one dead and two injured (DCM2, 151–152). With the councils extending, a certain unease also spread across the region.

The armed conflict accelerated and solidified the movement: in addition to the peasants, various social constituencies in the region realized the value of collective self-assertion for not just political but social rights. In the months following the conflict, the Turkmen council movement grew closer with the OIPFG. Hashemi and Hassanpour were called out and replaced by Esfandiar Karimi (Fereidoun). At this time, the OIPFG had no serious political rivals in the region and enjoyed unsurpassable popularity. Concurrently, while the OIPFG was popular among many social constituencies nationwide, nowhere else did it have the influence it had in Turkman Sahra. This probably explains why Fadaiyan took a leading role in the council movement — a grassroots movement that they certainly had not created by design or intention — and consistently reflected the movement's achievements and challenges in the pages of the weekly *Kar*, as did independent daily newspapers *Ayandegan* and *Peygham-e Emrooz*, before they were shut down by the regime on August 8, 1979 (Elwell-Sutton and Mohajer 1987). In this period, the OIPFG followed the strategy for promoting popular self-management and self-governance: the workers' councils and unions and the peasants' councils.

Just about two months into a revolution for freedom, the number of pro-regime pressure groups increased and spread all over the country; they attacked the offices, gatherings, performances, and rallies of any and all groups outside the pro-Khomeini orbit. These pressure groups — commonly called Hezbollah — guided by Komiteh and IRGC consisted of their elements in plain clothes that headed bands of local hoodlums, criminal thugs, and mobs of religious, alienated, and unemployed men. These men did not hesitate to destroy, injure, even kill. Their first significant public show of force was the demonic attack on the women's rally on International Women's Day (March 8, 1979). A case in point (with bitter irony) is the brutal assault during the April 17, 1979 rally to the Premier's Office in Tehran organized by the National Democratic Front that protested the continued pressure and infringements on freedom of speech and assembly. The repressive trend continued and reached its height in August 1979 (for details, see Chapter 5).

The clerics, under Khomeini's protection, pulled the strings, and after creating the IRGC and purging or expelling top-ranking generals of the Iranian army, Khomeini felt confident that he could defeat secular as well as any other opposition. He had placed the affairs of the state with veteran politician Mehdi Bazargan, the Premier of Provisional Government, and his cabinet that consisted of liberal-minded, Muslim or secular, personalities — a coalition of the Freedom Movement (Nehzat-e Azadi), National Front, and Iran Nation Party. They were charged with running the country in uncertain times. These politicians emulated technocrats. But it was Khomeini, his clerical network, and the IRGC that pushed the country's political scene in the direction they wished, unambiguously ignoring the Provisional Government. By design or not, this "dual government" caused much confusion within the opposition: while repressive Khomeini and his band trumpeted anti-imperialist slogans, which appealed to the radical opposition, moderate Bazargan tried to manage the affairs externally and internally through negotiations. The "anti-imperialist petite-bourgeoisie," an inept moniker given to Khomeini's clique by the Tudeh Party (and few other leftist groups) was thus contrasted with the "compromising liberals" of the Provisional Government. This was an inept application of Marxist class analysis to the Iranian situation in 1979.

As such, while the mob violently attacked free assemblies throughout the country with the implicit approval of Khomeini, the suppressed groups petitioned the Provisional Government with their grievance. Soon, one after the other the ministers resigned. Khomeini masterfully exploited the "liberals" to run the government until he could fill the state with trusted persons. Bazargan and company, in contrast, had agreed to serve, hoping that they could contain clerical radicalism and promote some democratic principles and rights. In short, while managing the country's affairs until the clerics and their associates were ready to occupy all positions of power, the Provisional Government also provided a wonderful decoy that shrouded the views of Fadaiyan and other "anti-imperialist" leftists into seeing the cunning and brutal nature of the clerics. Even a year after the Revolution, when the Provisional Government was already gone, in one of its rallies (on Friday, January 4, 1980, to be precise) the OIPFG, unable to break away from its inept "class analysis" of politics, still naïvely and distastefully demanded "exposure of liberal capitalists."

Just about ten days after the armed conflict ended, Persians and Turkmens in Gonbad Kavus met in early April, as *Kayhan* (no. 10681, 11 April 1979) reported, to brainstorm about the upcoming city council elections. Ministry of Interior delegate, Dr. Ali Rasuli was quoted as having stated that the meeting was amicable and that an agreement had been reached to hold the elections. He declared that there was no misapprehension by the two sides (DCM2, 148). A week later, Mazandaran Governor Dr. Tabataba`i confirmed the meeting (*Kayhan* April 21, 1979) in his speech in Gonbad Kavus, stressing that the council was a body to represent all of the people and had nothing to do with being Persian or Turkmen (DCM2, 148).

Between March and May 1979 there was a rapid expansion of the councils and associations, in town and country. In rural areas, many villagers wrote and signed petitions, addressed to the CHCPT, expressing their willingness to join the organization and naming their needs, and the CPCTP published several original petitions for proof (LSTP, 51–53, 99–104, 136–138). Each village termed specific demands. For instance, the council of Tatar Olya, one of the largest and most progressive villages, having confiscated lands and machinery, requested CHCPT's assistance in protecting their surrounding meadow, building roads, creating a Rug-Weavers' Council and an emergency fund, as well as a library, a public meeting venue, and the council office. This council had confiscated 850 hectares, and it was then joined with seven other councils. Together, they created the Union of Tatar Olya Councils. Hossein Jorjani played a key role in creating and leading this Tatar Olya council and was its representative to the Plenary Union of Councils (LSTP, 94–95; *Kar* 1980f: 3; see also Appendix 1). Jorjani was born to a farmer family and completed a certificate program from the Hamedan Institute of Agriculture. Tatar Olya demands are evidently ambitious and long term. As a result, the CHCPT created a "rural study committee" to evaluate the conditions of each village and propose recommendations (LSTP, 151). Also, it was made clear that land occupation did not mean that the councils distributed land. It meant that they confiscated land on behalf of the entire village as *collective ownership* (LSTP, 151). This aspect is important: land was deemed as commons, to be "owned" only collectively, which, in turn, is a key component of the Turkmen council movement based on their claim to *ancestral* lands.

In the towns, one of the first councils was notably the Turkmen Women's Association, established in the last days of winter. Created by the female students of Kamineh high school, it was housed in Pishgam's office and enjoyed the visible support of non-Turkmen women. Activists of the Women's Association often appeared in public in bright red traditional Turkmen apparel. These activists established literacy classes for women, advocating for support for rural rug-weaving girls and women. The CHCPT issued a May Day statement on behalf of the Rug-weaving Women's Council that specified that "The struggle of rug-weaving women of Turkman Sahra is not only against capitalist oppression but also against the traditions that segregates women from men, and peoples from each other" (LSTP, 108–109).

The Teachers' Association of Turkman Sahra was founded at this time by teacher-activists of Gonbad Kavus. Makhtoom was a prominent figure among them. The teachers, as well, championed ways to propagate Turkmen language, arts, and music, and held events (DCM1, 22–23), not only in Turkmen towns and villages but also in Tehran and other cities. Later, members of this association participated in the city council elections of Gonbad Kavus. The CPCTP also created the Arts and Folklore Centre of Plains of Turkmen to promote Turkmen culture. The Centre mobilized local artists and produced published works and recordings of traditional Turkmen music that were sold as cassettes around the country (Atabay 2023). These associations did have measurable impact. Bringing visibility to Turkmens and releasing them from Pahlavi-imposed segregation, these efforts introduced the Turkmen culture to the rest of the country in a celebratory way.

During the council movement but also after its decline (see Chapter 5), the OIPFG continued to promote Turkmen music by releasing tapes of Turkmen masters and bands under its own art centre, the Arts Workshop of Iran. A *baghshi* music concert in Tehran on International Workers' Day in 1979 was released by the Arts Workshop of Iran. The books published in this period in Persian and Turkmen by CPCTP/CHCPT or OIPFG included: *Makhtoomqoli, Goroghli, Invitation: Passages of Life and Struggles of Makhtoomqoli Faraghi, Turkmen Poet; The Origins of Turkmen People; Daikhan; Alphabet and Rules for Writing and Reading Turkmen Language; Adam and Dunya;* and *The Life and Struggles of Turkmen People.* During this period the CPCTP published periodicals, *Iel Guyji* (*The People's Power*) and *Turkman Sahra Newsletter,* and CHCPT the *Journal of Turkmen Women* (DCM2, 439, 442–443; DCM1, 527). The Pishgam students actively created libraries in towns and villages (Azad 1980, 26), the number of which exceed 100 rural libraries (Khajehnejad 2020, 209). Note that poet Makhtoomqoli Faraqi (1723 to circa 1790s) was to Turkmen language what Ferdowsi was to Persian or Shakespeare to English.

Speaking of the International Workers' Day of 1979: although it never was a national holiday (as in some European countries), in Iran this day was officially recognized in 1946 when in the critical context of the time, the young Shah appointed seasoned politician Ahmad Qavam (1256–1334) to form the government. At this time, socialist Tudeh Party was at the height of its social power, and in the immediate post–Second World War context, as occupation of Iran by Soviet, British, and American forces was expected to come to an end, Qavam decided to form a coalitional government by appointing three Tudeh leaders to ministerial positions. Under pressure by them, Qavam's government officially recognized International Workers' Day (May 1, or 11 Ordibehesht in the Persian calendar). After the 1953 coup, it was not possible to celebrate May Day (however, it was secretly celebrated in small, private gatherings). The 1979 May Day parade was therefore the historic moment of returning to the May Day celebration of Iranian workers. This particular day is symbolic: if previous assaults of the nascent state on social movements across the country were not indicative of the new rulers' true motives, this day marked a definite rift between the ruling Islamists and the workers and activists of the growing secular left spectrum. The Islamists held their own demonstration, attended by tens of thousands, at which the future (first) president of Iran, Abolhasan Bani Sadr (who escaped Iran in 1981 and died in exile in Paris in 2021), and influential ideologue of the Islamic Republic, Ayatollah Seyed Mohammad Beheshti (who was assassinated in 1981), addressed the crowd in Tehran. Islamist Ali Rabi'i spoke to the crowd as the "workers' representative" and threatened worker activists by attributing their efforts to the "enemy and counter revolution." Ayatollah Khomeini, too, sent a televised message (in his usual bad Persian), one filled with his usual empty rhetoric, using the vague religious designation of "downtrodden" (*mostaz'afin*) for the workers, stating that "work is the origin of all existents" and "the world is throughout the workers' day, not just one day!" (quoted in Radio Zamaneh 2023). All the while since the Revolution, the state pushed for dismantling independent workers' bodies and unions (a legacy of strike committees) and promoting its own "Islamic Associations" in factories to marginalize and persecute independent workers' activists, unionists, and syndicalists. The cunning rulers of the country had decoded the Machiavellian mannerism of simultaneously saturating society with populist rhetoric and dismantling opposition outside the public's eyes.

On May Day of 1979, however, a show of workers' power was prominently displayed when the OIPFG, Kurdish parties, the National Democratic Front, women's organizations, Teachers' Independent Association, Unified Oil Industry Workers' Union, and the Centre to Coordinate Workers' Unions, under the title "Coordinating Committee to Celebrate May Day," invited a rally to celebrate May Day across the country. I attended this rally, and it was the largest I had witnessed since the rallies of the revolutionary period. In Tehran, this rally was attended by hundreds of thousands, possibly even half-a-million people (*Peygham-e Emrooz* 1979, 2). Among other cities, the rally in the Kurdish city of Mahabad (home to the short-lived Mahabad Republic of 1946) was notably large and well attended. In Tabriz, too, tens of thousands rallied in the streets (*Kar* 1979d, 1–2). Almost everywhere, Islamist thugs attacked these rallies, insulting women, and injuring demonstrators. *Peygham Emrooz* (1979, 2) reported these attacks and registered how women and men participated in this rally shoulder to shoulder. In state propaganda, the conflicts in Kurdistan and Turkman Sahra were attributed to "ethnic disturbances" and intrigues of "international arrogance," but the May Day parade clearly indicated two diverging Irans: that of the authoritarian Islamists and that of the secular left as an inclusive defender of the weak and marginalized, notwithstanding the actual limitations of vision among leftist groups of the time. The 1979 Revolution was the mother of them both.

The councils and land issue both remained two of the government's unresolved hotspots. In Spring 1979, the pro-Khomeini mob was tasked with regularly attacking and dismantling the councils of factory workers and government employees from the outside, while the new regime's insiders regrouped and pushed to transform these councils into "Islamic Councils" (or associations) and thus ancillaries of the new regime. As a case in point, Peyman Jafari (2021) narrates the rise and decline of *showras* in the oil sector between 1979 and 1982. This trend also started cautiously in Turkman Sahra by propagating the idea of "Islamic Councils" that sounded more like "advisory councils" without any power ("On Councils" 1979, 29; see Chapter 5). In other words, the so-called "Islamic Councils" served as the ornamental bodies of empty populist claims of the Islamic Republic's rising ruling oligarchy, whereby concealing the real relations of power that disenfranchised the working people. Insofar as the CHCPT de facto governed the peasant councils, the regime's directive remained largely rhetorical at this time. The councils in Kurdistan (which needs a separate study) also resisted this push by the state.

Land continued to be a sensitive issue in the aftermath of a revolution that was manned, in its bulk, by economically disenfranchised populace. Huge numbers of them were previously landless peasants that, thanks to the land reform that had occurred over a decade earlier, had now been thrown to inhabit the shantytowns surrounding large cities in search of work. And it was not just in the Plains of Turkmen or Kurdistan that land had increasingly grown into the revolutionary government's nightmare. From Baluchistan to Khuzestan to Azerbaijan, the land issue persisted: a legacy of the Pahlavi dispossessive modernization. It was clear that sooner or later the state had to supply a legal, universal solution, which it eventually offered in the new constitution written by the Assembly of Experts and finalized on November 15, 1979, before it was ratified in the referendum of December 2–3, 1979. Article 7 of this constitution recognizes *showra* as decision-making and management organs of all levels of governance, from central government to villages, with the scare-note that the council's power is "to be decided by law," thereby rendering it possible to turn these councils into cosmetic appendages of the state. This principle reappears in Article 104 that recognizes workplace councils (with the same note!). Moreover, Article 44 recognizes cooperatives as one of the three sectors of Iranian economy (in addition to state-owned and private sectors), and of course, the same note persists here too. Article 46 states: "Everyone is the owner of their own legitimate enterprise and work (*kasb va kar*) and no one can prevent another from pursuing enterprise and work based on their claims of ownership of their own enterprise and work." The article contains a faint reference to the issue of land (and other disputed ownerships). In the decades to come, this article's ambiguity led to savage accumulation of land and businesses by the rentier, corrupt oligarchy, but in the 1980s it was interpreted as suggesting that the state recognized the grievances of dispossessed peasants.

After the armed conflict, leading Turkmen activists and organizations chose a clearly reconciliatory approach toward the government but without making unprincipled compromises. They had realized that the council movement's survival depended on *not* antagonizing the state and maintaining at all times the delicate balance between advocating and promoting the councils on one hand, and the unreceptive, if not intimidating, interventions of the regime's armed forces and local institutions on the other. The government's consistent refusal to recognize the councils complicated the situation. In late May 1979, Premier Bazargan issued an ultimatum that the peasant councils were illegal and should be removed (DCM1, 526).

Expectedly, however, in the Plains of Turkmen in April–June 1979, the government found itself pressed to take a position, however piecemeal, with regard to the grassroots land occupation. The spring harvest time was approaching in June, and so far, Turkmen peasants had successfully self-organized and managed to cultivate the land collectively. On May 25, 1979, the second congress of peasants' councils was held and it declared that "land belongs to those who work it" (LSTP, 209). Meanwhile, village councils held meetings to organize the harvest (Khajehnejad 2020, 219). In anticipation of harvest time, a "delegation of good will" of Turkmens, headed by respected Turkmen-Sunni cleric Arzanesh met with Ayatollah Khomeini and the Minister of Interior in Qom on June 13 or 14, 1979 (Khajehnejad 2020, 219). Although Arzanesh mentioned that the meeting was fruitful (Khajehnejad 2020, 222), for the Turkmens the outcome was notably underwhelming. Khomeini had made some repetitive, generic remarks about how revolutionary Iran had inherited problems from the Pahlavi reign. He was cunning enough to know not to address the Turkmens, only advising them that they had waited for a solution for fifty-odd years and could wait another couple of years (in Khajehnejad 2020, 219–222)!

A day or two after this historic meeting, the spokesperson of this delegation, Toomaj, held a news conference in Tehran (in *Ayandegan*, no. 3377, 17 June 1979, p. 3). He opened his remarks by stating that the Plains of Turkmens have the most fertile lands but Turkmen peasants have been living in misery. The Turkmens offered a solution to the land issue that they hoped would be useful as a model for other regions. He continued that while the government had not recognized the councils, "the government had not offered a specific policy regarding land issues" either. Characterizing the efforts of the peasants and CHCPT as an anti-imperialist move, he accused the government of trying to destroy the councils. Toomaj was quoted as stating: "in our negotiation with the government's representatives, I reached the conclusion that this year the produce from the lands of the despised Pahlavi family and their associates is to be harvested under the supervision of the representatives of the government, Central Headquarters [CHCPT], and peasants councils," with the revenue to be allocated to village improvements. Toomaj also asserted that the best solution to the "national issue" was self-governance (*khodmokhtari*) and he rejected the interpretation that this means secession (in DCM 1, 147–150; see also Khajehnejad 2020, 219).

A couple of days after this meeting, in response to the land issue arising from all over the country and following the new regime's motto of economic self-sufficiency (which, ironically, only unleashed a plunder neoliberal economy, feeding a gluttonous and corrupt ruling kleptocracy beginning in the 1990s), Ayatollah Khomeini declared Jahad-e Sazandegi or Reconstruction Crusade (Jihad or Effort; *Ayandegan*, no. 3377, 17 June 1979, p. 1). As we see, this emerging organ played a key role in addressing land issues across the country in favour of the government's central authority and assisted with the assimilation of the genuine councils.

But immediately after this meeting, Gonbad Kavus Islamic Revolutionary Prosecutor issued a curious order with two directives (*Kayhan*, no. 10734, 17 June 1979): "As regards the acquisition of that which rightfully belongs to the downtrodden (*mostaz'afin*), Gonbad Kavus Revolutionary Prosecutor advises the landowners to willingly submit 20% of their spring wheat harvest to Gonbad Revolutionary Prosecutor in trust," reads the first directive. "Because this 20% is in trust and belongs to public treasury (*beytolmal*) any abuse or infringement or waste will be against the law and Shari'a (*shar'*) and the perpetrators will be prosecuted" (in DCM2, 149). The second directive was even more curious: "If a person holds claims against another person's land and [consequently] should personally and directly cause disruption in harvest, his actions are null, and such persons should first contact the Revolutionary Prosecutor and seek advice" (in DCM2, 149).

By requiring landowners to submit 20 percent of their harvest in trust to the Prosecutor's Office (supposedly for future distribution among grieving peasants), this order practically turns the issue of *distribution* into one of *charity* overseen by the state. In its warning against disrupting harvest, the order also pointedly, albeit implicitly, refuses to recognize the peasants' land claims. This rushed, ill-advised, and ill-devised order carried no executive weight and never came into effect. It was a weak political posturing, although a telling one.

Immediately afterward, the CHCPT issued a counter-statement. According to the CHCPT, it was agreed in previous negotiations with the government delegation that the peasants had a right to harvest all lands of Amlak-e Pahlavi as well as those of now émigré large landowners. The negotiations with the government continued when another delegation came to Gonbad Kavus and spoke with the 500 delegates of councils. This second government delegation affirmed the previous agreement, but because it was in relation to the small landowners' lands for which the government delegates had proposed the 20 percent solution, the Turkmens still rejected this proposal (Atabay 2023; Khajehnejad 2020, 218–219; LSTP, 205–207). It should be noted that after the "peace," the Revolutionary Council issued a decree (*madeh-ye vahedeh*) stating that disputes over landownership should be settled through a special commissioner consisting of the delegates from the Ministry of Interior, Ministry of Agriculture, Ministry of Justice, and two local trustees (*mo'tamed*) nominated by the Governor of Gorgan and Gorgan Regional Bureau of Agriculture with the approval of the provincial governor. This commission was tasked to resolve land disputes and its decisions were final (Gorgani 1979, 114). The decree does not mention Turkmen representatives. So, one can deduce that this also was the composition of the team that negotiated with the CHCPT. Still, it seems that the CHCPT involved government representatives in its approach. For instance, the report of the meeting of councils of Kalaleh district (May 24, 1979) shows that the council decided to hold a next meeting to specifically discuss the "condition of harvest from dispossessed lands that are confiscated" in the presence of representatives from CHCPT and the government (Khajehnejad 2020, 349).

As harvest time approached, small landowners and representatives of the large ones intensified their lobbying of the government. In a newspaper interview, Toomaj reported on "the repeated visits of the feudals to Tehran, Ministry of Interior, Imam's Office, and other places…. [They] had even posted banners in Ministry of Interior [building] that we [the landowners] needed a brigade (*goruh-e zarbat*) to repress the counter-revolutionaries" (quoted in DCM1, 147). Meanwhile, though, the CHCPT mobilized the councils and instructed them to harmonize their next move. On May 18, 1979, 400 delegates of peasant councils, of all nationalities, gathered in Pishgam Youth Hall (former Scouts Hall) in Gonbad Kavus to discuss the challenges ahead and receive directives from the CHCPT (*Kar* 1979e, 6).

After a successful harvest in June, the CHCPT held Turkman Sahra's first Jashn-e Gandom or Wheat Festival on July 16, 1979, to celebrate the occasion (DCM1, 527). It was followed by a second festival in Yalmeh Saliyan village (DCM1, 451) a couple of months later. This festival was an old Turkmen tradition that had been abandoned during the Pahlavi reign due to land dispossession (see Allamehzadeh 1980). In the meantime, the councils continued to emerge in every profession and social group in the region. The expansion of councils and unions was met by occasional clashes. An example is the attack of Gendarmerie forces on a fishermen's rally in Ashuradeh on July 16 (DCM1, 527). Every day, hundreds visited the CHCPT office in Gonbad Kavus seeking directives or to dispute arbitration. Toomaj and Makhtoom were the key figures of CHCPT in matters pertaining to farming, land, and councils.

In July, a documentary titled, *Speak Turkmen* (*Harf Bezan Turkmen*) was released. Directed by Reza Allamehzadeh (1980), this 40-minute documentary was commissioned by the CHCPT. Allamehzadeh enjoyed a reputation among Iranian leftists and artists. He was a graduate of the Film and Television Institute. Charged with planning to take hostage the Royal Family, he was arrested in a SAVAK sting operation and tried in military court in 1974 along with a group of twelve artists and poets. His death penalty was commuted to life imprisonment (see Vahabzadeh 2010, 218). *Speak Turkmen* was widely screened in colleges and universities across Iran, mostly through Pishgam organizations. The documentary itself seems rushed and lacks artistic merits and even a coherent pictorial narrative. It is a montage of exotifying imagery of Turkman Sahra, while offering interviews with Turkmens, including Toomaj who curiously appears both as an interviewee and interviewer (of Turkmen peasants). In the film, Turkmen and Baluchi peasants speak about their conditions. Its shortcomings notwithstanding, *Speak Turkmen* brought into public view the tangible image of immiseration of rural Turkman Sahra: devastated, impoverished, uneducated. There is a cry for social justice in the film that found its audience in the young, secular left revolutionaries across the country. I was moved by the documentary when I saw it in the summer of 1979.

In the months prior to the documentary's release, Toomaj, Makhtoom, and Vahedi (a Turkmen lawyer), had made several visits to Tehran (and elsewhere) to promote the Turkmen cause nationwide, speak to pro-Fadai gatherings, negotiate with government officials, and, as one imagines, meet in secret with OIPFG leaderships. They gave interviews to, and appeared in, newspapers but as "Turkmen spokespersons," anonymously. *Speak Turkmen* rendered Toomaj a Fadai celebrity in the minutes he appears in the film: with his thick, black rectangular glasses, thin black moustache, boney cheeks, humble demeaner, and palpable rapport with the peasants, Toomaj became the epitome of a Turkmen organic intellectual in the imagination of the left. He rose in public consciousness as the face of the movement.

Conclusions

Hannah Arendt's astute and ageless observation (as discussed in Chapter 1) is hypostatized in Turkman Sahra in 1979; once top-down authority embodied by the state is weakened, the people spontaneously and quickly converge and build their bodies of self-governance and self-management. Such bodies — as in workers' and other councils across the world and in the townhall meetings of the American revolution — are egalitarian and participatory, or, in short, the truest expression of democratic life. The Iranian workers' strike committees and councils of 1978–1979, studied by Asef Bayat (Chapter 1), also weighed on the imagination of the Turkmen council movement. Arendt made two important observations: the spontaneity of councils and the expansion of the council system as if it were contagious. The Turkmen experience indicates both. Arendt is right that when out of these grassroots and participatory bodies institutions of permanent government arise, as their first step, such institutions curb and destroy the organs of popular self-governance — the councils. In a way, while the Turkmen council movement took its shape by the involvement of Turkmen organic intellectuals associated with the Left, it was an expression of necessity for the economically disenfranchised and culturally marginalized Turkmens. Insofar as it lasted, the council movement offered an alternative social imagination and body politic. The Turkmens offered something *new* by virtue of the "miracle of birth" (Arendt 1963, 211): the councils phenomenalized and offered an alternative order, and they suffered in the first few months in the hands of the rising authoritarian Islamist regime precisely because they had dared to envision something new, an alternative to existing political orders.

What is more, in her book *On Violence* (1970), Arendt differentiated violence from several overlapping or synonymous terms — power, strength, force, and authority. This allows us to see the often-overlooked aspect of the councils. To reiterate, I follow Arendt in stating that once the force of the state is slackened, as in the Iranian Revolution, the people collectively take the initiative to forge their own community — in schools, factories, universities, workplaces, or ancestral lands — and create the means of self-governance as diverse equals. A free people's convergence in creating their own body politic is a nonviolent moment of creating power. Once we take note of this, we realize that the state is the institution of violence (as Max Weber recognized long ago) that imposes itself through force to not only prevent the people's collective power from emerging but also to disallow a life driven by nonviolent power.

Iranians faced two possibilities in the immediate aftermath of the Revolution: one possibility was another patriarchal, authoritative, top-down, power-over political system that was now Islamist, discriminatory, and intolerant, one that emulated the toppled regime in being repressive, and was intent upon destroying meaningful social differences in favour of ruling over a forcefully homogenized populace. The second possibility was that Iran could have a participatory, nonviolent, self-governing body politic driven by egalitarian, power-with, and inclusive imagination that celebrated and supported diversity and was guided by the principle of equality and social justice. I argue that both visions were present during the Spring of Freedom. The first grew rapidly like metastatic cancer through waves of violent shocks. The second was genuinely and gently present, despite the serious shortcomings of its movements, and pushed for change, but was crushed by the violent force of the state.

The Turkmen council movement was for both land and culture and these two could not be viewed as separate concerns. The livelihood of rural Turkmens inescapably depended on occupying and managing the land at the grassroots level, the land that was stolen from them, and yet, this could not have been achieved without cultural revival, without establishing the long repressed Turkmen national identity. As such, the inseparable struggle for land and culture indicates the revival of a people: only within a (revitalized) cultural universe could the issue of secure and dignified livelihood be meaningful. Stated differently, both culture and land informed the vision of a free Turkman Sahra. Land occupation, however, came with popular force. This is how the movement's first body emerged as the CPCTP, and the CHCPT came later, but once the latter found its footing in the grassroots land occupations, it subsumed the former. In the absence of state funding and promotion of multinational cultures in Iran, the self-organized, grassroots organizations like CPCTP took over the task of constructing a new identity.

We have already seen that traditionally there was no tribal hierarchy, concentrated power, and ruling among the Turkmens (Lambton 1953, 160). This is an important cultural factor that contributed to the council movement. For the councils to take off, there was sufficient ancestral cultural background to immediately make village councils graspable by average Turkmen. And soon, as noted, with the efforts of educated activists, the traditional *yashuli* councils were transformed into modern-day, elected councils. The convergence of ancestrality and modern ideas in this context is remarkable — and it reminds us of the present-day struggles of indigenous peoples across the world. As the council system spread across the Plains of Turkmen, a new vision of Iran emerged and was articulated by CHCPT. The fifth article of CHCPT declaration (April 4, 1979) demanded a semi-autonomous Turkmen province within a federal system of unified and shared authority. This vision was not unique to this region: the Kurds were the first to speak of a federative system in Iran where Kurdistan could be a semi-autonomous province. But neither the monarchy nor the Islamic Republic would tolerate such a vision, thanks to their patriarchal and statist prejudices.

The relationship between Fadaiyan and the Turkmen council movement is best understood as an "elective affinity": each sought in the other what it lacked in itself; each gave to the other what the other needed. In the Turkmen council movement, the OIPFG had found its greatest grassroots ally, as in Turkman Sahra the OIPFG had no serious rival. In Fadaiyan, the Turkmen activists had found a strong ally that could propagate their cause nationwide. The grassroots Turkmen council movement gave a unique historic opportunity to Fadaiyan to champion the cause of a national minority. At this time, the OIPFG was generally an advocate of democratic rights and a defender of workers, peasants, and minorities, notwithstanding its limited (Third World Marxist-Leninist) ideological vista that cherished clashes with imperialism and as such strategically faltered on defending human rights, the rights of women, and freedom of speech. Fadaiyan's support for Turkmens in 1979 was a clear indication of their advocacy of the marginalized and on par with the original vision of the PFG (back in 1971) as selfless defenders of the underprivileged. Out of a small group of militants that had already rejected armed struggle by 1977 and that were struggling to find a way to formulate Jazani's ideas of popular mobilization, the OIPFG was catapulted by the Revolution into a dreamt-of popular support that had resolved their theoretical dilemma (inherited from Jazani) in practice. They had not planned for such popularity, but now they no longer needed to theorize mass mobilization; Fadaiyan already had it in their bosom. Because of the reactionary and autocratic nature of the new regime, they had been driven into the position of the defender of the rights of the secular, educated middle class, working class, poor people, peasants, and minorities. They had to fulfill their democratic duty. This is a paradox: while Fadaiyan defended democratic and popular institutions like councils and unions, they neglected the task of building nationwide democratic alliances. We should note that the OIPFG was the largest leftist party in the country at the time, and the second largest group outside of the ruling Islamists (after the People's Mojahedin). In all fairness, let it be noted, it was still very likely that even a wide alliance of political and social forces outside of the regime might have been crushed by the Islamists' fiendish violence. But such an alliance was the necessity of the moment, as was recognized back then and appears to us in retrospect. Alas, it was not realized.

Complications were unfolding by Summer 1979, and the Turkmen council movement was yet to face its greatest challenge: how to sustain what Turkmens had built: the councils.

Chapter 5

The Councils and Collective Life
Expansion, Repression, Assimilation

The Plains of Turkmen have never seen such an expansive national and class struggle.

...

Analyzing specifically how to connect the national (melli) and class struggles in the Plains of Turkmen with the nationwide (sarasari) democratic movement in Iran, and in particular with the growing struggle of Iranian working class, is one of [our] crucial tasks.

— Cultural-Political Centre Turkmen People and Central Headquarters of Councils of Plains of Turkmen

AS THE SPRING OF 1979 TURNED to summer, the Turkmen peasants' council movement emerged triumphantly from its most crucial challenges. Much pain had been inflicted on the movement as it had dared to bring something new to the world of Iranian subalterns. First, the movement was forced to go through a dramatic, bloody, and imposed confrontation with the new state's ideological paramilitary, just as the new ruling oligarchy gradually consolidated its power, organized its supporters politically and in new armed forces, and tried to repress the irreducible diversity of the participants of the 1979 Revolution. Next, through united, grassroots resistance to the state-imposed, albeit inconsistent, policies and regulations regarding harvest and landownership, the council movement managed to assert its collective will. Enjoying the steadfast and popular backing of Turkmen masses; attracting growing support from non-Turkmen residents; having the unshakable backing of Iran's largest leftist organization, the Organization of Iranian People's Fadai Guerrillas (OIPFG); and lastly, having unrivalled recognition by other grassroots movements and the Iranian Left in general, the Central Headquarters of Councils of Plains of Turkmen (CHCPT) and

Cultural-Political Centre of Turkmen People (CPCTP) had taken de facto control of the region without confronting the regime, especially in towns where their revolutionary, symbolic, and cultural presence appeared to be strikingly refreshing to the gaze of an outsider. At this time, Turkmen leaders and activists had realized that the survival of their movement, as the epigraph to this chapter indicates, depended on making mutual and lateral connections with the progressive elements and democratic movements in the country by building "relations of equivalence" (Laclau and Mouffe 1985) with other movements. They had realized that the Turkmen demands for cultural revival and land-related collective-legal rights, which defined Turkmen nationalism at this point, could only be met in the context of a democratic Iran.

In contrast, resolutely intent upon consolidating their power, the rising ruling oligarchy was unyielding. Agents and armed forces of the state continued to roam the region, trying to exert control in towns but more menacingly in rural areas. The landowners continued to actively lobby the Provisional Government and the clerical establishment while sending their hired cronies and Komiteh to harass rural Turkmens who had taken over their lands. The state had learned its lesson from the previous conflict with the Turkmens (back in March), as well as the continuing ones in Kurdistan, and the emerging commanders of newly established forces, Komiteh and the Islamic Revolutionary Guards Corps (IRGC), were devising new strategies to put these movements out of operation for good. The regime's strategists had realized that there were no sweeping options for resolving the "issues" of land, workers, and national and cultural minorities, and that each movement should be dealt with through combined and specific strategies. To this end, as history teaches us in retrospect, the Islamists had their dress rehearsal in suppressing social movements in Summer 1979.

Significantly, the "first war" and the council movement brought the Turkmens, one of Iran's most marginalized peoples up to that point, to nationwide spotlight. It was not just that only the OIPFG, the Kurdish parties, or other leftist groups advocated for the Turkmen cause. In independent newspapers and magazines, many non-Turkmens sympathetically wrote about the oppression and dispossession of Turkmens by the monarchy, as well as their inalienable right to restorative justice, land distribution, and self-governance. If in an imaginary alternative universe Iranians were not forced under authoritarian Islamists, it would have been likely that the Turkmen council movement had inspired the radical rethinking of Iran as potentially a world-class participatory, democratic, and federative system fit for such an irreducibly diverse nation.

The Structure of Councils

By late spring of 1979, the Turkmen council movement had clearly found its effective organizational form. What the Turkmens founded was an exemplary model of power-with, participatory, and democratic body politic — not to mention the fact that this model was nonviolent. This was achieved somewhat heuristically, since the entire movement shaped up rather intuitively, albeit collectively, as the process of its emergence shows (Chapter 4). But it must be noted that the movement's organizational shape and democratic structure was dialectically solidified and accelerated in the face of the growing threats of the rising authoritarian regime and the large landowners. The Turkmens' model of grassroots, participatory democracy was almost lost on the activists in the turbulent months of 1979 and on the historians ever since. This form of organization has much to offer to today's world, in particular for indigenous movements and those of peoples with ancestral collective roots in land. In fact, as the conclusion will show, there is a transnational significance to the Turkmen council movement that was completely overlooked until this study: at least in a couple of significant cases in the world after the Turkmen council movement, in Chiapas and Rojava, similar forms of participatory democracy were put in practice.

Accordingly, let us not forget that we are dealing with, literally, a grassroots movement, evidenced by the fact that originally a few councils (e.g., the Khojeh Logarkaz council in late February, which was *possibly* the first) were created by peasants and activists who drew on *yashuli* and *aq saqal* traditions — in short, the councils of trusted elders. With their initial success in land confiscation and peasant mobilization, and given the general discontent of pent-up rage of Turkmen peasants due to their prolonged dispossession and suppression under the ancien régime, the experiment of pioneering councils quickly spread through the region. In the next few weeks, this popular move caused rural and urban activists, especially the Turkmen intellectuals around the CPCTP, to understand the need for a coordinating body that culminated in the CHCPT. My emphasis is the *bottom-up* nature of this movement.

An illuminating and unique document (authored anonymously but jointly published circa November 1979 by CHCPT and CPCTP; in LSTP) speaks of how the councils were organized and became active, and it registers my aforesaid point. According to LSTP, "Soon, to manage their lands and maintain order in the process of working it, the villagers elected some village elderly (*rishsefidan*), but since their struggle contained a particular momentum (*taharrok*), the enthusiastic, energetic, and revolutionary youth promptly replaced the villages' elders and trustees" (LSTP, 268). This transformation, I surmise, was concomitant with the formation of CHCPT. As the document admits, the councils were indeed the outcome of "spontaneous" (*khodbehkhodi*) actions necessitated by the popular land occupation movement, but it evolved and was developed by being braided with revolutionary organic intellectuals (LSTP, 269). Right here, in this account, we witness the movement's theoretical significance, where Hannah Arendt meets Antonio Gramsci (1971); à la Arendt, we observe that when left to themselves, the Turkmen people came together and proved themselves as being capable of self-organizing and self-governing in an egalitarian and participatory fashion; à la Gramsci, we register how the Turkmen organic intellectuals that could articulate the demands of a popular movement were able to lead the movement in a sustainable, progressive way, giving it a long-term vision. The lesson of this study is that these two components — the possibility of egalitarian self-governance and the presence of organic intellectuals — constitute the fundamental condition of grassroots mobilization against the status quo and the joint, oppressive forces of state and land capitalism (see the concluding chapter of this book).

Given the fact that the councils were steadily threatened and harassed by the agents of large landowners and Komiteh personnel, the councils felt the need for mutual support and for coordinating their efforts. The CHCPT found its function — as the headquarters of Turkmen organic intellectuals — precisely here. The village councils of between five and seven members were democratically elected by all residents. The interesting aspect is that elected councillors could be replaced anytime by popular will (LSTP, 269). The common rule across the region was that all members of a village would participate in and share the cultivating and harvesting of wheat, while the cultivation of other grain or produce (and the land allotted to such) was assigned by lottery, with its initial set-up costs paid from the council treasury and then returned to the treasury by the assignees upon harvest. All villagers contributed to the treasury upon council and popular ratification. The common funds were diverted to developing the village: building and maintaining schools, public bathhouses, libraries, roads, and bridges. Also, a specific fund was allocated to taking the critically ill to the city for treatment (LSTP, 270). The transformation of for-profit, agrarian, or land capitalism to this model of communal ownership within such a short period is nothing short of miraculous. The secret in a nutshell? Mobilization and articulation.

Over the course of their development, the village councils were organized into regional unions of seven to fourteen villages, which held weekly meetings among themselves. Then these unions would elect two delegates to the plenary (*sarasari*) union that also met weekly, usually but not exclusively at a nearby town (Gonbad Kavus, Bandar Turkmen, Aqqala, etc.). By November 1979, 280 councils in twenty-five unions were organized under the Plenary Rural Union of Turkman Sahra (LSTP, 4, 271). Of course, these unions only gradually emerged throughout the region, mostly during the spring but even as late as May 1979, as indicated by one case (DCM1, 438–439). One of the primary tasks of these unions was to oversee the process of mechanization of farming (LSTP, 272). At each level, council members made decisions and discussed them at the higher council. The CHCPT would function as the coordinating body. With its members present at all three levels of councils, the CHCPT delivered not only expert agricultural advice but also legal and political training. A newsletter facilitated this process (LSTP, 273–274). Let us not forget that the body of peasants consisted mostly of under-schooled and illiterate men and women. Consequently, political education and expert assessment of the country's conditions that was supplied by educated members of CHCPT was necessary for the thriving of the council movement. This is a remarkable moment of Gramscian organic intellectuals at work, at the heart of a movement and managing its daily affairs. There is no doubt that without the presence of Turkmen organic intellectuals the councils would have never grown into a popular, regional movement that inspired this model of councils all over the country.

Figure 5-1 provides the organizational structure of the peasant council movement. The actual challenges of the village councils included both common issues, such as primarily land confiscation and management,

Figure 5-1. The Structure of the Council System

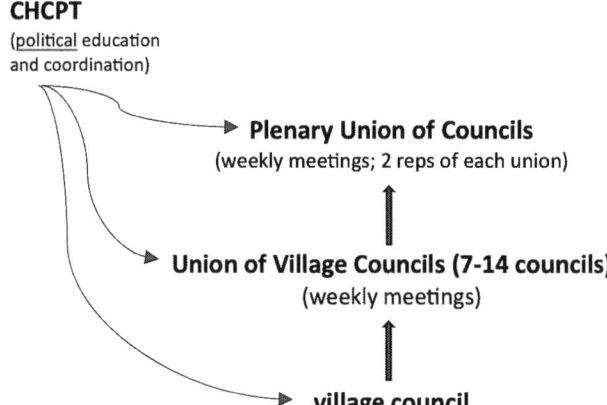

and specific issues pertaining to the locale of each village and its needs, the issues of women, agrarian workers, and non-Turkmen residents. Appendix 1 registers the cases of Tatar Olya and Qezeljeh (Marjanabad) villages. The challenges of these villages and the decisions of their councils exemplify the many facets and complexities of the council movement. A valuable window into the realities of Turkmen villages, Appendix 1 partially relies on the lived memory of village elders regarding land dispossession and provides the activists' picture of the concrete realities of self-governance faced by village councils.

As mentioned in Chapter 2, the councils grew out of the 1979 Revolution and thrived for a while. From factories to barracks, neighbourhoods, Kurdish towns and villages, the councils were the clearest expression of democratic and participatory popular authority. Having already realized that popular self-governance was a direct threat to its centrist and authoritarian rule, the rising Islamist state was intent on dismantling the grassroots councils through a pragmatic melange of repression and appropriation (Islamicization). The Turkmen councils, in my judgment, emerged as possibly the most coherent, elaborate, and programmatic council movement in 1979 Iran. The "first war" showed that the state could not simply dominate Turkmen popular self-governance. From the point of view of the state, a "dress rehearsal" was needed to appraise the state's strategies and tactics, as it consolidated its own ideological and dedicated armed forces.

The Bloody Summer of 1979: The State's Show of Force

The so-called Spring of Freedom (1979) came to an ominous close. On May 30 (later called Black Wednesday), on the directive of Khuzestan Provincial Governor, General Ahmad Madani, the IRGC troops under commander Mohammad Jahanara attacked the sit-in protesters at the Cultural and Political Centre of Arab People in Khorramshahr, shooting and killing protesters. The clashes between Arab nationalists and the regime's forces quickly spread to other Khuzestan cities and towns. Martial law was imposed, and the regime's masked armed men attacked, killed, injured, and detained hundreds of protesters, several of whom were executed in subsequent weeks.

The rapid political developments in Kurdistan immediately following the fall of monarchy drove Iranian Kurds into clashing with the state. Kurdistan was one of the most deprived and oppressed regions in the country. Due to this book's focus, it is not possible to do justice to the developments in Kurdistan, but a short overview of events should offer insights into the dynamics of the Kurds' movement for *khodmokhtari* — autonomy or self-government within a federal system. Following the Revolution, the Kurdish nationalist and social democratic party, the Democratic Party of Iranian Kurdistan (DPIK) — heir to the short-lived, autonomous Mahabad Republic (January–December 1946) and thus being present in the Kurdish collective consciousness — emerged as the leading and most popular party. With its key motto, "Federalism for Kurdistan, Democracy for Iran," the DPIK supporters and *peshmergas* (militants) soon managed to exert unrivalled control and influence over Kurdish regions (across three provinces). The second Kurdish party, the Revolutionary Organization of Toilers of Iranian Kurdistan, or Komala, had its roots in the (brutally suppressed) 1968–1969 Kurdish revolt. Aside from its limited number of university student activists with Maoist tendencies, it was dormant in the 1970s. Komala was officially founded in February 1979. It quickly attracted young Kurds and saw itself as a party of class struggle, accusing the DPIK of tribalism and representing Kurdish bourgeoisie. It regarded the new regime as the class enemy of the Kurds, thus advocating armed struggle to overthrow it — an ideological and unrealistic policy. The OIPFG was the third largest active party in Kurdistan, and while trying to implement its nationwide policy in Kurdistan, the OIPFG remained an influential non-Kurdish party in the region. One can easily see that from the very beginning, the new state faced the problem of authority in Kurdistan, as its Persian and Shi'i-centric ideology disregarded the regional grievances of national minorities.

Narrating the process of continued clashes between the Kurds and the state requires a separate study. Suffice it to say that the Kurds, seeking this historic opportunity to rectify the injustices of the past, suffered enormous injuries and damages by the army, IRGC, Komiteh, and pro-regime Kurdish militias. The unpredictable nature of the armed clashes hurt and imposed hardships on vast numbers of civilians. In the days of armed uprising against the monarchy — on 10–11 February 1979, just as in other cities or towns across the country — the Kurds, too, raided military barracks and police and Gendarmerie stations, confiscating loads of weapons. So much so that it was not uncommon in the local markets of Kurdish cities like Mahabad and Sanandaj during the first few weeks after the monarchy's downfall to see the army's weapons being bought and sold. Political groups, of course, took advantage and armed their supporters. During the Nawruz (Persian New Year) holidays (starting on March 20) of 1979, right before the "first war" in Turkman Sahra, a major clash between the Kurds and the regime broke out in Sanandaj. The conflict was the culmination of the movements and intrigues of the regime in the previous weeks. The army and air force descended on the city, only to encounter fierce Kurdish resistance. Soon after, peace negotiations between the two sides brought some calm to the region. Following this experience, the Kurds steadfastly boycotted the referendum (as did the Turkmens and the OIPFG). The situation in Kurdistan was complicated by a conflict between (predominantly Sunni) Kurds and (Shi'i) Azerbaijanis in the town of Naqadeh, where, on April 20, 1979, there was the confrontation between the DPIK militants and Azerbaijani militias. After three days of armed conflict, a truce was reached and all militants left the town, letting the army take over and maintain order. Occasional armed clashes between Kurdish parties and the state's forces continued throughout the spring and early summer of 1979. The height of clashes took place during the siege and occupation of the Kurdish town of Paveh by DPIK and Komala and the battle of Paveh on August 14–19, 1979. Outraged, as the (self-appointed) chief commander of the armed forces, Khomeini publicly ordered all military, IRGC, Gendarmerie, and irregular forces of the regime to crush the Kurdish militants.

Khomeini assigned the notorious cleric Sadeq Khalkhali, the regime's sadistic "hanging judge," to Kurdistan. In makeshift, minutes-long "trials" and without any solid evidence, he sentenced several dozen Kurds to death in Paveh, Marivan, Sanandaj, and elsewhere. The sentences were carried out immediately afterward by firing squad. As well, military-sanctioned but seemingly wayward actions of vengeful supporters of the regime spelled disaster in the region. On September 2, 1979, irregular militiamen, attached to Gendarmerie and backed by military, entered the Kurdish village of Qarna near Naqadeh and massacred the residents. The number of victims in various reports ranges between forty-seven and sixty-eight, most of them women and children killed by knives (see *Kar* 1979m: 1–2; *Kar* 1979l). The situation in Kurdistan continued to be extremely volatile within the first year after the Revolution. At this time, the Fadaiyan's headquarters in Tehran was also raided and evacuated.

The OIPFG's official declaration concerning Kurdistan (published in *Kar*, no. 30, 3 September 1979) reflects its policy regarding national minorities, which pertains also to the Turkmen council movement. The declaration points out correctly that by confronting the minorities, the new regime had lost its support among them. According to the article, "The Kurdish people (*khalq-e Kurd*) thought that in a liberated Iran they would attain their just ideals and demands, [a cause] for which they had fought for years and had dedicated many martyrs, and the new state (*hakemiyyat*) would recognize the national rights of this oppressed people within a free Iran" (*Kar* 1979l, 4). The article continued: "Because of its class essence, however, the ruling class (*hakemiyyat*) blocked the anti-imperialist struggles of the people half-way, making impossible the realization of the demands of the Kurdish people, like other peoples, leading the situation to creating a new formation of revolutionary and counterrevolutionary forces in the region" (*Kar* 1979l, 4). The repression of progressive forces, *Kar* announced, "will pave the way for the complete domination of imperialism" (*Kar* 1979l, 5). Analytical errors only create delusions. The OIPFG saw in all this the "conspiracy of reaction and imperialism against the people," thus blaming the "liberals," referring to Bazargan's Provisional Government (*Kar* 1979k, 1, 3), not Ayatollah Khomeini, the real puppet master.

Analyzing this passage as an exemplar reveals the pathology of the Iranian left's error in appraising the nature of the new ruling elite. The declaration identifies the promises of the Revolution but points at the wrong direction analytically because it *reduces* the totalitarian aspect of the fundamentalist ruling clerics to a presumed class essence. Only an erroneous system of assumptions based on a barren "class analysis" could makes this passage make sense. Still, connecting the Kurdish struggle for federative autonomy to "anti-imperialist struggles" of the nation indicates how the Iranian left in general viewed the Revolution: on par with the decolonizing and national liberation movements of the time. For the clerics, such was not the case. They wanted to overthrow the Shah and Islamicize society after their own retrograde *weltanschauung*. Accordingly, the clerics' assault on secular opposition could not be derived from the same leftist reading of the Revolution, and no class analysis could explain the new regime's repressive policy. The struggle for self-governance was a profoundly *democratic* struggle: it surely had a "class character," perhaps much greater in Turkman Sahra than in Kurdistan in this period, but the OIPFG failed to develop a democratic theory, since its views were derived from an uncreative and misplaced application of Leninist class analysis instead of offering an original analysis of the new ruling class and the social movements in the country. To be fair, the Fadaiyan do address the democratic aspect of these struggles (see next section) but only in a secondary fashion and only as it pertains to their own group and allies. In short, they lacked a democratic theory.

But Kurdistan had a much deeper impact on the OIPFG. In light of the nationwide wave of repression, the OIPFG held its first plenum in September 1979 (in four different secret venues) in which sixty members participated. Kurdistan overdetermined the debates. Disagreements over Fadaiyan's presence in Kurdistan boiled down to whether the OIPFG should defend the Kurds officially or unofficially. The attentive reader detects how each position clearly had serious implications for Fadaiyan's policy regarding how to deal both with the regime and with national minorities. This plenum marked the ominous formation (in Central Committee and body) of a majority (which later supported the regime), and a minority (which opposed it). I have illustrated the process of formation of the two factions leading to the schism of 1980 in a previous work (see Vahabzadeh 2010, 69–77), but it is important to mention that either position regarding Kurdistan had supporters among both of the emerging factions. The schism really shaped up regarding disagreement on the OIPFG's past. This also had policy implications. The November

1979 United States embassy takeover by pro-Khomeini students and the subsequent hostage crisis catalyzed the future split.

In the summer of 1979, the OIPFG issued a set of directives to its vast body of supporters. Fadaiyan recommended a decentered and more clandestine type of self-organization with emphasis on creating independent publishing cells to counteract state censorship and raise public awareness. In addition, Fadaiyan advised OIPFG supporters to connect with and organize "the masses" in neighbourhoods and workplaces. Amazingly, while the opposition was under attack by the Komiteh, IRGC, and Islamist brutes, the statement still insisted that the reactionary pressure groups (Islamist thugs) were attached to the old regime by blaming "the hireling SAVAK [Iranian intelligence] elements and bellicose hoodlums who are the same club-wielders of the Rastakhiz Party [the Shah's last political party]" (*Kar* 1979l, 5). Fadaiyan's self-deception in these lines cannot be exaggerated. While a sense of desperation reveals itself in this statement, it also implies that repression maybe transient. It was not: repression continued in ever-growing, destructive waves that by the mid-1980s had effectively eradicated all opposition, killing tens of thousands of people and sending tens of thousands more into self-exile.

This context is important to understand how Kurdistan's drive for federalism and resistance to the regime's totalitarian encroachment and assimilation overdetermined the new state's outlook and future relations with the national-cultural minorities. Although Kurdistan was the clerics' greatest challenge, the latter's continued presence in Kurdistan gave the new state the much-coveted confidence that its armed forces — old and new — were capable of crushing any internal movement, no matter how popular. It was now a matter of careful planning as to how to proceed with eradicating each specific movement. The use of force backed by mob-like mobilization had demonstrated its effectiveness where the regime's supporters enjoyed the upper hand, but elsewhere, force needed to be calculatedly exercised. The regime continued its assault on all opposition from August to September 1979. In succeeding to impose serious setbacks on the Kurdish opposition, a reign of terror descended on the country in the late summer of 1979. Scores of activists across the country and from very different affiliations were beaten, arrested, and tortured by various agencies of the regime. Many were executed or killed extra-judicially.

This period was not just one of repression of movements and the opposition. The regime found it a unique opportunity to attack critical journalism and shut down newspapers and publications. The daily publication, *Ayandegan* (est. 1967) was shut down at this time based on a series of unfounded accusations by the main Islamist newspaper, including its alleged links to SAVAK. In the months leading to the Revolution, *Ayandegan* had critically advocated freedom of speech, its journalists playing a key role in organizing the newspapers' strike, just as in the months after the Revolution *Ayandegan* had reflected the people's struggles through investigative journalism and fought against censorship, thus making itself a target of the regime's loudspeakers including Kayhan and *Jomhuri-ye Eslami* (official organ of the Islamic Republic Party). The closure of *Ayandegan* was accompanied by Islamist mobs raiding and ransacking its office and even distributors (Shahidi 2007, 27). Other newspapers and magazines were also shut down at this time — namely, the left-leaning *Peygham-e Emrooz* (Today's Message), left-leaning satirical weekly *Ahangar* (The Blacksmith), and weekly *Tehran Mosavvar* (Tehran Illustrated). In light of these events, political party organs and their printshops went underground.

The wave of repression alarmed the OIPFG, and in an important *Kar* editorial titled, "Fighting for Freedom and Democratic Rights Is the Essential Duty of All Revolutionary and Progressive Forces," Fadaiyan revealed their deep anxiety about the directions of the country. The editorial speaks of a "new dictatorship" run by the "monopolists" (of power; the clerical rulers): "they are intent upon implementing systems [of repression] within the social and legal fields that were not even possible in the age of Constitutionalism, [and] these systems do not match the existing social relations in Iran and will cause the society to suffer intense social and political contradictions" (*Kar* 1979l, 1, 2). Thus, the editorial advises a resolved defence of freedoms and democratic rights and a firm stance against dictatorship, calling for the convergence of "revolutionary and progressive forces, nationalist, religious, or supporters of the working class" to fight the dominant "monopolists" (*Kar* 1979l, 2). Although such a "convergence" against dictatorship was never realized, this particular stance of the OIPFG was a correct one. Except, once again, allusions to imperialist intrigue, revealing itself through the Islamicized imperial army, casts its shadow over Fadaiyan's delusional outlook. This misguided and schoolish notion of "anti-imperialism" caused the majority faction of Fadaiyan after the group's faithful split in June 1980 to take a reconciliatory tone in approaching the ruling clerics (due to their "anti-west" stance) and relinquish defence of the democratic rights of the people. We will return to this point, as this stance spelled disaster for the Turkmen council movement; in effect, the Turkmen council movement lost its greatest nationwide ally as the pro-regime faction within the OIPFG leadership had paralyzed itself when it came to protecting the Turkmen councils from being appropriated by the regime.

Clearly, what happened in August 1979 was not a confrontation of unruly, renegade militants and the state's armed forces, as the Islamic Republic "historiography" depicts this period — a version also echoed, albeit in different iterations and without much analysis, within meagre accounts dedicated to the subject in scholarly historiographies (see Abrahamian 2008; Amanat 2017; Behrooz 2000, 130–132;). What really happened was that a totalitarian closure on diverse Iranian political life was imposed, there was a wide-ranging assault on hard-won freedoms, and a glimpse into what was to come was offered: the dark decade of 1980 and the massacre and total eradication of all opposition.

To the dismay of freedom-loving Iranians, the colourful and enchanting Spring of Freedom ended in the black and traumatizing summer of blood and lead.

New Developments in Turkman Sahra

The first conflict in Sanandaj and the continued civil war overshadowed progressive initiatives in Kurdistan. Thanks to their profound wisdom, the leaders of the Turkmen council movement did not allow the "first war" to overdetermine their relationship with the new regime. They appreciated the fact that peace would immensely serve the grassroots movement they had organized. Time was on their side and peace would only contribute to their growing movement. They also knew that negotiation with government officials and maintaining delicate relations with the Komiteh and IRGC was key to the movement's survival. The OIPFG was the sole nationwide actor in the Turkman region (unlike Kurdistan) and could exercise measurable influence on the movement's general strategy. At this time, the OIPFG consistently avoided conflict with the regime to augment Fadaiyan's social base throughout the country.

Following the March 1979 referendum that officiated the Islamic Republic, the Revolutionary Council and Provisional Government planned to hold the Islamist version of a constituent assembly — now called the Assembly of Experts (Majles-e Khobregan) — to write the new constitution. Although the Turkmens had boycotted the March referendum, Turkmen leadership decided to offer candidates for this seventy-five-person Assembly elections, scheduled to be held on August 3, 1979, and to commence on August 19, 1979 (during the wave of repression). Assured of their popular support, CHCPT leaders Toomaj and Makhtoom announced their decision to run and be the voice of Turkmens in July (DCM1, 527). Bardi Dardipour also stood as a candidate (DCM1, 170). A meeting was held in Pishgam Youth Hall in Gonbad Kavus on July 25 organized by CPCTP. In its statement, the CPCTP declared that the future constitution must be created by the representatives of "the masses, that is, workers, peasants, toilers, and nationalities (*melliyatha*)" (*Kar* 1979i, 8). Arzanesh also spoke to the crowds, highlighting the fact that the proposed constitution draft (*pishnevis*) had completely disregarded the rights of national minorities, including the Turkmens. In the end, Toomaj spoke and announced that he intended to ensure that "the peoples' right to self-governance (*khodmokhtari*)" was included in the new constitution (*Kar* 1979i, 8). The constitution draft, published in daily papers, showed the undemocratic intents of the ruling elite: an indication of their attempt to control the outcome of the Assembly. *Ayandegan* (no. 3376; 16 June 1979) published the full constitution draft alongside the assurances of government officials, namely Minister Yadollah Sahabi, that the draft could be completely revised, and "non-religious" groups could be elected to the Assembly. Of course, both promises turned out to be lies. In the same issue, *Ayandegan* also published the serious concerns of the OIPFG and a few lawyers.

The Turkmens' decision was consistent with the policy of the OIPFG that also decided to offer candidates across the country for the Assembly of Experts (see *Kar* 1979h, 1–2). The Turkmens had realized that they could not remain a regional movement: the survival of their movement depended on the course of political development in the country. This decision might seem to contradict the referendum boycott, but the OIPFG — and, in fact, several other opposition parties at this time — had realized, if only intuitively, that this might be their last chance to participate in a nonrestricted election and possibly affect the future course of developments in the country through the only democratic means available to them. What alarmed all groups in opposition was the proposed draft constitution that was supposed to be debated and modified by the Assembly. As a *Kar* editorial explains, this proposal both undermined the hard-won freedoms and disregarded social justice–oriented demands of the people, in particular the working class and minorities. At this time, the editorial continued, it would be unwise to simply boycott the elections. The OIPFG also showed it had no illusions about the electoral process: "Clearly, the forces that want to rush an anti-people (*zedd-e mardomi*) constitution and impose it on 37 million citizens of Iran will try to limit the participation of the revolutionary forces and real representatives of the toilers" (*Kar* 1979g, 2). At this time, Fadaiyan's delegate in the region was Esfandiar Karimi (aka Fereidoun) who was tasked with harmonizing the Turkmen council movement with OIPFG policies. Dr. Ferdos Jamshidi Rudbari stood as the OIPFG candidate for the Assembly from Mazandaran province, and he was also supported by CPCTP. Reportedly, Makhtoom and Toomaj received 130,000 votes in the election (Atabay 2023; *Kar* 1980i, 11). They were not elected, which, given their popularity among the Turkmens, raised reasonable suspicions that the election was rigged. Instead, the low-ranking cleric named Kazem Noor Mofidi was elected (DCM1, 201–202).

Not surprisingly, with an Assembly dominated by pro-Khomeini members of the Islamic Republic Party, the retrograde, undemocratic, and discriminatory constitution of the Islamic Republic was put to referendum on December 2–3, 1979. Turkmens and the OIPFG boycotted this referendum. In a press release, the CPCTP appropriately criticized the way the entire three-pronged process (from March to December) of legalizing the new constitution was set up, pointing out the rampant repression and limitation on freedoms, the state's reactionary laws, and the "anti-imperialist" demagogy of the new rulers. According to this press release, "Clearly, a constitution created through an imposed assembly, a rigged (*farmayeshi*) and undemocratic election, and dogmatic, intolerant, and retrograde deputies, a reactionary and anti-worker (*zedd-e kargari*) constitution in which the most basic rights of our people are ignored, will not possibly be affirmed by our heroic peoples." The press release continued,

> Due to these reasons and since the principles of self-governance (*khodmokhtari*) and the peoples' right to determine their destiny — despite the surface acceptance of the ruling group in recent days, which directly resulted from the failed policy

of repressing the Kurdish people — had not been included in this constitution, the Turkmen people, shoulder to shoulder with other oppressed peoples, workers, and toilers of our homeland, will not participate in the new constitution's referendum. (DCM1, 201–203)

This process shows the increasing convergence of the Turkmen council movement with Fadaiyan's policy pertaining to nationwide issues. But before this decision, a "good will delegation" of Turkmens, headed by cleric Arzanesh, met with Ayatollah Khomeini in Qom. The meeting should have been unsuccessful, as Toomaj announced in a news conference shortly after the decision to boycott the referendum. He also revealed that the CHCPT and CPCTP had proposed an eight-article plan for self-governance and communal management of land, which the government had ignored (DCM1, 148–150). This indicates the Turkmens' proactive approach to self-governance and the land issue: they did their best to find a compromise, a solution with the government. The problem, of course, was that the state had no interest in listening.

Let's go back to the summer: the National Democratic Front of Iran, a small group of intellectuals with democratic-left tendencies, held a three-day "People's Solidarity Conference" in Tehran on July 18–20. Several Kurdish, Arab, and Turkmen delegates, from different affiliations, participated in the conference, while representatives from Azerbaijan and two groups from Baluchistan also attended as guests. The conference offered a model for a federal and democratic system (*Kar* 1979g, 1–2). Subsequent to the conference, a special issue of *Kar* was dedicated to the "peoples' question" (*mas'aleh-ye khalqha*), advocating self-governance and federalism (*Kar* 1979j), echoing the resolution of the conference. In my present-day judgment, the conference's proposal erred grossly in assuming that the nationalities within Iran were homogeneous and their regional boundaries were fixed, not to mention that there is an unmistakable patriarchal tone to the document. Nonetheless, the conference offered a model for a federal system within Iran (*Kar* 1979j, 2), proving that post-Revolutionary Iran contained many diverse and progressive ideas that did not survive due to escalating repression. It also proved that diverse underrepresented and subaltern nations within Iran had common grievances and similar visions. The proposed federal model (see Appendix 2) was generally progressive and democratic, and it aimed at decentralizing the state, as centralized state power in modern

Iran has been breeding one dictatorship after another, feeding off preferential distribution of natural and other resources among ruling classes in an oligarchic capitalist system, and exacerbating social, gender, and cultural inequalities.

Since I have spoken of the National Democratic Front, I must add that it was a unique and visionary leftist organization that (in contrast to dominant liberationist and "anti-imperialist" views of the Iranian left at the time) had correctly identified the formation of a democratic, popular front as the only possible and viable means to challenge the monopolization of power by the Islamists. The group's theorist was Shokrollah Paknejad (1941–1981), a lawyer from the generation of the founders of the OIPFG and a political prisoner under the Shah whose publicized defence statements in the military court had made him a renowned figure. The National Democratic Front was raided in 1981, in the first round of the regime's all-out assault on opposition, and Paknejad was arrested and executed shortly afterward (see Faghfouri Azar and Nasiri 2023).

While the country was grappling with the new regime's unleashing of its wholesale repressive force on opposition in the last part of the summer, the Plains of Turkmen were relatively quiet. Of course, local scuffles between Turkmens and the Komiteh or other forces (including disgruntled landowners) took place almost consistently. Still, the Turkmen council movement and its organizational leadership had managed to maintain relative stability in the region. The regime's agents, however, worked to stir up conflict. At the time of conflict in the Kurdish town of Paveh (August14–19), Mazandaran governorship issued an ultimatum: the Turkmens must evacuate all occupied government buildings. These included the offices of CHCPT (stationed in the Governor's Building), CPCTP (located in Gonbad Kavus library), and Pishgam Youth (in Scouts' Hall). The IRGC, now fully stationed in the region, was waiting impatiently to enforce the ultimatum. At this time, eager to depict the Turkmens as warmongers, the pro-regime *Jomhuri-ye Eslami* newspaper reported on August 21 that the Turkmens were planning to resist the governor's decision (in DCM2, 152). Another report holds that at one point Turkmen activists raided the pro-regime Cultural-Islamic Centre, destroyed its books and posters, and confiscated its printing machine (Khajehnejad 2020, 215). An absurd report by *Jomhuri-ye Eslami* claimed that weapons intended for Turkmens had been smuggled from the Soviet Union, and the CHCPT had stashes of over a thousand assault rifles hidden in the hills (Khajehnejad 2020, 230–231). This newspaper also reported on October 10, 1979, that the army had managed to collect more than two hundred illegal weapons and countless rounds of ammunitions (in DCM2, 153–154). Such inflammatory reports, impossible to verify, were meant to prepare the public and sway opinion for an impending conflict with the Turkmens.

Intelligent and prudent Turkmen leaders, however, understood the situation perfectly. Turkmen leaders and four OIPFG delegates (Fereidoun, Qasem Ja'fari, Karim, and Ghadir) — a total of thirteen men — held a secret meeting. According to an insider's report, the four OIPFG delegates voted against evacuating the buildings, thus inviting potential conflict, while all Turkmens voted in favour. Their decision was supported by the movement's moral authority, Turkmen cleric Arzanesh (Atabay 2023). By evacuating the government buildings and moving to their new locations, the Turkmen centres wisely avoided unnecessary confrontation at the time when the regime's forces were only too eager to deal with them with a heavy hand. The meeting showed two important aspects of the movement: that Turkmen leaders were not submissive to OIPFG policy and made their own decisions; and that the irresponsible OIPFG delegates were clearly unfit for carrying out pro-Fadaiyan activities in this region. Indeed, as we see, Fadaiyan's adventurist policy was partially responsible for the demise of the movement.

In light of the "first war," the question of legitimate self-defence was raised by both Turkmen and Fadaiyan activists. By this time, Fadaiyan had already abandoned the idea of armed struggle and emerged as a political party, but they still adhered to the principle of legitimating self-defence. The OIPFG's Kurdistan chapter had already organized groups of militiamen. So, in the summer it was decided that a select number of trusted Turkmen and pro-Fadai activists be secretly deployed, in two separate groups, to receive military training at the OIPFG's Kurdistan training base located near the Iraqi border (DCM1, 31; Khajehnejad 2020, 212). Sometime in the summer, Fadai member Bahman Jabal Ameli was arrested while transporting weapons and ammunition from Tehran to Gonbad Kavus (Naderi 2011, 33).

This decision remains baffling. Considering the previous conflict and given the regime's intent upon dismantling the movement, the Turkmen leaders' concern about a possible conflict is understandable. It is not clear what number of Turkmen activists, as opposed to pro-Fadai activists (Turkmen or not), actually took part in this training. This information, it seems, is relegated to secrecy. However, the mere idea that a regional movement has any viable and long-term chance to stand up to the country's armed forces sounds impractical and irrational. It indicates that the Fadaiyan were still tethering some of their (now misplaced and obsolete) ideas from their years as a guerrilla group. While self-defence against arbitrary exercise of force is the right of every citizen, let alone movement, it remains unclear what a few dozen militants could offer to, and how they could protect, a movement that involves hundreds of thousands of people, a movement that could only thrive by carving its own space within an inhospitable, even impossible, political context. In the end, the short-sighted military training might have influenced the disastrous course of events in the winter of 1980 (see the next sections).

Meanwhile, in the Autumn of 1979, Turkmen peasants successfully managed their fall harvest, collectively and cooperatively, through their councils and under the coordination of the CHCPT. Following the harvest, the collective tilling of land and sowing for spring harvest continued until January 1980. The relations between Turkmen peasants and their organic intellectuals around the CHCPT was further reinforced (Kor 2013). Once again, the council movement proved its efficiency. And that frightened the regime.

The Organization of Iranian People's Fadai Guerrillas and Its Program

It is not surprising that in the official "historiography" of the Islamic Republic's so-called research agencies, the Turkmen council movement is depicted as an appendage of the OIPFG and merely an instrument at the latter's disposal to exercise pressure on the government through "regional disturbances." For its part, existing scholarly historiography, with its power- and state-centric narratives, has hitherto relegated this world-historical movement to oblivion, inadvertently letting the regime's ideological and distorted narrative dominate public memory about the Turkmen council movement. Most unfortunately, the approach that recognizes only institutional powers has also permeated the collective memory of aging Fadaiyan activists to the extent that at times they echo the regime's "official" discourse (see Hamidian 2004). The Turkmen council movement was anything but that.

As mentioned, the convergence of the movement and the OIPFG was one of elective affinity, and the Turkmen leaders, mostly Fadaiyan supporters, had decided to have the OIPFG defend their cause and be their nationwide voice. Before the disastrous split of 1980, and notwithstanding their analytical errors and disturbing silences — especially (and with emphasis) with respect to the regime's discriminatory policies regarding women and religious minorities — during the first turbulent year after the Revolution, Fadaiyan were steadfast defenders of the people's democratic rights and the rights of the subaltern to social justice. Of course, what the OIPFG lacked, and badly needed, was a democratic theory of the kind that the National Democratic Front was in the process of developing before its demise. Therefore, shedding the epistemic preference to focus on centres of power (state or political parties) from my gaze, here I review the impact of the Turkmen council movement on Fadaiyan's programs and policies.

As mentioned, the Turkmen council movement was a grassroots initiative rooted in old Turkmen traditions and propelled and organized by left-leaning and pro-Fadaiyan Turkmen organic intellectuals. Thus, the OIPFG played no part in shaping the movement's initial formation. During the 1978–1979 Revolutionary months, the councils were rooted in the strike committees in factories and in government offices (Chapter 1). Immediately after the Revolution, councils also appeared in neighbourhoods, cities, and even among personnel in the armed forces. The Turkmens were the first to create a sustained and successful peasant council. As such, discussions about councils in the pages of *Kar* initially hinged on workers' councils. Gradually, the land issue and peasant councils also appeared in *Kar*, often reporting the successes of Turkmen councils.

In light of Turkmen experience and clearly influenced by it, the OIPFG's theoretical organ, *Nabard-e Khalq*, published a short article titled "On Councils" ("On Councils" 1979). Unlike the limited (shop floor) concept in certain socialist traditions (Chapter 1), this article defines councils as "a new *form* or more accurately a new *type* of government that emerges from the initiative of the masses. In truth, the masses have innovatively created their own type of democracy" ("On Councils" 1979, 27; original emphasis). This is an expansive view of councils and surprisingly akin to Arendt's view. Unlike the factory councils that, if not connected to a federation-type organization, remain limited in scope and activity, this view regards the councils as a form of participatory and democratic self-governance. The article contrasts the popular councils with parliamentary democracy as an expression of class domination. The councils, the article argues, are formed during unusual crises: wars, revolutionary upheaval, the conditions where people must inevitably defend themselves ("On Councils" 1979, 27–28). Note how the spectre of Arendt reappears. As a result, the article continues, councils are bodies of revolutionary governance and have nothing to do with specific types of revolution. The examples include revolutions in France, Russia, China, and Vietnam ("On Councils" 1979, 28). Accordingly, "The councils are the outcome of people's own initiatives and do not have general rules and emerge out of necessity" ("On Councils" 1979, 28), or they emerge from workers' strike committees or out of abandoned factories, lands, or military units ("On Councils" 1979, 28). Referencing Kurdistan and Turkman Sahra, the article states that the post-revolutionary government did not recognize the councils but then acquiesced to them because of the pressure from below. But, then, the government asserted that these were only "advisory councils" so that these councils would be transformed into bodies of "class reconciliation" ("On Councils" 1979, 29). The fact, however, is that councils are organs of popular democracy with executive power ("On Councils" 1979, 30). In an uncanny fashion, as if issuing a warning against the (future) hijacking of the councils, the article advises that the revolutionary groups must try to send their "real, radical, and assertive representatives to the councils," table appropriate demands (sho'arha), propagate them, and advance them in existing councils. At the same time, though, the councils are the means of pressuring the government to submit to grassroots demands. They allow for democratically debating different views, and constitute the embryo of popular self-assertion that in future will create a new form of government ("On Councils" 1979, 30). The article clearly shows that, on par with the council and national minorities' movements, the OIPFG did not regard the regional councils as the cores of separatist movements. Rather, it correctly viewed the councils as democratic bodies of popular self-assertion within a federal and democratic Iran.

Moreover, considering the movements across Iran and the OIPFG's involvement with many of them, Fadaiyan offered a Minimum Program on the occasion of the first anniversary of the 1979 Revolution (*Kar* 1980b, 4–5; Appendix 3). The six-section program exceeds our expectations from a Marxist-Leninist group. Notwithstanding its omissions and some of its conventional principles (e.g., nationalization of economy), from a social and political standpoint, the program depicted a democratic Iran driven by the principle of social justice. In its recommendations for dismantling the old system (Section 1 of the program), the program has nothing new to offer: it generally speaks of decolonizing and dismantling the imperialist institutions. The same goes for Section 6 on foreign policy that reflects the bipolar Cold War world. Section 3 offers a state-controlled economy, while it also refreshingly speaks of the workers' rights. These sections speak in a wholesale fashion and without regard to the specific conditions of Iran or lessons learned from related global experiences and their successes and failures. Obviously, the OIPFG remained uninformed about and lacked expertise in the economic field.

In Section 2, however, the council system is proposed as the supreme model for national governance. Clearly, this idea was influenced by the Turkmen model, since the Turkmen council system was the most sustained and sophisticated model of self-governance unlike many other councils across the country and in the factories that due to circumstance became ineffectual. The idea of popular militia to defend the self-governing council system must have been inspired by the Turkmen's ability to defend themselves in the "first war" (as well as Kurdistan). Section 3, Articles d and e are also clearly influenced by the Turkmen council movement. Section 4 speaks of democratic, political rights and defends the rights of women and argues for equality of women with men (Article e), but textually and discursively the section on women's rights comes only after other political rights, which indicates the androcentric and patriarchal bias of the writers of the program. Article f in this section, clearly influenced by Kurdistan, speaks of a federal system and the right to self-governance. Some conditional clauses of Section 4 — such as Articles a and c — are indeed alarming and indicate a group that does not actually believe in full-fledged democratic freedoms. These clauses give a free hand to the state to suppress its opposition by mere allegation. Section 5, on the welfare of people, demands free education and healthcare for all.

Noting that this is a "minimum" program, it is nonetheless somewhat schizophrenic: on the one hand, it contains unstudied and bookish applications of old (and clearly failed, even to the 1979 gaze) socialist axioms (e.g., nationalization of industries) alongside otherwise immortal and necessary steps (e.g., nationalization of natural resources and the environment), on par with most decolonizing, national liberation movements. On the other hand, the program contains the element of federalist, participatory democracy when it comes to governance — in a way a genuine return to the tradition of *anjomans* in the early twentieth-century — although, again, the application of the council system to national governance is not properly perceived. The OIPFG's imagination of democratic governance was certainly influenced by their involvement with the councils in factories and in Kurdistan, but above all the Turkmen council movement. In their vision, the council system could be the foundation for a nationwide, federal system. Whether the council system — in fact the successful system in Turkman Sahra — had the capacity to be applied nationwide remains a topic of debate, theoretically and practically.

Gradually, a stealthy and wily current in the OIPFG Central Committee was secretly and quietly steering the once honourable Fadaiyan and their supporters toward shamefully supporting the reactionary ruling Islamists, which grew full-fledged in the months to come. Just before this program, the OIPFG had issued a press release (dated January 21, 1980) wishing a speedy recovery for Ayatollah Khomeini who had been hospitalized to treat his heart condition. The OIPFG was clearly attempting to ingratiate themselves with the regime's murderous Supreme Leader all the while it was drafting its progressive Minimum Program in early February.

The extent of the OIPFG's (unacknowledged) indebtedness to the Turkmen council movement cannot be exaggerated.

The Autumn of the Councils

Thanks to the wisdom of Turkmen leaders, the movement in Turkman Sahra largely avoided the reign of terror in August (indeed summer) of 1979 and potentially another disastrous confrontation with the state. While the regime's cronies and press tried to instigate clashes at this time, the Turkmen activists cleverly evaded a disaster. By the time Autumn arrived, the movement was solidly in place and seemed unshakable. The peasant councils had spread roots in the region, and the participants in these councils as well as the people had gone through several months of hands-on, practical training under CHCPT guidance. Councils had appeared in assorted collectives, from workplaces to high schools.

Now the councils continued to spread in other sectors of the economy. Examples included Bandar Turkmen and Ashuradeh Fishermen's Council, Rug-Weavers' Council, and Gonbad Kavus Brick-Kiln Workers' Council (Atabay 2023). In October, fishermen staged a rally and called on the government to meet their demands that included issuing fishing licences to professional fishermen, cancelling the fishing licences of companies, terminating fishing guard units, and paying unemployment insurance to fishermen (Khajehnejad 2020, 231). Fishermen's precarious status had been the subject of some CHCPT reports (LSTP, 117–122).

By this time, participatory and democratic collective life had been socialized among the Turkmens and non-Turkmens in the region for months. In major towns, energetic pro-Fadai Pishgam student and youth organizations drove forward cultural and social life, propagating progressive values. The CPCTP published ten issues of the bilingual (Turkmen-Persian) periodical *Iel Guyji* (as expressed by Arne Goli during email correspondence in 2023), beginning in Spring 1979 and shut down after the February 1980 assault on Turkmen organizations. The issues of this periodical have not survived.

In the meantime, the nationwide solidarity between Kurds and Turkmens grew stronger. Just as the Kurdish groups had expressed their support for Turkmens during the Nawruz conflict in Gonbad Kavus, Turkmen organizations also supported the grievances of the Kurds. This is reflected in many allusions to Kurdistan in the statements and interviews of Turkmen leaders. Of particular mention is the three-hour music performance organized by CPCTP and held on November 2, 1979, in Kamineh high school in Gonbad Kavus. The event reflected the inclusive and "multicultural" attitude of the Turkmen council movement: the event featured the performances of Kurdish, Azerbaijani and Turkmen musicians and choirs, including a group of Kurdish Pishgam students from the University of Tabriz (DCM1, 200; *Kar* 1979n, 4). To introduce Turkmen culture to the rest of the country and give more visibility to the Turkmen cause, the CPCTP had been organizing performances by Turkmen musicians and bands, since Spring 1979, in university campuses or high schools of cities and towns across the country, where they were mainly hosted by Pishgam student groups. Music festivals proved to be a popular medium for connecting the Turkmen council movement to other subaltern movements. The Turkmen Bakhshilar band played in the Folks Music Festival organized by the OIPFG on the first anniversary of the Revolution held in Tehran, Mahabad, Bukan, and Sanandaj (February 1980). Their performance in Tehran (February 8–12, 1980) was recorded and the recordings sold. In this particular event, which I personally attended, in addition to the Turkmen artists, other performers included the Coiron band from Chile (affiliated with MIR, the urban guerrilla Marxist-Leninist Movimiento de Izquierda Revolucionaria, or Revolutionary Left Movement) and the Palestinian-Swedish band Kofia, which provide evidence of the OIPFG's transnational solidarity network. Other performances included that by the Roja band from Mazandaran, and musicians and dancers from Lorestan and the Qashqai tribe, as well as the pro-Fadai Arts Workshop of Iran (Kargah-e Honar-e Iran) choir (*Kar* 1980e, 12). The recordings of Turkmen traditional music (Baghshi or Bakhshi) in this event were released on cassettes in 1980 by Arts Workshop of Iran.

The unrivalled popularity of CPCTP and CHCPT is registered in the Gonbad Kavus city council elections in Fall 1979. The election indicates the unwavering democratic attitude and inclusive approach of the Turkmen council movement. The far-sightedness and perceptiveness of Turkmen leaders and activists can hardly be exaggerated. As mentioned earlier, Gonbad Kavus was a multicultural town where the Turkmen majority lived alongside Azerbaijani Turk, Persian, Mazandarani, and Sistani settlers. At this time, Dr. Tabataba`i was still the Provincial Governor of Mazandaran, while Tolami was the Governor of Gonbad Kavus. Appointed by the Provisional Government, they were both liberal-minded Muslims. The city council consisted of seven seats. Through the campaign, two solid blocs emerged: the CHCPT Turkmen candidates supported by Turkmens and non-Turkmens and the non-Turkmen Islamist candidates backed by Komiteh and IRGC. The election results were overwhelmingly in favour of the Turkmen candidates who won all seven seats, each winning more than 60 percent of the votes: a clear majority. While the election process was properly observed and its outcome fair, the Turkmen candidates recognized the value of inclusivity. As such, three elected Turkmen councillors stepped down to allow three runners-up (by significant distance) to represent certain minorities in the council. As a result, elected Turkmen councillors were Vahedi, Ahangari, Haji Tatari, and Ghafur, while the Islamists were cleric Hosseini, Ebrahim Jajormi, and Azhdar Fahim. Lawyer and CHCPT leader, Vahedi, was elected as the Chair of the City Council (Atabay 2023; DCM2, 375–376).

This move was so original that even the Islamic Republic's commissioned historian could not deny or distort it (see Khajehnejad 2020, 233). Notably, this move was made in the absence of Karimi, the OIPFG representative of the region (Atabay 2023): a testament, once again, to the wisdom of Turkmen leaders. The OIPFG, however, seemed to acquiesce to this move, stating: "Let the dogmatic monopolists [fundamentalists] see the revolutionary approach of the Turkmen people and learn from it! Although their reactionary essence will not let them [learn]" (*Kar* 1979n, 1). The CHCPT press release indicates a different view: "To accept such an alliance (*e'telaf*) indicates exactly our view about the importance of democratic approach to solving municipal issues and respect for the rights of all toilers" (in *Kar* 1979n, 5). Of course, in retrospect, the word "alliance" sounds like a huge stretch, as the Islamists felt no association with the Turkmens.

The council election stands out to indicate the deep understanding and democratic attitude of self-didactic Turkmen leaders whose analyses arose from concrete conditions. Turkmen leaders had no illusions about the totalitarian intentions of the regime, but they had realized that shunning their rivals from bodies of governance would further alienate them from, and position them against, their movement. They had hoped that by keeping their adversary close they might positively influence the state's policy in the region. One might disagree with this decision by reading it from the viewpoint of the movement's unfortunate future fate (see next section), but in my judgment, this brilliant move was necessary for the process of socializing one's challenger into one's worldview. This was a genuinely political moment, as Arendt would say.

In stark contrast to the inclusive efforts of the movement at this time and focusing on dismantling the movement, the regime had also finally ensured its solid footing in the region, not only by reinforcing and spreading local IRGC units but also by mobilizing segments of non-Turkmen, Shi'i residents that it had managed to inculcate through religion. One must acknowledge the diversity of non-Turkmens too: in fact, the majority of Azerbaijani Turks in the Turkmen region (and in Azerbaijan and other Turk-majority provinces) were followers of Grand Ayatollah Kazem Shari'atmadari, and after the latter's fallout with Khomeini (1980–1982; he was accused of sedition and forced into televised confessions; see Abrahamian 2008, 181), the majority of Azerbaijanis withdrew support for the regime.

The regime had learned its lessons from the "first war" already and was intent on a new strategy regarding the Turkmen council movement. Komiteh and IRGC reports of so-called disturbances in Turkman Sahra were incessantly dispatched to both Khomeini's and government offices. So much so that Khomeini issued an order (note he has no official authority!) dated October 30, 1979, assigning two clerics to station themselves in Gonbad Kavus and Gorgan and resolve the regional issues including land disputes (in Khajehnejad 2020, 231). But those familiar with the region's delicate issues had other, more strategic, plans: in Fall 1979, a government commission accompanied by the Reconstruction Crusade personnel began contacting the peasant councils and offered to help them with care of the land. The CHCPT representatives, including Toomaj, also contacted these personnel (Atabay 2023). The growing involvement of the Reconstruction Crusade in the Turkmen council movement clearly indicated the state's new strategy, which was not necessarily to destroy but to assimilate, distort, and scaphize the council movement, or viewed from another angle, to cunningly "support" the councils and render the CHCPT redundant.

The Reconstruction Crusade (Jahad-e Sazandegi) was founded on June 17, 1979, on Khomeini's orders. It originated with some University of Tehran Muslim student activists who, aiming to achieve agricultural self-sufficiency (*khodkafa'i*; a key buzzword of the new regime), wished to develop so-called deprived, rural Iran and help peasants produce more scientifically and efficiently. In a way, the Reconstruction Crusade was originally meant to undo the adverse effects of the Shah's land reform and industrialization plans that had heavily damaged the already feeble structure of rural Iran (Chapter 2). But its originators did not — in fact could not conceptually — understand the land question through a critique of capitalism (as Marxists would), and as such, they ultimately betrayed the rural poor. Soon, the Reconstruction Crusade became the much-needed instrument of the regime for killing softly rural councils and resistances, and "resolving" the land question in favour of the state's neoliberal policies and in the interests of the gluttonous rising ruling oligarchy. The Reconstruction Crusade's first nationwide campaign was to organize volunteer "harvesting work parties" of university and high school students and deploying them to farms that lacked proper harvesting machinery. Long story short, in 1983, the Reconstruction Crusade was formalized into a ministry that would win state contracts (without any competitors) to build infrastructure (through subcontracts and subsidies). Like all such ministries in Iran, this too became a source of corruption and concentration of wealth in the hands of the ruling oligarchy.

Meanwhile, on November 17, 1979, Ayatollah Khomeini issued a press release addressed to "Kurdish brothers and sisters." In a reconciliatory tone, Khomeini acknowledged the oppression of the Kurds, asked them to stop the fight, and promised, rather vaguely, that "the right to manage internal and local affairs and removal of cultural, economic, and political discriminations belonged to all groups of the nation including the Kurdish brothers" (in *Mardom* 1979, 5). At this time, the conflict in Kurdistan was continuing and the several meetings between Kurdish parties and government delegations had produced no tangible outcome. The OIPFG did not acknowledge the Ayatollah's press release; instead, the next issue of *Kar* (1979o) dedicated an editorial to supporting Kurdistan's federalism and proposing a peace platform. It asked the government to remove warmongering hardliner troops from Kurdistan. The Ayatollah's press release, as future events proved, was a subterfuge, and the civil war in Kurdistan only continued. The February 1980 conflict in Turkman Sahra also verified this. The continued solidarity between Kurds and Turkmens was once again affirmed through the support statement of the Kurdish negotiating team to the congress of Turkman Sahra village councils (*Kar* 1979p, 12).

The OIPFG still had other plans to pursue: according to T. Atabay (2023), by Summer 1979, Fadaiyan had managed to establish themselves as the third strongest group in Kurdistan (after DPIK and Komala). Now the OIPFG representatives in the region, Karimi, Qasem (in charge of western Turkman Sahra), and Karim (in charge of peasant issues) wished to boost OIPFG's status in the Turkmen region in the same manner (in DCM1, 31), although one wonders how else they could improve their uncontested status. The dubious military training of a few dozen Turkmen activists (mentioned earlier) was one step in that direction.

It is interesting to note that the regime's historiography uses the interrogation records (highly questionable and acquired under duress) of Hassan Ameli, a Fadai prisoner, to indicate the ulterior motives of Turkmen leaders. According to this record, Toomaj and Ameli stole a herd of sheep from the farm registered to the former Imperial army, sold them on the market, and gave the proceeds to Karimi. Ameli also allegedly confessed that he had stolen and then sold 30 tons of barley and 100 tons of wool from former imperial army and Royal Family lands and given the money to the OIPFG (Khajehnejad 2020, 210–211). This deposition, of course, cannot be verified, but it shows the regime's effort to smear the Fadaiyan, depicting them as thieves.

On November 4, 1979, a large group of Islamist university students, calling themselves Muslim Student Followers of the Imam's Line, occupied the embassy of the United States in Tehran and caused an international, diplomatic, and hostage crisis that lasted for 444 days. The occupation's simultaneous overdetermination of multiple subsequent political processes was immense and a unique gift to hardline clerics. The takeover unwaveringly elevated Khomeini as an uncompromising anti-western leader with global ambitions and reach. It caused the Provisional Government and Premier Bazargan, moderate Muslims, to resign in toto, and the collapse of the liberal Muslim government solidified the hardliners around Khomeini, thus taking Iran to more radical moves nationally and internationally, forging a new ruling oligarchy that would take the country into disastrous kleptocratic neoliberal policies after the war with Iraq (1980–1988).

Moreover, significant to our study, the embassy occupation overdetermined the Iranian left. A binary, "anti-imperialist" tendency largely defined the Iranian left (and in other countries) at this time: this was an ideologically misguided but global position that was situated within the context of the Cold War. The embassy takeover fed this particular anti-imperialism, literally forcing the leftist parties to take a firm stance with respect to it: the embassy takeover was symbolically anti-imperialist — but actually, anti-American — but it produced discursive intimations about the regime's (supposed) radical political substance. The ruling clerics' reactionary and fundamentalist hostility toward the United States connoted liberationist anti-imperialism, which the Islamic Republic was not. Conflating these two very different phenomena produced a tragic slippery slope. The Tudeh Party was the first to jump on the bandwagon and identify the reactionary clerics with (delusional) progressive anti-imperialism, thus disgracefully becoming the Islamists' unwavering apologist until the regime turned against Tudeh and destroyed it in early 1982. Most other leftist groups saw the plot and avoided the pitfall. After some delay, though, the OIPFG emerged to support the students' embassy takeover, committing what proved to be a tragic strategic error. On par with Fadaiyan's new policy, the CHCPT staged a rally in Gonbad Kavus in support of the embassy takeover (*Kar* 1980c, 4). But an even more appalling error was the OIPFG's insistence that the occupying students (who obviously had their own agenda) should publicize the embassy's secret documents that would prove that the Provisional Government Ministers were agents of the United States. This position blinded Fadaiyan to the totalitarian nature of the clerics (see *Kar* 1980a). After the schism of June 1980, the majority wing of Fadaiyan declared its support for the regime in the May Day rally of 1981. From a popular, leftist, social justice–oriented group that advocated democratic rights and self-governance within the first ten months after the Revolution, the OIPFG's majority faction devolved into becoming the shameful apologist for, and collaborator with, the repressive machine of Islamic fanatics (as in the majority faction's documented collaboration with the army to repress the Kurdish resistance who were the OIPFG's previous allies [Behrooz 2000, 115–116]), before the regime finally crushed the majority faction by 1983. Turkmen region's Pishgam organizations in large part followed the majority wing. The split and the subsequent policy changes of Fadaiyan adversely affected the Turkmen council movement, contributing to the Reconstruction Crusade's assimilationist policy.

Women's Participation in the Movement

A key concern for me, writing about this forgotten world-historical movement almost forty years later, is to uncover the extent of the participation of women in the movement and register women's impact and contributions. Turkmen society has been a patriarchal society, structured in that way, and in agrarian Turkmen society women lived within the domestic realm and familial bonds. They contributed significantly to the family economy by farming, but importantly, also through rug-weaving. In olden times, they held much of the family savings in the form of their personal gold ornaments. Traditionally, Turkmen society was led by men collectively (as in *aq saqal* councils) and without women's participation. The leaders and activists of the Turkmen council movement whose names have been made public were invariably men. I did not find a single record of women having been a member of a village council, even after these councils were transformed by young activists from their traditional (elderly) set up. Even the lists of casualties of armed conflicts report only men, with a couple of exceptions of murdered women; for example, Bayram Bibi Mellati and her 6-month-old infant were killed by the Imam's Komiteh gunmen when they raided her home on March 28, 1979 (LSTP, 246), and Safar Gol Khaledzadeh, a rug-weaver in her twenties, was also killed in similar circumstances (DCM2, 404). So, it is crucial for me to explore if the Turkmen council movement actually managed to improve gender relations. Alas, publications pertaining to the struggles of Turkmen women and their achievements in this period are scarce. Details have to be gleaned from a few reports in CPCTP publications. The issues of *Kar* were completely silent about this subject. In fact, a survey of the pages of *Kar* (numbers 1–60) published within 15 months after the Revolution show that the OIPFG spoke of women's issues and freedoms *only once* on the occasion of International Women's Day (in issue no. 2 of *Kar*, dated 15 March 1979), right after the women's march against discrimination and impending forced veiling in Tehran that was attacked by an Islamist mob.

Reports indicate that in many CHCPT and CPCTP meetings and rallies, Turkmen women in colourful (red) traditional apparel would read poetry and statements (a clip in Allamehzadeh's *Speak Turkmen* also captures this). One can surmise that these women were mostly associated with Pishgam. High school student activists associated with the pro-Fadai Pishgam Youth Organization were at the forefront of promoting the Turkmen council movement mostly in towns. According to Atabay, Turkmen Women Centre (Kanun-e Zanan-e Turkmen) was founded in February–March 1980, but it originated with the student activists of Kamineh high school in Gonbad Kavus. Through most of 1979, young Pishgam women had created literacy classes for women, supported rug-weaving women and girls in villages and towns, and actively participated in rallies and meetings (in DCM2, 323). The focus on rug-weaving women is reflected through some activist reports on their conditions (LSTP, 105–113). Advocating the cause of rug-weaving women, the young Pishgam women associated with CHCPT declared, "We, Pishgam women … support the defenceless women who were robbed of their rights in capitalist society and express that we detest all elements that subject to agony and oppression the working, homemaking, and peasant women and regard these elements as the enemies of humanity" (in LSTP, 108).

Following the "second war" (see the next section in this chapter) in February 1980, Pishgam students boycotted schools, notably in leftist-dominated high schools such as Kamineh and Bizhan Jazani in Gonbad Kavus, and female students created a campaign to clean or paint over the pro-regime graffiti on street walls (DCM1, 297). The Turkmen Women Centre, under CHCPT, declared that "its aims hinged on achieving the interests of toilers and specifically the rural toiling women" (DCM1, 423). The Turkmen Women Centre created a Rural Research Committee to advocate for the female rural workers and rug-weavers. It created a Rug-Weavers' Council and began negotiating with the Ministry of Labour representatives to alleviate the conditions faced by these women, but to no avail (DCM1, 419–423). With the decline of the movement, the women's efforts also diminished, and many activists left the region.

The council movement did not significantly address or noticeably uplift the status of Turkmen women, especially in rural areas. While in towns, especially in a multicultural town like Gonbad Kavus, young Turkmen women had the option to participate in the ranks of Pishgam and experience social freedom alongside non-Turkmen activists, rural women were largely relinquished to the age-old patriarchal milieux, and women activists' efforts to advocate for them did not seem to have produced any measurable or enduring progress. It seems that the CPCTP and CHCPT recognized the importance of women's advocacy, but they clearly had no serious plans in the area of enhancing the visibility and participation of Turkmen women. It appears that any strides taken toward women's issues were pushed on CHCPT by young Pishgam women. Sadly, the movement failed to create an enduring legacy for augmenting the status and rights of Turkmen women.

The Winter of the Councils: The February Clash

The "second war" of Turkman Sahra between the activists and the regime's forces occurred in early February 1980. Its consequences were disastrous, as the clash signalled the beginning of the end of the Turkmens council movement. As discussed earlier, in the months building up to February, the region continued to be noticeably volatile: the CHCPT was at its zenith, fully established and popular, and so was the OIPFG, in part by virtue of its association with the Turkmen council movement, while the IRGC was intent on regaining full control, ending the semi-autonomy of the councils, and dismantling the bodies of participatory decision-making that the new state regarded as a threat. To that effect, the state's forces had been planning and waiting for the right moment to implement their premeditated and much-calculated crackdown. The Turkmen leaders had perceptively managed to avoid a conflict in late summer. Meanwhile, as the regime was still steadfastly intent on destroying this exemplary movement, and indubitably in response to the CHCPT's peaceful leadership, the state's multiple institutions — in particular, IRGC and Reconstruction Crusade, aided by new laws — had devised an overarching plan to achieve their objective. The dry tinder of the situation needed only a spark, one that the brilliant Turkmen leaders had hitherto circumvented. Fadaiyan's surprising and irrational decision provided just that, a decision for which they never took responsibility.

Despite their failed previous attempts at electoral politics, both Fadaiyan and Turkmen organizations decided to nominate candidates for the upcoming election for the first post-revolutionary Majles to be held on March 14, 1980. The OIPFG offered its own list of candidates, while Toomaj and Makhtoom stood as Turkman Sahra candidates (DCM1, 255) — another indication of the convergence of CHCPT and OIPFG on nationwide policies.

Given the success and persistence of the CHCPT during the past year, the OIPFG decided to stage a rally to celebrate the ninth anniversary of its founding operation (19 Bahman in Persian calendar; February 8, 1971) in Gonbad Kavus. Without a doubt, this was planned as Fadaiyan's show of popular power contra the regime. But before attending to the actual events, it is important to register the conflicting reminiscences of how this particular rally led Turkmens to the second armed clash between Turkmens and the state.

According to Atabay (2023), who expressly blames the OIPFG for the demise of the movement, in the months prior to the rally (December 1979 and January 1980), Fadai members in charge of the Turkmen region — Karimi, Qasem, and Karim Nazer — moved the Fadai members with "moderate" views out of the region and recruited more militant members; they did the same with Turkmen members. Atabay calls this "an invisible coup" (Atabay 2023). This claim has never been echoed by anyone else, but no one else has ever denied it either, not even Fereidoun Karimi in his rejoinder to Atabay (Karimi 2013). While this claim remains contestable, Kor reflects that at the time political manoeuvring and avoiding the second conflict was quite possible. He rightly asks: "The question is, what specific policy was dominant at the time in the leadership of the Fadai Organization? Why did the Central Committee of the [Fadai] Organization at that time, when … they had the option of negotiating with, and directly contacting, the government, [let the events] lead to armed conflict in Gonbad?" (Kor 2013) He continues, "What I clearly remember is that the [Fadai] Organization's member in charge of Turkman Sahra [Karimi] insisted on the necessity to show power" (Kor 2013).

Not so much the Turkmen activists but Pishgam Youth activists were tasked with taking on the bulk of preparations for the rally (Kor 2013). Let us recall, once again, Fadaiyan's strange decision to deploy a select (small) group of Fadai and Turkmen activists to Kurdistan for military training a few months earlier. Is there a pattern here? It should be noted the at least some Turkmen leaders objected to Fadaiyan's "show of power": Turkmen cleric Arezanesh recollects how on his way back from the funeral of three Turkmens killed by Islamist thugs in a nearby village, he noticed how the streets of Gonbad Kavus were covered with the tracts and posters of Fadaiyan's upcoming anniversary. He recalls professing his worries about this to Turkmen leader Vahedi: "These [Fadaiyan] only think about showing their power and taking pointers from the government at the expense of our [Turkmen] nation, and in case of a catastrophe, we will be the ones who must shoulder loads of misfortunes" (Arzanesh 2008). Arzanesh (2008) further warned that "we will be the ones responsible for the Turkmen peoples in case of any incident, not these [Fadaiyan] who not only do not live here, they will not hesitate to leave the region in case their lives are in danger." His far-sightedness is undeniable. One should only recall the bloody Summer of 1979 — just a few months earlier — a clear warning to anyone paying attention. The OIPFG certainly was not.

With respect to this conflict, we encounter two (opposing) versions. One is of the state's agencies and the other my reconstructed one based on all the evidence available to me. Based on the state security's released documents, on February 4, 1980 (Monday), the CHCPT applied to the Provincial Governorship for a rally permit for Friday February 8 (19 Bahman), but because the CHCPT was not a registered organization with the government (which shows the state never "recognized" it), the Governor's office declined and asked that individuals apply. The CHCPT's leader and lawyer, Vahedi, applied by pledging to the conditions of the police (that demonstration must be unarmed, and it should not bear banners or voice slogans against the Islamic Republic). Upon agreement of the Governor of Mazandaran, the permit was issued in his name (Khajehnejad 2020, 244). Subsequently, printed tracts, signed by OIPFG-Turkman Sahra, announced the rally for Friday February 8 at 10:00 a.m. at Ettehad (Yadbud) Square in front of the town's Education Ministry office (Khajehnejad 2020, 244).

I must slightly jump ahead of my narrative: the "second war" led to a debate between the OIPFG, the IRGC, and the then President Bani Sadr that was broadcast on national television, to which I will return. An hour-long version of this 4-hour debate is available on YouTube ("TV Debate" 1980), which lacks certain key information but some of those eliminated sections appear in the work by Khajehnejad (2020). I draw information from this after-the-fact televised debate to offer some important information that shed light on the two versions surrounding the clash.

Let us first attend to the regime's version of the events leading up to the armed clash. In its "analytical" summary of the events — filled with omissions (note the oxymoron!) — written a few days after the clash, the IRGC Gorgan Command held that the permit for the rally was issued provided it met the aforementioned conditions. In anticipation of possible clashes (as if the IRGC knew), the Gonbad Kavus IRGC unit set up checkpoints on the roads entering the town prior to the rally and reportedly managed to confiscate a dozen or so weapons from a white Toyota (we do not know who it belonged to, however). On Friday, the rally began at 10:00 a.m. with 8,000 to 10,000 people marching starting at Ettehad (Yadbud) Square. Reportedly, the CHCPT had advertised in surrounding villages that there would be a rally for the first anniversary of the Revolution and bused Turkmen villagers to town (Khajehnejad 2020, 252). Adding to the "credibility" of IRGC's version of events, the report suggests that the Turkmen villagers were duped into believing they were going to celebrate the Revolution's anniversary, not that of Fadaiyan's foundation.

In any case, earlier, at 8:00 a.m. on the same day, a certain "reactionary cleric (*akhund mortaje'*) and a crony of a Persian feudal" (the words of the IRGC report) amassed some "religious extremists and ignorant (*naagah*) elements" and provoked them to attack Turkmen protesters. The IRGC is clearly trying to distance itself from the counter-protesters. But Seyed Ebrahim Derazgisu, Governor of Gorgan and Interim Governor of Gonbad Kavus, pointed out an "ethnic" element to the affair

The Councils and Collective Life 197

The ruins of the last office of the Central Headquarters of Councils of Plains of Turkmen (CHCPT) after it was attacked by the Islamic Revolutionary Guards Corps (IRGC) and army tanks and rockets in February 1980. (Source: DCM2; image courtesy of Arne Goli)

(absent in the IRGC report), stating that when the Turkish and Persian peoples (the counter-protesters) heard that the Turkmen demonstrators were shouting slogans against the Islamic Republic (which is surprising, because the condition of their rally permit barred them to do so), the counter-protesters got irate and attacked them ("TV Debate" 1980). At this time, the head of police asked Turkmen protesters to change their route and avoid conflict, but they did not. Subsequently, the two columns of protesters clashed. The attempts of police officers to disperse protesters led to the police being attacked and at this point the IRGC forces entered the scene. When that happened, several Turkmen protesters took sanctuary in the Education Ministry's office. "Meanwhile," the IRGC report claims, "the Centre [Turkmens] attacked the other (opposite) protesters by throwing grenades and firing shotguns," as a result of which two persons were killed and twenty-eight injured. All protesters dispersed at this point. The Gonbad Kavus IRGC personnel still stayed away from engaging in the conflict. Some Turkmen protesters staged a sit-in protest in the Education Ministry building until noon of the next day, Saturday. Then, around 1:00 p.m. AK-47 shots were fired from the other barricades (supposedly those of Turkmens) and the armed clash broke out (Khajehnejad 2020, 247).

The Governor and cleric Noor Mofidi contacted the CHCPT via phone, inviting them to meet and announce a ceasefire at 4:00 p.m. on Sunday, but at 4:15 p.m. on Sunday the pro-Fadai Turkmens attacked the Communications Ministry building and fighting resumed (Khajehnejad 2020, 245–247). The number of sit-in protesters was only 300 to 500 people (Khajehnejad 2020, 248). Interestingly, in the TV debate (Khajehnejad 2020, 253), IRGC commander Mahmoud Darvish claimed that the cause for the casualties of the first day (Friday) was a grenade thrown by sit-in protesters in the Education Ministry building. Subsequently, the exchange of fire continued on Sunday and into the next days. According to Derazgisu, on Monday, Turkmen cleric Arzanesh phoned cleric Noor Mofidi, Khomeini's delegate in Mazandaran, to negotiate another ceasefire (Khajehnejad 2020, 256–257; 270–271). The regime's troops were prepared this time around for a clash of this sort; the IRGC immediately received support from the army. Darvish admits that the IRGC forces fired 50-calibre machineguns at Turkmen barricades and houses (Khajehnejad 2020, 254), pointing out that the Turkmens had created permanent concrete barricades in buildings in the Turkmen district, suggesting their hostile intentions ("TV Debate" 1980). The IRGC troops managed to take over the Turkmen positions by advancing in the cover of army tanks (Khajehnejad 2020, 255). Evidently, this was an organized, full-fledged military operation. The "second war" ended on Tuesday, February 12 (Khajehnejad 2020, 255).

In the TV debate, Mohsen Reza`i, an IRGC commander, showed some documents to prove that the Turkmens had already planned for a clash, although he stopped short of pointing out what purpose an armed insurrection of the Turkmen minority against an entire state machinery would serve. He stated that these documents had been retrieved from the CHCPT headquarters, confessing that the CHCPT office was raided and ransacked by state troops. Most interestingly, he said that if they could, they would have acquired more documents but they (the Turkmens) had destroyed them! ("TV Debate" 1980). According to Reza`i, the Turkmens of Gonbad Kavus had brought a "deluge of weapons" from Bandar Turkmen and Pahlavi Dezh ("TV Debate" 1980). A mass exodus of Turkmens from Turkmen quarters of the town took place during the clashes.

The regime's propaganda against the Turkmens continued. Once again, the (worn-out) claim that Turkmens had attempted to disarm Gendarmerie posts at the Soviet border appeared in President Bani Sadr's *Enqelab-e Eslami* (*Kar* 1980c, 4). This is an interesting report, though. The way *Enqelab-e Eslami* reported this "news" was clearly meant to sensationalize the alleged "threat" of Fadaiyan. The title on the first page reads: "Three Gendarmerie posts at the border with the Soviet [Union] were disarmed by People's Fadai Guerrillas," but the detail on the last page reads: "In another telephone contact that we had with Brother Mazinani, a *Sepah* [IRGC] official in Tehran, he said, 'an unconfirmed report indicates that three Gendarmerie posts near the Soviet [Union] border were occupied by the People's Fadai Guerrillas'" (*Enqelab-e Eslami* 1980, 1, 16; my emphasis). The newspaper certainly meant to agitate against the Turkmens and Fadaiyan.

Let me offer my researched, alternative version that is certainly truer to the actual events than the version propagated by the regime's various agencies. Aside from many omissions, in all state-official versions of the conflict the most important piece is missing, a key incident indeed that allows for decoding the entire affair, and it will not corroborate the official version. Quite the contrary, this piece provides damning evidence of the planned conspiracy of the Islamic Republic to crush this movement and indeed encouraged a clash of this type, and the OIPFG's short-sightedness played right into the regime's long-awaited strategy. This piece is the kidnapping, illegal confinement, and assassination of four Turkmen leaders. When state-sanctioned history inevitably speaks of the murder of Turkmen leaders four decades later, it still tries to spread a shroud of mystery over what is well-known by now. To this effect, this type of salaried "historiography" holds that: "Regarding the circumstances surrounding their arrest and fate (*sarnevesh*) there are multiple claims and stories, and parts of the realities behind this affair is still wrapped in ambiguity" (Khajehnejad 2020, 272). Note how the Persian "*sarnevesht*" (here translated as "fate" to stay with the author's intent, but it actually means "destiny") lexically serves to omit the term "death" or more accurately "assassination." Eventually, this "historiography" cannot evade the reality but frames the kidnapping of the Turkmen leaders as an accidental arrest (Khajehnejad 2020, 275–276) and attributes their death to cleric Khalkhali's wayward verdict (Khajehnejad 2020, 279–280) and his sadistic personality, thereby exonerating the regime and covering up the state's entire plan (recall that Khalkhali was the "hanging judge" deployed to Kurdistan to execute Kurdish militants).

I wish to remind the reader that, at this point, all independent (liberal- or leftist-minded) newspapers such as *Ayandegan* and *Peygham-e Emrooz* had already been shut down for months and state-run newspapers such as *Kayhan* and *Ettela'at* as well as the ruling clerical clique's *Jomhuri-ye Eslami* dominated the news discourse, and, along with the state-run radio and television, they constantly fed the public with (at times racist) misinformation about Turkman Sahra. Even President Bani Sadr's "centrist" or liberal newspaper, *Enqelab-e Eslami* did not reflect the news impartially (as we saw earlier). Movement activists and supporters in Kurdistan and elsewhere were now dubbed "counter-revolutionaries." Hence, newspapers and media played their role in demonizing the Turkmen council movement in nationwide public discourse. Only the opposition political party papers (printed underground) survived to offer alternative versions of events, but often from their specific, often ideologically informed, points of view.

In the context of vastly propagated misinformation by state media, the OIPFG published three special issues of *Kar* to offer the Turkmen's and its own version of the conflict. Relying on the reports of its members on the ground, *Kar* blamed the followers of Ayatollah Shari'atmadari (implicitly Shi'i Turks) of Gonbad Kavus for being hostile toward the Turkmen council movement and collaborating with the agents of former large landowners (*Kar* 1980c, 1) — again, excluding the IRGC and the state's agencies. But another piece of evidence points at another culprit: in the TV debate, OIPFG's Farrokh Negahdar read out a tract — indeed, the smoking gun — that was distributed on Thursday February 7, a day prior to the Fadaiyan's rally: "We announce that any conspiratorial rally is condemned by Revolutionary Guards Corps and Revolutionary Prosecutor, and we ask Muslim brothers and sisters to stay alert and neutralize any rallies organized by supporters of imperialism and social imperialism. Obviously, the Guards Corps will stop any intrigue due to its divine and national duties" (Khajehnejad 2020, 264). The tract tells it all: it clearly threatens to shut down the Fadaiyan's demonstration.

Kar reports that prior to the day of the rally, the IRGC personnel mostly stayed in their bases and were not present for long in town (*Kar* 1980c, 1). This report estimates the number of demonstrators on Friday to be 35,000 to 40,000 people. Reportedly, following the assault of club-wielding pro-Shariʻatmadari demonstrators, the Chief of Police approached and informed them that the Fadaiyan's rally had a permit and that they should disperse, but to no avail (contrary to the state's version). This report attributes the casualties of the initial clash to the accidental setting off of a grenade in the hands of pro-Shariʻatmadari protesters who apparently were armed with handguns and grenades (*Kar* 1980c, 2). After the attack, the pro-Fadai crowd dispersed, but about 400 Turkmens staged a sit-in protest in the office of CPCTP. At this time, CHCPT's attempts at contacting the city's Governor were ignored by him and he was replaced by the Governor of Gorgan, Derazgisu. At the same time, the Revolutionary Guards still roamed the streets peacefully. At 8:30 a.m. on Saturday (February 9), the pro-Shariʻatmadari supporters started shooting at Turkmen districts from behind their barricades in the Turkish district and by 10:00 a.m. the police's attempt to stop them failed. The provincial governor insisted that the sit-in protest must stop. By 2:00 p.m., after receiving advice from the IRGC and police, the sit-in protesters left, while firing from the Turkish district continued. This is when the IRGC 50-calibre gunfire and mortars began to pound the buildings in Turkmen neighbourhoods, to which the Turkmens responded with gunfire. The exchange of fire continued until Sunday (February 10). Cleric Noor Mofidi and Turkmen cleric Arezanesh agreed on a ceasefire at 4:00 p.m. on Sunday so the army could move in and bring order to the city, but that did not happen (*Kar* 1980c, 1–3). Monday, February 11 marked the first anniversary of the Revolution, and once again a ceasefire was agreed upon, but on this very day, military tanks advanced in the city, providing cover for IRGC foot soldiers. By Tuesday (February 12), the Turkmens had left the town en masse. The IRGC occupied the offices of CHCPT and CPCTP and turned them into their operations headquarters (Fereidoun 2001, 46); apparently, this happened on February 12 (Khajehnejad 2020, 284), and it effectively terminated the official presence of Turkmen organizations.

Khomeini nominated a delegation to investigate. His deputy, Ayatollah Hossein Ali Montazeri, also assigned the notorious cleric Khalkhali to investigate (*Kar* 1980d, 1–2). The clashes effectively ended on Wednesday, February 13, when the army and IRGC took control of the entire town (Khajehnejad 2020, 285). According to one report, twelve IRGC personnel were killed and an unspecified number injured in the clashes (Khajehnejad 2020, 281). Sources on Turkmen casualties are scarce: one count of confirmed cases indicates sixteen Turkmens (based on DCM2, 366–367). This is because after the "second war" Turkmen organizations fell into disarray and collecting such information became virtually impossible. To this list must be added Bandar Turkmen activists who were kidnapped after the conflict and subsequently assassinated: the mutilated bodies of Parviz Iranpour, Nazdordi Nushin, and Yousef Qarajeh were found in the Gonbad Kavus shrine on February 18 (DCM1, 527; DCM2, 417).

Previously, I spoke of the assassination of the four Turkmen leaders — the smoking gun that shows the "second war" was premeditated by the regime. Around 2:00 a.m. on February 8 (19 Bahman rally), Toomaj, Maktoom, Vahedi, and Jorjani were kidnapped as they were returning from CHCPT headquarters. Decades later, the IRGC commander who had admittedly arrested them, stated that they were captured in a roadblock because they refused to identify themselves, thus making their arrest appear to be accidental. According to him, the four leaders were taken to the Revolutionary Tribunal of Gonbad Kavus at 3:00 a.m. and were then sent to Tehran for investigation (in Khajehnejad 2020, 276). However, the IRGC's official statement at the time holds that the four Turkmen leaders were arrested on February 8 "in the course of Gonbad conflict" and sent to Tehran. On February 17, they were sent back to the region for "further investigation." Accordingly, "On the road between Aliabad and Gonbad [Kavus], the vehicle containing the arrestees was attacked by armed assailants. In the shootout two [IRGC] Pasdars were injured and the assailants managed to take the vehicle containing the four arrestees and flee. After a few days the cadavers of these four were discovered in the road to Bojnord" (in Khajenejad 2020, 278).

The fantastic gangster imagination of the author of these lines cannot be exaggerated. Clearly, by linking the arrests to the "conflict," the IRGC wanted to implicate the four Turkmens as the instigators of the "second war" before it actually happened!

A *Kar* Special Issue (1980f) states that late night on Thursday, February 7, the CHCPT leaders had a meeting with the five-person delegation of the Agriculture Ministry to discuss the issue of land distribution and conflict resolution. The meeting lasted until 2:00 a.m. (early hours of Friday, February 8). The ministry delegation and Turkmen leaders left the CHCPT building together but in different vehicles. The IRGC roadblock stopped both cars, letting the ministry's vehicle drive on and leave before arresting the Turkmens (*Kar* 1980f, 1). A subsequent *Kar* report (March 5) actually showed the scans of documents of IRGC Operations Unit that indicated the four Turkmen leaders were in Tehran prisons (1980h, 2–3), suggesting that Fadaiyan had supporters or contacts even within the IRGC.

Here, the memoir of Turkmen cleric Arzanesh about what happened that night proves valuable: recall his being staggered by the Pishgam's tract campaign for Fadaiyan's rally and his words of warning to Vahedi on the way back to Gonbad Kavus. Alarmed, they both decided to invite Toomaj and Makhtoom to Arzanesh's home on the same night (February 7) to discuss the issue. According to Arzanesh, Vahedi and Maktoom came to his home, and Vahedi called the CHCPT office to ask Toomaj to meet with them, but reportedly a voice unknown to him answered the phone, stating that Toomaj was not there. Two hours later, someone called and informed Arzanesh that Toomaj was now in the office and asked to meet Vahedi, so he left. Then, another call from CHCPT office said that Makhtoom had a visitor from Tehran; he also left. Arzanesh called the office but could not recognize who it was that was answering the phone (since he knew all CHCPT office personnel), but he was told that none of the three were in the office. The next morning, he went to the CHCPT office and did not find any of them. At that time, apparently, Jorjani was there too and was captured with the rest of them (Arzanesh 2008).

The strangest piece of the puzzle is this: given the tract that indicated the IRGC was ready to shut down the rally (as Negahdar exposed it in the TV debate later), and given that the Turkmen leaders had gone missing by the morning of February 8, why did the OIPFG leadership (including its regional leadership — namely, Karimi) not cancel the rally? The decision not to cancel the rally (and avoid another conflict) strongly suggests that Fadaiyan's leadership relied heavily on its Pishgam Youth foot soldiers for this affair, using them as a cohort to aggrandize its power and reach, and had made its decision regardless of the Turkmens' input. Yousef Kor is correct when he states that the "show of power" should have been cancelled immediately and steps taken to calm the situation and follow up on the whereabouts of the Turkmen leaders. In his opinion, "our popular support was strong and therefore the conditions for advancing peaceful measures were agreeable" (Kor 2013).

The maimed bodies of the four Turkmen leaders were found on February 18 under a small bridge in the vicinity of Chaman Bid village on the Gorgan-Bojnord highway, near Bojnord. Their deaths crushed the Turkmen council movement, but it also made national headlines, proving that the Turkmen council movement had become a part of nationwide public discourse: a cause célèbre for leftists and dissidents, a nuisance for the regime. The regime's misinformation campaign continued. *Jomhuri-ye Eslami* newspaper attributed these murders to Fadaiyan-e Turkmen (DCM2, 199), suggesting internal purges. No organ in the regime took responsibility. Several "rumours" at the time indicated that the "hanging judge" Khalkhali had arrived in the region, thus attributing the murders to his "rogue" verdicts and whitewashing the fact that he was Ayatollah Khomeini's murderous henchman. Interestingly, in a long statement (dated February 23, 1980) published in *Ettela'at* daily (no. 16083; 25 February 1980, p. 4), Khalkhali expressly denied he had any involvement in the death of the Turkmen leaders (Khajehnejad 2020, 278). Strangely, though, as if taking pride in his murderous verdicts, Khalkhali confessed in his memoir (written twenty years later, when he had served his purpose and had been dumped by the ruling oligarchy) that he was deployed to the Turkmen region where he "executed 94 persons, especially Makhtoom, Toomaj, and Vahedi" (Khajehnejad 2020, 279). The IRGC's first top commander Javad Mansouri offered a more elaborate version that was televised in Iran and vastly circulated on the internet. He stated that on the official ceremony of the Revolution's first anniversary (on February 11) in Tehran, sitting next to him, Khalkahli murmured to him that he wanted to go to Gonbad Kavus and execute the Turkmen leaders, but President Bani Sadr was against it. So, the two agreed that Khalkhali should go, and that he would tell the local IRGC that he had orders from Mansouri. Then, Khalkhali left the ceremony, travelled to Gonbad Kavus, and executed the Turkmen leaders by midnight before returning to Tehran (in Khajehnejad 2020, 279). Derazgisu also confirms that Khalkhali arrived in Gonbad Kavus one day after the conflict had ended and issued verdicts in absentia, without trials, and solely based on the "evidence" fed to him (in Khajehnejad 2020, 268). These two recollections are also blurred in that they miss the fact that the four leaders were taken to Tehran first (as the documents in *Kar* indicate) and then executed, although we do not know where or how. In retrospect, though, the plot is clear: the IRGC kidnapped the Turkmen leaders in the middle of the night a few hours before the OIPFG rally and had intentionally provoked pro-Shari'atmadari demonstrators to attack the rally and divert the nation's attention to the subsequent clash while the Turkmen leaders were being murdered.

The four Turkmen leaders, murdered callously and in secret, immediately became the martyrs of the great causes of land, culture, and language, thanks to the relentless campaign by the OIPFG. With his combed-back hair, Dallas moustache, and thick, black, rectangular glasses, Toomaj had been the most visibly recognizable figure of the Turkmen council movement and its most vocal spokesperson. The Fadai poet Said Soltanpour (1940–1981; he was kidnapped from his wedding and executed in prison) wrote a poem in his honour (*Kar* 1980f, 2). Later, the artists at the pro-Fadaiyan Arts Workshop of Iran wrote a catchy, fast-rhythm song about Toomaj. Sung by a female vocalist with a high-pitched voice, the song kept the memory of Turkmen council movement in an artistic way: "Turkmen sows your name in the body of the plateau / so that tomorrow they seek their red path from your name." One year later, to commemorate the Turkmen leaders and with the initiative and collaboration of Soltanpour, the Arts Workshop of Iran, associated with the minority wing of OIPFG also released an album on cassette in honour of the Turkmen council movement and its leaders.

The movement that these four leaders and other organic intellectuals of Turkmen people led had been deeply rooted in the region. And knowing this, the Islamic Republic immediately began to hunt down Turkmen and Fadai activists in the region. In addition to the aforementioned cases, Hakim Shahnazi was killed in Gonbad Kavus in February (DCM2, 391–392). Many Turkmen activists were arrested in subsequent weeks, and some of them were executed in the early 1980s. These included Ane Galdi Goklani, a cofounder of CPCTP (d. 1982), Abdollah Qezel (d. 1980), Halli Hallizadeh (d. 1980), Morad Galdi Bidar (d. 1983), and Gorkan Behkeleh (d. 1983; DCM2, 382–384, 385–388, 389–391, 392–393).

Right after the "second war" and the murder of Turkmen leaders and activists, the OIPFG launched a campaign to pressure President Bani Sadr into a fact-finding debate about Turkman Sahra. The campaign was successful: the liberal-minded Bani Sadr agreed. He had just been elected (February 4, 1980) as the first President in Iranian history and wanted to gingerly distance himself from the clerical hardliners and appeal to the increasingly discontented middle and educated classes, both religious and secular. Bani Sadr was deposed by the hardliner-dominated Majles on June 22, 1981. He then fled to France and lived as an exile until his death in 2021. The first free televised political debate in Iranian history, the debate aired on March 1, 1980. In addition to Bani Sadr (sitting in the middle, to suggest his impartiality), the attendees were Farrokh Negahdar, Ali Keshtgar (Ali Mohammad Farkhondeh Jahromi), and Jamshid Taheripour of the OIPFG, Army Chief of Staff General Valiollah Fallahi, IRGC commanders Mohsen Reza`i and Mahmoud Darvish, Mazandaran Province Governor Mr. Moshef, Gonbad Kavus Governor Ebrahim Derazgisu, and a moderator. The key information in this debate has already been discussed. This debate brought the OIPFG into the nationwide spotlight: if its presence in the Turkmen council movement had not already been noted, the televised debate was indeed a show of Fadaiyan's power: by virtue of the fact that they had successfully pressured the hubristic commanders of the IRGC to answer to them in public, they were a force to reckon with. The Turkmen council movement was now in irreversible decline, while the OIPFG planned to increase its nationwide status; it achieved it through subsequent editorials and discussions in *Kar*. Still, history's workings are often bizarre: the OIPFG's historic moment came only at the expense of the Turkmen council movement. It is extremely hard *not* to see the events in this sequence. Sadly.

In a rare moment in the debate, Negahdar asked the most pertinent question that attested to the profound marginalization of the Turkmen people: "Why isn't a Turkmen present [in this debate] on television and I should speak in his place?" ("TV Debate" 1980).

Aftermath: Decline and Assimilation

The prosecution of Turkmen activists followed the "second war". With their offices shut down and their key activists murdered, arrested, or on the run, the CHCPT and CPCTP effectively disappeared as civil society organizations, although they lived on for a while in tracts and press releases. Many activists, Turkmen or not, gradually left the region as it became increasingly unsafe for them. The Pishgam organization continued but rather demurely. With Toomaj and Makhtoom — candidates for the upcoming parliamentary election — murdered, the CPCTP announced it would boycott the election (DCM1, 277; *Kar* 1980h, 12). The OIPFG, in contrast, decided to put its own nationwide interests ahead of its solidarity with the Turkmen council movement and run for the elections that also turned out, by OIPFG's own admission, to be rigged (*Kar* 1980j, 1, 7; *Kar* 1980k, 14). In retrospect, this was not just an *unprincipled* decision; it also showed Fadaiyan's growing illusions about the ruling clerics as well as their own nationwide popularity. The OIPFG held demonstrations in Tehran and Tabriz to commemorate the Turkmen leaders in late February and early March. The Kurdish negotiating team also relayed a solidarity message to the Turkmens (*Kar* 1980g, 6, 7). As well, a Fadai faction led by Ashraf Dehqani (Iranian People's Fadai Guerrillas that had split from the OIPFG in Spring 1979) held a demonstration in Azadi Square in Tehran in April 1980 to protest the repression of the Turkmen council movement (DCM1, 315). As a testament to the ongoing popularity of the councils, notwithstanding the militarization of the region, people travelled in the thousands to Toomaj's birthplace, Yalmeh Salian village, to commemorate their four lost leaders on the fortieth-day of their passing (an important day in Muslim custom), where statements of the OIPFG and the CHCPT were recited (*Kar* 1980l, 16, 10), just as they did in the Wheat Festival of 1980 (Atabay 2023).

In response to nationwide grievances and struggles of peasants, especially in Turkman Sahra and Kurdistan, in March 1980 the Revolutionary Council finally ratified a land reform law of sorts. This law identified three types of land: (1) natural resources, (2) cultivated lands confiscated by the Islamic courts, and (3) large lands (i.e., triple the size one cultivator can operate according to local customs) that belonged to the agents of the previous regime. The first two categories were placed under "the auspices of the Islamic government," but the lands in category 2 could be transferred to "eligible persons" or charity. As regards category 3, uncultivated lands of large landowners were to be taken over by the government and assigned (*dar ekhtiar*) to peasants or eligible persons. Large landowners who actively cultivated land were entitled only to the area cultivable by small landowners (depending on regional ecology), but if the cultivator was a subcontractor, they would be entitled to the land. The rest of the plot in these cases would be taken by the government and given to eligible persons "according to the interests of society" (*maslehat-e jame'eh*). The decision in each case were to be made by a 7-person "Land Assignment Committee" (consisting of delegates from Agriculture Ministry, Interior Ministry, Reconstruction Crusade, Justice Ministry, and village council). Land assignments would be for specific but renewable terms, and they could not be sold.

Assigned lands would be cooperative or joint cultivation. Lastly, "the farmers (*zare'in*) did not have the right to take any land other than the one assigned to them by the Islamic government" ("Details" 1980, 2). Obvious flaws in this "reform" are clear: it simply is not intended to distribute land to peasantry permanently. Instead, as it turned out to be the case, this "reform" allowed for "eligible persons" (i.e., not peasants) close to the state to apply, be assigned, and over time own, confiscated lands (located in the best areas) almost for free, before they turned them into sources of income (villas, resorts, rental property). This is the origin of post-revolutionary lucrative land kleptocracy, and an obvious continuation of land capitalism through yet another land reform. In practice, in an arid plateau like Iran, this law killed small landownership and pushed the already battered peasantry out of land and unto city margins. This law was revised many times in the next few years as Iran embarked on implementing neoliberal economic policies. Up to 1988, according to a source, approximately 1.5 million hectares of land (of all three categories) were distributed among 250,000 peasants ("7-Person" 2023). While under the Shah the land reform served to bring agriculture into the capitalist relations and transform the large landowner class into a class of industrialist and mercantile entrepreneurs and proletarianize the peasants in the process, under the Islamic Republic the so-called land reform served the rising oligarchy feeding off a rentier state to grab the best lands for the purpose of wealth and resource accumulation in a rapidly privatized, neoliberal capitalist economy.

The state's Islamic land reform also served yet another political purpose: propagated nationwide by newspapers, radio and television, and locally by the Reconstruction Crusade field personnel, it gradually replaced the leftist rhetoric of genuine, social justice–oriented land reform in public discourse. As soon as this land reform law was made public, the OIPFG, attributing such a lame land reform to the struggles of Turkmen peasants, wrote, rather superficially, that "the land reform ..., if implemented, will benefit the peasants" (*Kar* 1980h, 13). It did not. Instead, the confiscated lands of the Royal Family and absentee landowners were taken over by the Mostaz'afan Foundation (founded after the Revolution and tasked with collecting all confiscated property and distribute them among the poor), which gradually and in due course, allotted these lands (and other confiscated property including factories) to persons close to the ruling elite and commanders of the armed forces who, through a vast nepotistic network, had applied to "cultivate" some of the best lands in the country, but in fact, turned them into sources of income.

But the Islamists' land reform duped Fadaiyan into vocally advocating for the implementation of the land reform's category 3 (distribution of large lots), famously at the time known as *band-e jeem* (the "C clause"). This rhetorical shift from genuine, grassroots, Turkmen-style "land reform" to insisting on the implementation of this vague clause, pushed Fadaiyan away from being the defender of people's rights and into a reformist path that regarded the new regime as "anti-imperialist" and thus worthy of their support. In fact, a cursory review of the issues of *Kar* after the US embassy takeover indicates the increasing shift in supporting the cleric's "anti-imperialism" and exposing the "liberal" cliques within the regime that were hesitant about it. Strange statements emerged in the pages of *Kar*: "Reactionary clerics ... show their animosity toward progressive and anti-imperialist clerics and peasants" (*Kar* 1980j, 4). What catalyzed this metamorphosis was a major split in June 1980 in the OIPFG ranks that created an increasingly pro-regime majority wing, under the influence of the Tudeh Party and its unwavering support for the clerics, and an anti-regime minority that resisted this delusion (see Vahabzadeh 2010, 69–77). But even before the split, and even while the Fadai leaders vehemently defended the Turkmen council movement in the TV debate and continued to do so in the pages of *Kar*, the tendency to support the "radical clerics" was simmering within the OIPFG leadership. The metamorphosis within Fadaiyan's leadership that had started with the embassy takeover was complete with the so-called land reform. Perhaps this explains why the OIPFG never acknowledged the extent of damage to the council movement because it would not serve its new sycophantic strategy in relation to the ruling clerics. The pages of *Kar* after February 1980 propagated lies and began to blame unidentified "black gangs" (*bandha-ye siah*) for the continued repression and murder of activists across Iran, while every Iranian at the time, as I recall vividly, knew that these brutes were the regime's own Brown Shirts.

A cunning move right after the attack on the Turkmen councils, the Islamic land reform justified the transformation of the fabric of rural Turkmen society in the coming months. With the regime's victory, within the next months the activities of the remaining CHCPT activists immensely diminished. The village councils were still solidly in place, but the movement was clearly withering away. The regime could not just wish the councils away: for about a year, Turkmen peasants had been socializing into collective self-management, and the councils were a part of their everyday life. In the absence of young, enthusiastic CHCPT activists in village councils, the Reconstruction Crusade stepped in as the primary agent. In fact, the Reconstruction Crusade copied the idea of village councils, but under its own directives and certainly not autonomously (I saw this first-hand in my travels to rural Iran in the 1980s), and implemented it across the country to improve crop production and contribute to the country's food self-sufficiency (*khodkafa'i*), a buzzword of the rulers during the war with Iraq. The infiltration of the Reconstruction Crusade into villages and village councils represented an updated, Islamicized version of the appointment of village *kadkhoda* under the Pahlavis: an attempt at regulating village life under the state. At this revolutionary time, according to Atabay (2023), many Reconstruction Crusade personnel in the region had radical, social justice–oriented views; they were against large landowners and actually wished to preserve the councils in a modified fashion. But such elements were gradually replaced by conservative personnel subservient to the whims of the increasingly corrupt ruling oligarchy.

What happened to the councils and activists after the "second war" is scarcely documented. The pages of *Kar* of the majority faction of the OIPFG contain some information, but one cannot verify or finetune them. The minority faction's *Kar* was silent about the Turkmen affairs until it published a single report about the region in December 1980 (*Kar-Minority* 1980, 7). In a process that took several months, the councils were transformed and depoliticized so that they would be annexed to the state. They were renamed "Islamic Councils," organized under an assimilated version of the CHCPT, "Central Headquarters of Islamic Councils" (Fereidoun 2001, 46). Other councils, too, underwent a similar process: with their key activists stepping down or on the run, they were staffed by Islamists. Just like the Islamic Association of Teachers of Gonbad Kavus, many of the former grassroots councils became "Islamic Associations" or "Islamic Councils" and attached to the state's institutions. The regime's scheme was to strip the council model of its radical self-governance. To that effect, while some villagers reportedly resisted the newcomers, the Reconstruction Crusade, accompanied by the Gendarmerie and IRGC, held meetings with village councils to inform them of the changes ahead and required electing new councils as some council members had already been arrested (*Kar* 1980m, 6). In Spring 1980, reports emerged that former large landowners had returned to their lands (previously confiscated by councils) and claimed them with the permits issued by Gonbad Kavus Governorship (*Kar* 1980l, 11). On May 2, though, the 11th Congress of the Plenary Rural Union of Turkman Sahra, organized by CHCPT, took place in Aq Degish village. Given the persecution of Turkmen activists, one assumes that this congress must have taken place in secret, and oddly, *Kar* reports it as if it was all business as usual (DCM1, 482–485; *Kar* 1980n, 4), thus concealing the repressive atmosphere that dominated the region. This was the time of wheat harvest once again, and the CHCPT, possibly in hiding, issued directives to the village councils about the harvest, recommending that they not forget American imperialism (OIPFG's new buzzword), avoid conflict, maintain solidarity across Turkmens and non-Turkmens, and harvest collectively and through the councils (*Kar* 1980o, 7). How realistic or even useful such advice was, given the repressive conditions, remains unknown.

In the eventful spring of 1980, a new military assault on Kurdistan was taking place and continuing throughout the year, and in June the IRGC and Islamist goons attacked universities — dominated by leftist and radical students — through a "Cultural Revolution." Shutting down universities for the next couple of years, the regime purged tens of thousands of students (this author included!) and thousands of professors. Thus, the regime effectively shut down one of the most important bastions of progressive values in the country. The eradication of the university student movement certainly had a ripple effect: many student activists were pacified while others joined their chosen movements, but without a strong, progressive student body, social justice–oriented movements lost considerable support. In September 1980, Iraq invaded parts of southwestern Iran, and that led to an eight-year war, which justified the increased repression of political activism, especially in Kurdistan.

Facing new conditions, a thirty-five-person delegation of Turkmen councils from several towns travelled to Tehran (May 21–22, 1980) to meet with the Deputy Minister of Agriculture, Revolutionary Council office, and some parliament deputies to insist on their previous demands: land distribution, recognition of councils, and an existing five-person conflict resolution committee. Reportedly, they returned home feeling ignored (*Kar-Majority* 1980a, 9), clearly because there was no movement behind them. To persuade the councils into the directions of the regime's land reform, the Reconstruction Crusade used agricultural loans as incentive to villagers to elect new councils (*Kar-Majority* 1980b, 5). Meanwhile, the government ratified new regulations regarding councils in workplaces that were an attempt at transforming genuine, democratically elected councils and unions in factories and companies (and village councils across Iran) into ineffective, Islamic Councils attached to the state. In rural Iran, seven-person committees gradually succeeded in settling land disputes through a mixture of restoring land titles (at time partially), distributing land to individual peasants (thus gradually eradicating collective ownership), and confiscating land through various state foundations like the Mostaz'afan Foundation. Tasked with accumulating the confiscated assets of the ancien regime, these "foundations" grew into economic powerhouses and privatization agencies in the next decades. They sold the confiscated lands at preferential, bargain prices to the cronies of the ruling oligarchy. One report holds that huge stretches of Turkmen lands were taken over by the Mostaz'afan Foundation (*Kar-Minority* 1980, 7). Short reports one year after the "second war" indicate continuing sporadic clashes between Turkmen villagers and landowners or agents of the state in late 1980 and 1981 (*Kar-Majority* 1981a, 20; *Kar-Minority* 1980, 7). As late as 1986, a CPCTP tract warned the peasants about plans to sell the confiscated lands back to them (in DCM1, 493).

By 1982, the Marxist-Leninist OIPFG-Majority was fully in support of the Islamic Republic, the Turkmen activists were in disarray, and the movement was practically gone. Assimilation of once grassroots Turkmen organizations was complete, and a report in *Kar* speaks precisely of a symbol of defeat: a delegation of the Islamic Association of Gonbad Kavus Teachers that visited Khomeini. But more saddening was the report of creating a union of councils in Aqqal region on the *initiative* of the seven-person conflict resolution committee (*Kar-Majority* 1981a, 7).

As mentioned, the majority of Pishgam activists in Turkman Sahra joined the majority wing of the OIPFG after the split, and their subsequent activities were aligned with it. They continued to hold limited events with great caution until 1983 when the Islamic Republic security descended on the group (that had supported the regime up to this point) and arrested hundreds of its activists across the country. At this time, all open activities ceased and Pishgam activists went into hiding or moved elsewhere.

After the "second war", many CPCTP and CHCPT activists gradually left the region and the members of both the bodies gradually went "underground." In the subsequent months and years, many Turkmen activists left the country into exile where they revived the CPCTP, which underwent several reshapings. Around 1989, the activists of the refashioned CPCTP (in exile) severed links with Fadaiyan for good. Other activists formed new Turkmen groups outside the country and published several periodicals in the 1980s and 1990s including *Turkmenistan*, *Iel Guyji*, *Il Gün*, *Genkesh*, and *Tazeh Yol*. Websites and weblogs of Turkmen activists also emerged in the twenty-first century. Efforts to refashion the CPCTP with more nationalistic outlooks continues to this day. These efforts of Turkmen intellectuals contribute to debates about the future of diverse cultural-national populations in Iran.

Conclusions

Iran's Turkmens succeeded in creating the most sophisticated and organized form of a grassroots, democratic, self-governing council movement in the country in post-revolutionary times and, without a doubt, the most elaborate regional land-based council movement in modern Iran. Despite continued adversities brought on by the state that wanted to crush the de facto authority of the organic bodies of CHCPT and CPCTP, the Turkmen council movement managed to peacefully direct the affairs of some 500,000 to 800,000 residents of the Plains of Turkmen in various economic sectors — above all and with particular emphasis, the peasants with whom the entire council movement originated. The key to this movement was the Turkmen claim to ancestral lands and the cultural distinctness of Turkmens as a people. The movement thrived by mobilizing the population through a refined council system and with the guidance of Turkmen organic intellectuals. With its emphasis on social justice and the popular, peaceful, and nonviolent power from below, the Turkmen council movement succeeded in creating collaborations and alliances across different sectors and classes within the region, as well as nationwide solidarity with oppressed groups, above all the Kurds. The Turkmen organic intellectuals were successful in overcoming the long "ethnic" divisions within the region — in particular, the ones between Turkmen peasants and migrant workers and Turkmens and other nationalities in towns — that was a legacy of the Pahlavis and amplified by the Islamic Republic that promoted the Shi'i-Sunni disunion. The movement's wise leadership created relations of equivalence between Turkmens, Azerbaijani Turks, Baluchis, Sistanis, and Persians living in the region. The elaborate organization of the council system, as discussed earlier in this chapter, provides an exemplary model for participatory, democratic, and grassroots organization of the people (see the concluding chapter).

Rising as a heavy-handed authoritarian system, the Islamic Republic was in its raison d'être entirely alien to the democratic and grassroots aspirations of the Turkmen and other movements. Given the specificities of its formation, the Turkmen council movement found the OIPFG its most steadfast supporter in the country. The movement allied itself with the OIPFG's national policies and participated in certain elections to register its legal presence, even though the state did not recognize or licence the Turkmen bodies as political or cultural organizations. The OIPFG fruitfully brought the plights and the successes of the movement into the nationwide spotlight in 1979–1980, giving the Turkmens visibility and promoting the Turkmen culture and the social imagination of the council movement across diverse social justice–oriented movements in the country. While the CHCPT and CPCTP were mostly harmonious with Fadaiyan on nationwide politics, these bodies managed to maintain their autonomy in their regional affairs. It is not an exaggeration to claim that Fadaiyan's bookish knowledge of councils was indeed enriched by the practical field experience and knowledge of Turkmen organic intellectuals and council activists and participants. In fact, as I argue, the OIPFG was immensely influenced by this movement, as reflected in their early 1980 Minimum Program. The Turkmen council movement was larger than life: it inspired councils across the country, created multinational solidarity within the Iranian diversity, and contributed immensely to OIPFG's policies.

The Turkmens' alliance with the OIPFG, however, protected the movement in as much as Fadaiyan could exercise social power under the Islamic Republic. Observed in retrospect and from the Turkmen point of view, Fadaiyan's unreasonable and rash insistence on holding their rally in Gonbad Kavus in February 1980 inadvertently brought about the demise of the movement. In the end, it was the Turkmens who suffered the brunt of this avoidable calamity. But why did Fadaiyan not have the wisdom to avoid this conflict that the regime was only too eager to create? Whether they were naïvely played by the elaborate plot of the regime's intelligence, whether their conceit and hubris blinded them to seeing how limited their power actually was contra the state's sheer force, whether they failed to hold a consistent policy, or all of the above: these remain up for speculation. The OIPFG nevertheless remains responsible for the damage it caused the very movement that was its ally. The catastrophic metamorphosis of the OIPFG diminished the group that was once Iran's largest most popular leftist group to defend the democratic rights of peoples (despite their serious policy and ideological shortcomings) and transformed it into a shameful apologist for the Islamists by the OIPFG-Majority. Indeed, fascinated by the aura of the state, the majority wing betrayed the movements that once constituted the pillars of its democratic, social power. In retrospect, it appears that the repression of the Turkmen council movement proved to be a convenient solution for the OIPFG's growing dilemma, in late 1979 to early 1980, of how to support *both* the Turkmen's democratic council movement *and* the reactionary but supposedly "anti-imperialist" clerical regime that was intent on eradicating the councils. The fact that the OIPFG-Majority gradually relinquished speaking of the plights of the Turkmens after the "second war" and clearly "naturalized" in its discourse the imposed process of Islamicization, assimilation and the gradual demise of the councils stands as evidence to my claim. History is a severe judge: no one wanted to own the Turkmen council movement, not even its closest ally, the OIPFG, and the shame of disowning the movement stays forever with the OIPFG-Majority.

The regime was now in the region with clear plans to assimilate the councils in the regime's policy and appropriate the Turkmen's ancestral lands. And the death of key Turkmen architects of the movement left no chance for this marvellous exemplar of popular and democratic movement to rebuild. However, the praxis and legacy of the councils were so deeply ingrained in the everyday lives of Turkmen peasants that repression alone could not suppress the movement and the council's assimilation through Reconstruction Crusade was equally instrumental (and repressive) in eradicating this movement. A forgotten world-historical movement thus came to an end, but as the conclusions to this study argue, its legacy has important lessons to offer for today's popular struggles for social justice and democratic self-governance as an alternative to the tripartite oppressive force of state-capitalism-patriarchy.

Conclusions

A World-Historical Movement
Turkmens' Radical Democratic Experience

Every nation is entitled to the right of living within its own homeland and decide its own destiny. Every nation is entitled to speak and write in its [mother] tongue, preserve its customs and traditions and decide its preferred political and economic system.... While having cultural and ethnic (qowmi) particularities, the peoples of Iran have many common characteristics that has made them into an integrated (yekparcheh) entity called the Iranian people.... Safeguarding the right to true self-governance (khodmokhtari) within a democratic and free Iran not only guarantees the indivisible integrity of our country, it will make it deeper and more robust.
— Cultural-Political Centre of Turkmen People
Press Release (July 15, 1979)

IN 1979, THE TURKMEN COUNCIL MOVEMENT shone brightly in a particular historic moment as Iran was rapidly transitioning from an imperialist-backed dictatorship to the long dreamt-of freedom and popular self-assertion. That moment, as it sadly turned out, was brief. Soon, the country's rising retrograde and autocratic oligarchy, monopolizing and wielding the sheer force of the state supplemented by cunning manoeuvrings, drove the country into a prolonged, fundamentalist darkness that has lasted to this day and ruined and taken numerous lives and destroyed the possibility of an ecologically sustainable future. The sweet taste of freedom was fleeting. History has tasted bitter ever since.

What the Turkmen organic intellectuals articulated back in 1979 — as included in the epigraph to this chapter — resonates with today's declining world. What they imagined as a humane, democratic, participatory, nonviolent, and rights-based collective life; what they regarded as a people's fundamental rights; what they wished to be realized not just for Turkmens but for all peoples of Iran, we can find in the United Nations' fundamental declarations in the past decades, in today's indigenous movements for land and autonomy worldwide, in the prevalent discourse of human rights as the undeniable rights of every living person on this planet, and in the struggles of hundreds of millions of people today for equality, equity, and social justice across the world.

A historically marginalized people within Iranian modernity, the Turkmens gifted Iranians with a most sophisticated land-based, culturally informed, grassroots, and democratic alternative for a better life. Their unique gift was relegated to oblivion, perhaps because it was simply too original for framed minds: academics ignored the movement, and the state's salaried historians distorted it as an anomaly and an ethnic disturbance. The Turkmen council movement succeeded to manage the complex affairs of a region with a diverse and large population (of 500,000 to 800,000 people) surrounded and permeated by belligerent forces that were intent upon destroying the newly-found, meaningful collective life of the region's residents with justice, fairness, and inclusivity.

In these concluding remarks, I offer analyses and discuss the Turkmen council movement's many overlooked contributions to both theory and practice, hoping that this world-historical movement will be viewed for what it gifted to our ever-deeply connected world. This book is a work of counter-memory and counter-history, as I refuse to subscribe to dominant, ideologically sanctioned narratives. This book intentionally points out and disturbs the silences in history.

A Transnational and Anticipative Movement

Orientalist historiography of Iran (and elsewhere) in general bears a tendency to restrict its subject to "area study" and thus objectify and view it as a regional phenomenon marginal to the grand (European) World History. In this case, the Orientalist approach isolates and reduces the Turkmen council movement to a "regional" or "minority" issue, thus not only clouding our view of the movement's impact on the Iranian social imaginary and history, but also concealing its transnational connections and potential contributions. It thus contributes to the marginalization of the subject matter. Moreover, for the most part, the existing historiography of modern Iran, the Iranian Left, and Iran's social movements has produced works that lock up these phenomena in a bygone past, almost like a dead weight that the Orientalist wishes to disown and drop quickly by enumerating its "failures." As such, mainstream, Orientalist historiography tears the people's movements from their historical contexts and presents them in scholarly works without any connection to and implication for present-day struggles. A phenomenological gaze such as mine allows us to reactivate origins from under layers of sedimented events, interests, and interpretations, and unearth and explore the potential contribution of past movements and struggles to those of the present.

The Turkmen council movement stands at the nexus of a myriad of transnational histories and incessant borderland influences. In its autochthonous, grassroots self-organization, it arose from the long, ancestral Turkmen traditions of *yashuli*, while the modern iteration of the peasant councils through Turkmen activists emerged as an inadvertent heir to *anjomans* of the Constitutional Revolution, the *anjomans* whose conceptual inspiration and historical moment came from the councils of the 1905 Russian revolution via the Caucuses. Furthermore, the participation of leftist Turkmen activists that gave new momentum and directions to the traditional councils is evidence that the Turkmen council movement was also obliquely linked to the long European and global socialist and anarchist tradition of factory and workers' (red) councils as well as to the *showras* of Iranian workers during the revolutionary months of 1978 and 1979. The movement registers a brilliant articulatory amalgamation of traditional and socialist council worldviews by Turkmen organic intellectuals. Still, the Turkmen council movement was a direct response to the Shah's American-advised land reform and peripheral capitalism. The birthplace of the Cultural-Political Centre of Turkmen People (CPCTP) in Gonbad Kavus — a modern city designed by Germans — was the public library that was founded by a man from the American Peace Corps, and some activists in 1979 had gathered, in their adolescence, around this library and learned English from this American. As university students, the key leftist activists of the movement such as Toomaj were supporters of the Organization of Iranian People's Fadai Guerrillas (OIPFG), a group deeply inspired by the urban guerrilla movement in Latin America as well as conventional, global iterations of Marxism-Leninism and liberation movements in Africa and Asia. In showcasing the Turkmen culture nationwide in the music festival of 1980, the pro-OIPFG organizers placed Turkmen Bakhshi/Baghshi alongside music from Chile, Palestine (via Sweden), and the rest of Iranian cultural diversity. Turkmen national self-consciousness was in part a response to the post-revolutionary domination of Shi'i Islam and its discriminatory policies regarding religious minorities.

What is more, the Turkmen organic intellectuals, the minds and faces of the movement, had come from a particular historical junction where they had received education outside of Turkman Sahra in one of the country's emerging or expanding universities as a part of a state-centric developmentalist project. In a dialectical fashion, the Turkmen intellectuals were the products of higher education (from state universities) that was designed to produce technocrats and intelligentsia for a growing bureaucracy and industry while the inclination of activists toward social justice (from the leftist discourse) turned them into their people's organic intellectuals. Educated and dedicated, these intellectuals became the articulators of the council movement, giving it vision, coherence, and strategy.

The wisdom granted by hindsight and a knowledge of global social movements will reveal that by creating a three-tiered structure of the councils (Chapter 5), and unbeknownst to the activists of the time, the 1979 Turkmen council movement theoretically albeit inadvertently "anticipated" the grassroots, participatory, decolonizing, and social justice–oriented autonomous movements of the Zapatistas in Chiapas, Mexico, and Rojava in north and east of Syria, movements with similar participatory structures. My claim here is not that this movement was foundational or unique; rather, I argue that the movement revealed the elements of democratic, participatory resistance to colonial-capitalist modernity, the elements that in our day have become signatures of emancipatory and autonomist movements. The Turkmen council movement belongs to the history of autonomous movements *within* the boundaries of the modern nation-state. Unlike the Zapatistas and Rojava that have grown into inspiring world-class movements, sadly, the Turkmen council movement was defeated and then relegated to oblivion, removed from the known tradition of global autonomous movements.

Governing roughly a quarter of a million indigenous Mayan peasants in an area about one-third of the state of Chiapas in Mexico since 1994, the Zapatista Army of National Liberation has organized rebel communities through grassroots participatory community councils and in a system where every proposal of the Revolutionary Clandestine

Committee must be debated and conclusions reached by *all* communities. In the rebel-controlled zones, the private ownership of land has been abolished and all land is treated as commons and worked collectively. Schools, healthcare centres, and community offices manage and educate the daily affairs of the communities. One-third of Zapatistas and the Zapatista army are women and communities are required to protect women's rights and protect women against domestic violence. In fact, the Zapatistas call the Zapatista women's revolution (1993) their first revolution.

Since the 2012 nonviolent revolution in war-torn Syria and under the directives of the Democratic Union Party, Rojava or the Autonomous Administration of North and East Syria has created livable conditions for about 2 million Kurds, Arabs, Syrians, Assyrians, Yazidis, Armenians, Chechens, Turkmens, Circassians, and Nawars in self-governing, autonomous cantons (now regions) in polyethnic and multinational arrangements. Four levels of councils — namely the commune, neighbourhood/village, district, and the People's Council (parliament) — each tasked with governing the issues of the residents, are governed through the principles of cochair (of genders) and mandatory 40 percent membership of either sex in each council. Situated in one of the most hostile regions in the world and under constant occupation or threat by Turkey, Syrian government, the Jihadists, and Kurdish Regional Government (in northern Iraq) and under economic embargo, the women and men in Rojava are organized in separate People's Defence Units (YPG) and Women's Protection Units (YPJ). In Rojava's council system, it is not mandatory for lower councils to act on the ratifications of higher councils. TEV-DEM or Movement for a Democratic Society is created as an organization of activists from different political parties who participate in all councils to promote democratic input and educate the citizens. The region is governed according to a Social Contract. Private property is abolished, and all land is confiscated by the councils. Lands are cultivated through cooperatives. Businesses and houses are governed by the principle of use ownership.

Like the forgotten Turkmen council movement, both for the Zapatistas and in Rojava the grassroots participatory council movements have made significant strides to neutralize the devastating effect of capitalism and private landownership. Their important differences, situations, and challenges notwithstanding, the family resemblances among these movements are undeniable: they offer alternatives to the present destructive, capitalist order. In our profoundly connected world today — an oppressive, exploitative, and colonial world on the brink of an irrecoverable collapse of the human species at the expense of other species and regional ecologies — one can no longer speak of any movement as distinct or "regional": we are all heirs to the actions and movements of others.

From Arendt to Gramsci and Back

The Turkmen council movement stands witness to the ageless Arendtian thesis that, once left to themselves and released from the force of the state, the people — as diverse equals due to the human capacity of beginning something new collectively — are capable of "acting in concert" and self-governance (Arendt 1963, 1969, 1970, 1985b; Vahabzadeh 2019b, 121–139). Despite its great strides in creating a participatory, democratic self-organization and regional arrangement, the Turkmen council movement was short-lived due to the constant menacing and ultimate repression (led by the Islamic Revolutionary Guards Corps; IRGC) and assimilation (through the Reconstruction Crusade) by the rising Islamist state. This fact, in addition, attests to the Arendtian thesis — based on her observations of councils in American, Russian, or Hungarian revolutions — that once the state becomes powerful it will not tolerate the people's genuine power. The Turkmen councils were short-lived, as were the experiences of German *Räte*, Italian *Bienne Rosso*, the Russian soviets (1905 and 1917), and Iranian factory councils (1978–1979). As a practical alternative arrangement of human collective life and contrary to the existing colonial and hierarchical forms of power, councils are repressed because they point to the possibility of a liberated, better, world. Chiapas and Rojava stand witness to the longevity of new ways of political life. Perhaps one can infer from these two cases — and many similar movements across the world today — that the age of the nation-state is coming to an end.

Let us not forget that from its inception the Turkmen council movement was about both land and culture. The Turkmen peasant's dependency on land is conceptually significant for our study. We need to recognize the difference between peasants' and workers' councils: being a product of modern capitalist industrialization, workers are able to move from one factory to another and still remain within the working class and participate in workers' movements, initiatives, unions, and councils. In contrast, peasants are literally attached to ancestral lands. Once they leave their land, they potentially lose their particular class-belonging and traditional community by becoming agricultural workers (as with the Zabolis in Turkman Sahra) or unskilled workers living on the marginalized edges of industrial boomtowns. In other words, for the Turkmens, land had a significant cultural significance. This is how traditional and cultural attachment to ancestral lands, the taking back of dispossessed lands collectively, and managing it through the updated tradition of councils identify Turkmens as a people.

The Arendtian moment in the Turkmen council movement, however, entailed the "social question," a component Hannah Arendt (1963) disavowed in her comparative study of French and American revolutions. Let me point out the theoretical significance of the Turkmen council movement. As mentioned (Chapter 1), in the Turkmen council movement, Arendt meets Gramsci. Left to themselves within the brief period of transition of state force from one regime to another in February 1979, and in the context of the decades-long land dispossession through repressive development, the Turkmens in Iran converged as a people and created something new, registering that they were capable of self-organizing and self-governing in a participatory manner. This is the Arendtian moment. The initial, spontaneous council movement and land takeover quickly converged with the Turkmen organic intellectuals. It was the unique and momentous ability of these intellectuals within CPCTP and CHCPT to articulate the economic and social demands of the Turkmens that enabled a sustainable, progressive movement. These organic intellectuals — Toomaj and Makhtoom, above all — gave the movement a long-term vision, directed it toward a new de facto "body politic," and supplied Iran (along with Kurdistan) with an alternative, federalist vision. This is the Gramscian process. We should note that the fact that Kurdistan and Turkman Sahra championed the cause of federalist arrangement for a new Iran, in contrast with dominant state-centric views in 1979, attest to the uneven political and economic development across the country. This unevenness was the basis of nationalist movements but at the same time made the regional minorities' demands for nationwide recognition and constitutional status unfulfilled due to the privilege of other regions and their power. For that to happen, the idea of national-cultural distinctness needed to be socialized nationwide through public discourse, a step taken by many secular parties within the first year after the Revolution (as in the People's Solidarity Conference held in July 1979), but the regime's repressive force intentionally silenced this discourse by descending on the diverse, and vastly secular, voices of the 1979 Revolution and imposing the retrograde values of Shi'i clerics. The success of the Turkmen experiment was entirely dependent on the expansion and victory of the democratic movement in Iran. Today some blame the movement for its "radicalism," but this is a distorted view. The movement weighed toward democratization and gifted a model for a new Iran. Yet history played its cards, and the force of the new regime ultimately crushed all opposition.

The lesson of this study is that these two components — the possibility of participatory self-organizing and self-governance in a new "body politic" and the presence of organic intellectuals as the articulators of the social question into sustainable political formation and demands — constitute the fundamental condition of grassroots mobilization against the colonial status quo and the joint, oppressive forces of patriarchy, state, and capitalism, including land capitalism. In what they achieved by careful design despite all adversity, the Turkmens of Iran showed a new mode of power: instead of "taking power," in the old revolutionary way (which in this context would mean a secessionist movement), they engaged in "making power" (Smith 2017) from below. Making power is always the endowment of a collective and of social movements.

Ancestrality and Collective Democratic Life

The concept of *ancestrality*, to which I have alluded in this book, has been inspired by the discourse of CPCTP: in registering the Turkmen peasants' inalienable right to the land on which the Turkmens have lived for a millennium or so, the CPCTP used the Persian expression, *aba va ajdadi* (literally, "fathers and ancestors") to capture the relationship between the Turkmens and their homeland in the Plains of Turkmens. The discursive deployment of this expression was meant to register the collective right to land as commons that historically and morally precedes any present-day (capitalist) landownership. Ancestrality connects a people to land. Because my concept of ancestrality is owed to the Turkmen experience in 1979 and the political articulation by the Turkmen organic intellectuals, this concept should be regarded as the contribution of the Turkmen council movement to theory and potentially to the struggles of landless peasants in the world. Ancestrality draws on common ancestry bound to a particular place; in the context of the internally colonizing modernization of Iran (through the laws of land registry that turned land into private property), ancestrality connects a historically rooted collective's land claim to the cultural revival of a dispossessed and subaltern people, such that the ancestral relations to land refuses the turning of land into (capitalist) property ownership of individuals. This is in contrast to private ownership that treats land as property, which, then, is the object of exploitation and a source of profit, and is also in sharp contrast to the state that regards land as territory, which is the field of exercise of the sovereign's hubristic domination. Thus, an ancestral worldview regards land as life.

Stated differently, in the manner in which the concept rose from the Turkmen experience and the way I developed it in this work, ancestrality registers a particular relational ontology of land that radically diverges from the matrices of state and capitalist domination. In this context, culture allows ancestrality to surface, as it enables the movement to sustain itself. Accordingly, understanding land as commons is important here. By definition, ancestrality is connected to a cultural-national collective identity of a people, and as in the Turkmen council movement, its organic mode of land claim and collective governance was embodied by the councils. As evidenced by the council movement, ancestrality denotes a particular, ethical relation to a place that a people call their homeland. The people residing in this place, then, regard themselves as the caretakers of land, being responsible for it but also caring about the future of themselves as a culturally distinct people. This historical approach to land, place, or homeland, has affinities with Glen Coulthard's (2014) concept of "grounded normativity" as an ethical relation of Indigenous Peoples in Canada to land. In the case of Turkmens, they resisted the capitalist plundering of land by the Pahlavis as well as the incipient Islamic Republic. Their decades-long legal battles against Pahlavi land grab, and their year-long reclaiming of land after the Revolution, in short, their resistance, was indeed motivated and invigorated by a deeply rooted collective identity driven by ancestrality. Theirs was a resistance against private landownership that deprives others of a place to live that they call home. The collective ownership of Turkmens offered a noncapitalist form of landownership. A movement based on such a profound conception of land defends collective ownership and rejects capitalist private property, although, inevitably, it is connected to a world dominated by capitalist economic relations. Situated within a capitalist economy, this form of ownership could not take a conventional legal form due to the property laws of the state and must create its own laws.

The junction between the (ancestral, social, cultural, communal) collective and the (economic) commons takes the political form of participatory, democratic decision-making, in a council system, and the inclusion of minorities within the region. These qualities were all present in the Turkmen council movement (as they are in Chiapas and Rojava). The lesson of the Turkmen council movement is that ancestral claims cannot be exclusionary and monopolizing. On the contrary, due to communal ownership and self-governance, a people's connection to ancestral land will necessitate the socialization of others into this relational and participatory model.

Viewed in this way, ancestrality has common bonds with the indigenous movements of our time and offers shared struggles. There are about 350 million indigenous peoples living in seventy countries on this planet (Alfred and Corntassel 2017, 132), and their struggles are deeply connected to both land and decolonization, as well as cultural revitalization. In much of Asia and Africa (and elsewhere), the many waves of invasions and mass migrations throughout history have caused the movements and settlements of peoples who, having been uprooted from their origins, had spread roots for millenniums in their current lands. Ancestrality speaks to this common reality of hundreds of millions of peoples across the world. We can now clearly see why I called this movement world-historical and stressed its affinity with the indigenous movement in Chiapas and with that of the Kurds in their ancestral Rojava: the struggles for land, culture, social justice, and democratic, collective life create solidarity among land-based movements of peoples in our world.

(Re-)Collecting the Past

The Turkmen council movement shone bright in its time, giving its participants dignity and an alternative collective life, while giving the rest of the country a vision of a better Iran. The fact that the movement was short-lived due to incredible adversities does not detract from the value of its potential contributions to visions of a better future for Turkmens and for Iranians. The future of the Turkmen council movement depended on the future of democracy in the country, a dream of Iranians for many, many decades, a dream that, after the consolidation of power by the ruling Islamists, turned into a nightmare.

If nothing else, this study shows that at the moment when the councils emerged and the pace of life changed in Turkman Sahra, the Turkmen people stopped being subaltern and became active, decolonizing agents of their own destiny. Viewed from our present-day standpoint in this colonial and rapidly declining world, the Turkmen council movement was one of our possible global futures. This work of counter-memory and counter-history re-collects the movement in the spirit of the emancipation of the oppressed.

Appendix 1

Reports from Turkman Sahra Villages

Author's note: this Appendix provides a first-hand, activist narrative of the realities and challenges faced by the peasants of Turkman Sahra. There are not many reports like this. The issues of land dispossession, land registration, collective mobilization, ethnic plurality, rural challenges, the role of law enforcement, and the councils are all discussed here.

Tatar Olya

With a total of 520 families, of which 320 families are Turkmens and the rest non-Turkmen, this village is located 20 kilometres outside of Gonbad Kavus. Its population stands at 5,000, and according to the region's map, it covers an area of approximately 3,500 hectares. Before 1932, the issues of the village were addressed under the supervision of village seniors and elders. The elders' decisions were based on consulting with the villagers and residents, and the problems were resolved according to religious laws and customs. The Properties and Registration Law (approved on February 11, 1931), allowed Reza Khan [Reza Shah] to transform all the lands of Gorgan and Gonbad [Kavus] as his private estates, and by 1938, except for a few northern pastures, all the villages of Gorgan, Gonbad [Kavus], and Rasht were registered [to his name] in the same way.

On September 21, 1941, all private estates were transferred to the government, and after that, on June 3, 1942, a law was approved to return these [Royal] estates to their original owners. According to this law, the owners of these lands were given a six-month deadline to apply to take back their lands. After a while, seventeen villages, including Tatar Olya, were taken back by Ms. Youfak Marama`i, Haji Arazgholi Rastegar, Khedra Qecheli, and Ane Movakhed Vahedi. On October 18, 1950, the villages of Tatar Olya and Tatar Sofla were sold by the aforementioned persons to misters Araz Jorjani, Poruq Jorjani, Aq Oveyli Tatari, Yelfi Bardi Tatari, Aman Dordi Tatari, Sa'at Jorjani, and Aman Tatari. These eight persons sold these two villages to the residents of the village on

December 7, 1957 in 553 shares. As of this point, the ownership in this area has been in the form of small holders (*khordehmaleki*). However, cultivation and harvesting was done by the villagers collectively. During this period, animal husbandry was the main occupation of the villagers. Then, exploiting the undivided nature of landownership, the land-grabbers (*zaminkharan*) started rushing to the villages and competing with each other in doing so.

The land grab in the village of Tatar Olya began through two persons named Haji Jom'eh Babrqojaqi and Haji Amanverdi Qojaqi. Haji Jom'eh Babrqojaqi (the current large landowner of the village) who had purchased 60 hectares of lands for animal husbandry from the four aforementioned large landowners was the first claimant and usurper of the lands although he was aware that the land had not been divided. He had a land title record registering 60 hectares and, by using it and the assistance of Gendarmerie, he took several lots amounting to 60 hectares and registered the lands to his name. The villagers visited Colonel Goudarzi who at that time held 270 hectares of land rented to the villagers to grieve their lost titles to the land. From this point onward, military men, lawyers, etc. passed the [grieving] villagers on to one another while they amassed lands for themselves. For example, Colonel Goudarzi referred the villagers to Colonel Faghani who grabbed 250 hectares of land without doing anything. Apparently, through his son Reza Faghani (who was a lawyer), Colonel Faghani took the matter to the court. In the meantime, his son also acquired 140 hectares of land. In light of the villagers' efforts to take back their lands, Qajaqi families plowed the lands that the villagers had already cultivated and were planning to harvest in an effort to destroy the last indication of the villager's right to the land. Aware of this plan, the villagers started guarding their lands to prevent Qajaqi's tractors from entering their lands. The resistance of the villagers against Qajaqi families caused the Qajaqis to seek assistance from Major Aqili, the Gendarmerie Chief of [the town of] Shahpasand, Lieutentant General Toomaj, the [Parliament] Deputy from Gonbad [Kavus], General Mo'ezzi and his representative Mahmoud Khosravi to suppress the villagers.

One day, when some villagers had gone to their farms to block the entry of Qajaqi's tractors that were sent to destroy the villagers' crops, they found themselves confronted by four Gendarmerie vehicles. The Gendarmes first shot at their horses, and then they started shooting at the villagers. In this clash, two persons named Ane Goldi Jorjani and Araz Jorjani were killed and seven others wounded. The women were attacked by Gendarmes too, and some people were arrested and sent to prison. The outcome of this collusion between the Qajaqis and the armed forces, and consequently the repression of the villagers, was the transference of some land titles to administrative and military officials, including Mahmoud Khosravi. In this way, Turkmen and non-Turkmen usurpers [of land] established their solid footing in Tatar Olya. From this point onwards, the usurpers mechanized most of the land and used the Zabolis or Baluchis, who were migrating en masse to Turkman Sahara in this period, as daily paid labourers. This phenomenon had exacerbated the situation of village residents.

Currently, the majority of village residents are small-scale landowners and each household owns between 1–2 and 30 hectares of land.

…

During the days of the Revolution, some village residents held a meeting in which they decided to rectify the [past] injustices against the peasants. After the overthrow of the Shah's regime, the village residents held a meeting in which they elected eight persons to represent the residents and form the village council. In its first order of business, the council announced the demands of the villagers as follows:

1. Taking back the 450 hectares of usurped lands of [local] residents.
2. Cooperating with the villagers of Qorchay, Oghli Pa'in, and Oghli Bala to take back the 400 hectares of usurped lands in these villages.
3. Seizing farming machinery and equipment that belonged to the land usurpers.
4. Cultivating reclaimed lands cooperatively.
5. Protecting pastures against unauthorized use, marking their boundaries, and repairing the roads.
6. Resolving local disputes and establishing continuous communication with other villages for cooperation and consultation.
7. Forming a rug-weavers' council through free elections.
8. Creating a cooperative fund to help those in need (noncash).
9. Constructing and running library, lecture hall, and rural council office.
10. Digging wells with the cooperation of the residents to provide drinking water and a public bathhouse.

After the usurpers fled the village, the rural council and the residents occupied some of the dispossessed lands. It totalled about 850 hectares, which as described above, belonged to the villages of Tatar Olya and Oghli Bala, Oghli Pa`in. These repossessed lands were planted collectively by the villagers, and it was decided that the crop would be divided among the villagers. It should be noted that collective work is rooted in the traditions and lived experience of the Turkmen (the term *yavar*, used by Turkmens in the past means "collective work"). After reclaiming the lands, the usurpers' machinery was also confiscated by the council, and the villagers surrendered these machines along with their own to the village council.

In an effort to fulfill the demands and rectify the lost rights of the villagers, the village council invited the Zabolis and Baluchis to cooperate and participate in the collective work of the village. But this invitation was not accepted by the Baluchis and especially by the Zabolis. Despite this, the village council has been trying to keep the Zabolis and Baluchis on par with the collective efforts of the Turkmens. Therefore, the members of the council have recently published a statement announcing the dissolution of the council and calling for re-election, so that the Zabolis and Baluchis can participate in the new election and have their representatives in the council. (In the previous election, the Zabolis and Baluchis participated in the election, but despite the insistence of the Turkmens, they did not nominate any candidates for the council).

Currently, the Tatar Olya council is under the Central Headquarters of Councils of the Plains of Turkmen [CHCPT], and it has joined with the councils of seven other villages to form a Union of Village Councils. This union holds regular meetings of councils. These meetings are tasked with the responsibilities that are greater than any council alone can handle by itself, and they also address the common issues of all villages. Each of the councils deals with the daily issues of the villagers and settles legal claims. In effect, the councils have eliminated the villagers' need to approach the Gendarmerie and other government departments [to seek solutions].

The government has tried to meddle with the affairs of the councils and create obstacles in the councils' work. For instance, according to a council member, when [the villagers] needed to purchase seeds to sow in the reclaimed lands, the [sale of] seed was blocked [by the government]. Previously, seed was sold to villagers at a price of 22 rials per kilogram by the Department of Agricultural Development. [This time,] the villagers went to the Department of Agricultural Development and requisitioned seed. The department responded to the villagers that if they brought a confirmation of their right to the reclaimed lands from Anaqelich Naqshbandi (the head of club-wielding supports of [monarchical] Constitution [see Chapter 4] and defender of the feudals [large landowners]), the department would sell the seed to villagers. The villagers were forced to purchase the 22 rials/kg seed at the market price of 45 rials/kg.

Report from the Rural Council of Tatar Olya

It has not been long since the councils were formed, but because the councils belong to the ordinary people, the people do not hesitate to offer work and support to advance its programs. The shining record of the council of Tatar Olya stands witness to the truth that by relying on their own power, the people can effectively and in a short span of time solve many problems that governments had never solved. The councils frighten the enemies of the masses because they cut off profits of the plundering landowners. When the masses achieve happiness and contentment through the power of the councils and taste it, no force could take it from them. The enemies of the people who are the agents of the former regime and the large landowners of the Turkman Sahra region tried to destroy the councils by creating a war [March 1979] so that they could dominate the people again. But if yesterday they succeeded in deceiving naïve Pasdars [IRGC personnel] and young, innocent men and positioned them against the people, today everyone has understood what the people say and want, and why and how the enemy conspires against the people.

...

(Source: LSTP, 85–97)

Appendix 2

The General Principles of Self-Governance Plan (July 1979)

The General Principles of Self-Governance Plan

Proposed by the Iranian Peoples' Solidarity Conference — a 3-day "People's Solidarity Conference" held in Tehran on July 18–20, 1979.

Article 1: Iran is a multinational (*kasirolmelleh*) country and its main nationalities include Baluch, Turk, Turkmen, Arab, Fars [Persian], and Kurd.

Article 2: The Iranian state consists of a congregation of self-governing (*khodmokhtar*) regions with equal rights and duties and shall be governed as a federal state (*hokumat*).

Article 3: Self-governing regions shall be determined through common language, culture, land, and economic characteristics.

  Section 1: The self-governing regions shall be solely determined by the vote of the people in contested areas.

Article 4: The Consultative Assembly (Majles-e Showra) of self-governing regions shall be elected through the free, direct, and secret ballots of men and women residents of the region, and it shall be tasked with legislating the laws and social and economic relations of the nation residing within the region.

  Section 1: Legislated laws and rules of the regional Consultative Assemblies shall not contradict the Iranian Federal Constitution.

Article 5: The Consultative Assembly of the self-governing region shall oversee the implementation of the regional laws.

Article 6: The Government (*hokumat*) of the self-governing region shall be elected by the Consultative Assembly of the region and in turn the Assembly shall be responsible for the correct implantation of all legislations.

  The self-governing government shall be responsible for all police (*entezami*), economic, educational, and health institutions.

Article 7: The Legislative Power of the self-governing region shall be independent according to the principle of separation of powers.

Article 8: The languages of the nations within self-governing regions shall be the official languages of these regions and shall be used in social, administrative, judicial, and educational institutions.

The Persian language which is the official language of the entire country shall also be taught and used alongside the languages of self-governing regions.

Section 1: The national minorities within self-governing regions shall have cultural autonomy while administratively under the government of the self-governing region.

Article 9: All affairs pertaining to foreign policy, national defence, monetary and foreign exchange, and trade policies as well as long-term plans shall be within the auspices of the federal government (*hokumat-e federal*). The implementation of national long-term plans shall be consulted with the regional governments and carried out by the federal government.

Article 10: In order to reach a national balance and compensate for the economic and social underdevelopment (*aqabmandegi*) of self-governing regions, the federal government shall be tasked with supplying extra and necessary budget to the regional governments.

Article 11: While tasked with managing the affairs of the region, the regional self-governing government shall be responsible for implementing the general policies of the federal government that had been ratified by the federal National Assembly, and it shall use all its efforts to reinforce solidarity and cooperation among all peoples of Iran.

(Source: *Kar* 1979j, 2)

Appendix 3

The Fadaiyan's Minimum Program (February 1980)

1. The depended capitalist system must be destroyed
   a. All related assets in all fields such as banking, industry, agriculture, etc. should be immediately confiscated and nationalized.
   b. All imposed, imperialist contracts and trades in all economic, political, military, and cultural fields must be immediately disclosed and cancelled.
   c. All advisers and agents of imperialism must be expelled immediately.
   d. The counter-people (*zedd-e mardomi*) army was created to protect the interests of imperialism and dependent capitalism, and the way it is organized and commanded, its hierarchy, training programs, and weapons and equipment are all in line with the interests of imperialism and dependent capitalism. This army, along with other administrative institutions left from the Shah's regime, must be replaced with a people's army and a new administrative apparatus that functions in the interest of the masses.
   e. The parties and groups of capitalist class must be resolutely suppressed, and the spy networks and black imperialist gangs must be continuously dismantled.
2. The democratic governance of the masses must be established
   a. The basic organs for establishing democratic governance by the masses are the People's Revolutionary Councils, which emerge during the struggles in factories, farms, and other areas of productive activities.
   b. The Supreme Council of the People of Iran, which is composed of revolutionary councils, is considered the highest body of government.
   c. All executive bodies tasked with the administration of the affairs of the country are appointed by the Supreme Council of the People of Iran. The task of defending this authority (*hakemiyyat*) rests with

the armed mobilization of the masses, namely the People's Army. Against potential invasion by global imperialism led by the United States and its domestic allies, namely, the capitalist class, the workers, peasants, and others must, in addition to their daily life activities, receive military training and be armed. What ensures the people's self-governance (*hakemiyyat*) and protects our democratic homeland will be the armed mobilization of the people.

3. The country's economy must be rebuilt according to the interests of the working class
   a. General economic planning must be planned and implemented by the government with emphasis on creating and expanding basic industries in order to augment national production and meet the needs of the people.
   b. To assist with augmenting national production and expanding infrastructural industries, foreign trade must be fully controlled by the government.
   c. All underground and natural resources must be nationalized.
   d. The lands of large landowners must be seized immediately and allocated free of charge to the councils of peasants who work on them.
   e. Peasants and smallholders must join in agricultural production cooperatives and be supported by the distribution of quality seeds, chemical fertilizers, financial aid, and the supply of agricultural machinery. They must also be supported by guaranteeing the purchase of their products at reasonable prices and by banning the import of similar foreign products. All debts of the peasants must be immediately forgiven.
   f. Large manufacturing plants must be managed by employees and workers councils within the framework of general economic planning. Permanent and suitable work must be allocated to all workers. Pension, disability, and unemployment insurance must be guaranteed for all. 40-hour work week, 2-day weekend, and one-month annual vacation must be upheld as a legal right of the working class.
   g. All anti-labour laws must be repealed immediately, and new labour laws must be drafted by workers' real representatives.
   h. The minimum wage must be continuously adjusted according to the cost of living and the level of national production.

4. The democratic rights of the people must be guaranteed
   a. The complete freedom of activity of progressive political and revolutionary organizations must be guaranteed.
   b. Freedom of writing, expression, belief, and religion must be guaranteed to people.
   c. Freedom of assembly, convention, rallies, and holding demonstrations that consolidate the rule of the masses, must be fully guaranteed.
   d. Freedom of activity of syndicates, unions, other guild organizations must be guaranteed.
   e. Full equality of women's rights on par with men must be guaranteed at all political, social, and cultural levels.
   f. All discriminations against nations (*setam-e melli*) must be eliminated. The right of all of Iranian peoples' self-governance (*khodmokhtari*) must be recognized. Except in matters of national defence, foreign policy, general economic and foreign trade planning, the administration of other affairs must be relegated to the self-governing people's councils.
5. The welfare of the toilers must be ensured
   a. Housing must be provided for all toilers, first through the confiscation of the buildings of capitalists and secondly through government investment.
   b. All toilers must be provided with education. Education up to the high school diploma must be made compulsory. All levels of education from kindergarten to university must be free.
   c. Education of the toilers must count as working hours. Those who do not know how to read and write must be schooled in offices, factories, and school.
   d. Healthcare and medical services must be made available sufficiently and free of charge to all Iranians. Providing medical services to villagers must have priority. All hospitals, clinics, and healthcare facilities must be free and run by the government.
6. Foreign policy must serve the interests of the Iranian people and the fight against global imperialism
   a. The foreign policy of a free and democratic Iran must take on the task of defending the sovereignty of the masses and preserving the national independence and territorial integrity of the democratic homeland and economic progress.

b. In the global scene, socialist countries, liberated nations, the working class of imperialist countries, and the people of colonized countries are all allies, united against global imperialism led by the United States, the main enemy of all the peoples of the world. Iran's foreign policy must strengthen the relations between allies in the global struggle against imperialism and capitalism, and it must offer active support of the working class around the world, oppressed peoples, and revolutionary forces.

(Source: *Kar* 1980b, 4–5)

Bibliography

"7-Person Land Assignment Committees" ["*Hey`atha-ye Haft Nafareh-ye Vagozari-ye Zamin*"]. 2023. *Wiki Feqh*. <https://shorturl.at/ewxFN>.

"A Document Regarding Gorgan Lands" ["*Yek Sanad darbareh-ye Zaminha-ye Gorgan*"]. 1979. *Ketab-e Jom'eh* 1 (July 26): 128–131. British Archives registration: F.O. 271/18992.

Abrahamian, Ervand. 1982. *Iran between Two Revolutions*. Princeton: Princeton University Press.

———. 2008. *A History of Modern Iran*. Cambridge: Cambridge University Press.

Afary, Janet. 1996. *The Iranian Constitutional Revolution, 1906–1911: Grassroots Democracy, Social Democracy, and the Origins of Feminism*. New York: Columbia University Press.

Aghajanian, Akbar. 1983. "Ethnic Inequality in Iran: An Overview." *International Journal of Middle East Studies* 15: 211–224.

Alfred, Taiaiake, and Jeff Corntassel. 2017. "Being Indigenous: Resurgence Against Contemporary Colonialism." In *The Movement of Movements, Part 1: What Makes Us Move?* edited by Jai Sen. New Delhi: OpenWord.

Allamehzadeh, Reza (dir.). 1980. *Harf Bezan Turkmen* [*Speak Turkmen*]. *YouTube*. <youtube.com/watch?v=jONoTrPLDsQ&ab_channel=chapgard>.

Amadori, Massimo and Giuliano Brunetti. 2020. "*Biennio Rosso*: Italy's 'Two Red Years.'" *Socialist Alternative*. June 5, 2020. <socialistalternative.org/2020/06/05/biennio-rosso-italys-two-red-years/>.

Amanat, Abbas. 2017. *Iran: A Modern History*. New Haven: Yale University Press.

Anderson, Benedict. 1983. *Imagined Communities*. London: Verso.

Anderson, Kevin B. 2010. *Marx at the Margins: On Nationalism, Ethnicity, and Non-Western Societies*. Chicago: Chicago University Press.

Angus, Ian H. 2001. *Emergent Publics: An Essay on Social Movements and Democracy*. Winnipeg: Arbeiter Ring Publishing.

Ansari, Ali. 2019. *Modern Iran since 1797: Reform and Revolution* (3rd ed.). New York: Routledge.

Arakelova, Victoria. 2015. "On the Number of Iranian Turkophones." *Iran & the Caucasus* 19, 3: 279–282. <https://doi.org/10.1163/1573384X-20150306>.

Ardavan, Anahita. 2012. "*Beh yad-e chahar akhtar-e foruzan-e khalq-e Turkmen*" ["Commemorating the Four Shining Stars of Turkmen people"]. *Turkmen Talk*. <shorturl.at/kosx4>.

Arendt, Hannah. 1955. *Men in Dark Times*. Orlando: Harcourt Brace & Co.

———. 1958a. *The Origins of Totalitarianism*. Orlando: Harcourt Brace & Co.

———. 1958b. *The Human Condition*. Chicago: The University of Chicago Press.

———. 1963. *On Revolution*. New York: Penguin Books.

———. 1969. *Between Past and Future*. New York: Penguin Books.

___. 1970. *On Violence*. Orlando: Harcourt Brace & Co.
Arzanesh, Vali Mohammad Akhund. 2008. "*Avalin Adamrobai-ye Rezhim-e Jomhuri-ye Eslami-ye Iran*" ["The First Kidnapping of the Islamic Republic of Iran"]. *Kanoon*, February 13, 2008. <kanoon6.blogpost.com/2007/02/blog-post_09.html>.
Asefi, Soheil. 2018. "The Formation of Workers' Councils in the Abode of the Islamic Republic's Chicago Boys and the Striving of Democracy Promoter Vultures in Iran." *Counter Punch*, October 31, 2018. <https://www.counterpunch.org/2018/10/31/the-formation-of-workers-councils-in-the-abode-of-the-islamic-republics-chicago-boys-and-the-striving-of-democracy-promoter-vultures-in-iran/>.
Atabaki, Touraj. 2018. "*Tarikh va tarikhnegari-ye kar va tabaqeh-ye kargar dar Iran*" ["History and Historiography of the Working Class in Iran"]. *Naqd Eqtesad Siyasi*. bit.ly/3sudBnk.
Atabay, T. 2023. "*Yad va khaterehi az dowran-e bepakhizi-ye borumandtarin farzandan-e mellat-e Turkmen*" ["A Memory of the Era of Uprising of the Brightest Children of Turkmen Nation"]. *Turkmen Talk*. shorturl.at/jtDGL.
Atayev, K. 1987. *Jonbesh-e rahibakhsh-e Turkmanha-ye Iran (Qiyam-e salha-ye 1917–1925)* [*The Liberation Movement of Iranian Turkmens (The Revolt of 1917–1925)*]. Tudeh Party of Iran.
Azad, Shahrzad. 1980. "Workers' and Peasants' Councils in Iran." *New Left Review* 32, 5: 14–29.
Bayat, Asef. 1987. *Workers and Revolution in Iran: A Third World Experience of Workers' Control*. London: Zed Books.
___. 1997. *Street Politics: Poor People's Movements in Iran*. New York: Columbia University Press.
___. 2017. *Revolution without Revolutionaries: Making Sense of the Arab Spring*. Stanford: Stanford University Press.
Behrooz, Maziar. 2000. *Rebels with a Cause: The Failure of the Left in Iran*. London: I.B. Tauris.
Benjamin, Walter. 1968. "Theses on the Philosophy of History." In *Illuminations*, edited by Hannah Arendt. New York: Schocken Books.
Bertrand, Charles L. 1982. "The Biennio Rosso: Anarchists and Revolutionary Syndicalists in Italy, 1919–1920." *Historical Reflections / Réflexions Historiques* 9, 3: 383–402. <www.jstor.org/stable/41298794>.
Chaqueri, Cosroe. 1995. *The Soviet Socialist Republic of Iran, 1920–1921: Birth of the Trauma*. Pittsburgh: University of Pittsburgh Press.
___. 2001. *The Russo-Caucasian Origins of the Iranian Left: Social Democracy in Modern Iran*. Surrey: Curzon Caucasus World.
___. nd. "The 'Perfect Crime': An Inquiry into the 'Perfect Crime' that Changed the Course of Iran's Modern History." Unpublished Manuscript.
Coulthard, Glen Sean. 2014. *Red Skin, White Masks*. Minneapolis: Minnesota University Press.
CPCTP (Cultural-Political Centre of Turkmen People). 1980. *Zendegi va mobarezeh-ye khalq-e Turkmen* [*The Life and Struggles of Turkmen people*]. CPCTP & CHCPT.
___. 1985. *Peydayesh-e khalq-e Turkmen* [*The Origins of Turkmen People*]. CPCTP.
Dabashi, Hamid. 2015. *Persophilia: Persian Culture on the Global Scene*. Cambridge: Harvard University Press.

Debray, Régis. 1996. "A Guerrilla with a Difference." *New Left Review* 218 (July–August): 128–137.

"Details of Land Distribution in Iran" ("*Joz'iyyat-e taqsim-e arazi dar Iran*"). 1980. *Kayhan* 10942 (March 1): 2.

Dolack, Pete. 2018. "Workers' Councils in the Prague Spring." *Socialism and Democracy* 32, 2: 32–55. <https://doi.org/10.1080/08854300.2018.1515405>.

Elwell-Sutton, L.P., and P. Mohajer. 1987. "Āyandagān." 1987. *Encyclopaedia Iranica*. <iranicaonline.org/articles/ayandagan-newspaper>.

Enqelab-e Eslami. February 10, 1980, 187.

Errejón, Íñigo, and Chantal Mouffe. 2016. *Podemos: In the Name of the People*. London: Lawrence and Wishart.

Faghfouri Azar, Leila, and Shahin Nasiri. 2023. "*Paknejad va tajrobeh-ye jebheh-ye Demokratik-e Melli: Darshai baraye emruz*" [Paknejad and the Experience of National Democratic Front: Lessons for Today"]. *Naqd Eqtesad Siyasi* April 4. bit.ly/41BpSoJ.

Farajollahi, Kazem. 2021. "*Jonbesh-e kargari-ye Iran: Negahi as darun*" ["Iranian Workers' Movement: A Glance from Within." *Akhbar-r Rooz* April 25. www.akhbar-rooz.com/111173/1400/02/05/.

Fatapour, Mehdi. 2023. "*Kanun-e Farhangi-Siyasi va Showraha-ye Khalq-e Turkmen modaf'eh khastehha-ye melli budand*" ["The Cultural-Political Centre and the Turkmen People's Councils Defended the Demands of the People"]. *Kar Online* February 15, 2023. www.kar-online.com/node/6011.

Fereidoun (Esfandiar Karimi). 2001. "*Jang-e dovvom-e Turkman Sahra*" ["The Second War of the Turkman Sahra"]. *Arash* 79: 45–46.

Fowkes, Ben. 2014. *The German Left and the Weimar Republic: A Selection of Documents* Leiden: Brill.

Gluckstein, Donny. 2018. "The Development of Workers' Councils: Between Spontaneity and Organisation." In *Council Democracy: Towards a Democratic Socialist Politics*, edited by James Muldoon. London: Routledge.

Goli, Arne (ed.). 2019a. *Turkmenha dar asnad va mokatebat-e tarikhi doreh-ye Qajar va Pahlavi (1256–1356)* [*Turkmens in the Historic Documents of Qajar and Pahlavi periods (1878–1978)*]. Sweden: Turkmen Study Center.

___. 2019b. *Asnad-e jonbesh-e showrai-ye Turkman Sahra (1356–1396), 1* [*Documents of the Council Movement of Plains of Turkmen (1978–2017), Vol 1*]. Sweden: Turkmen Study Center.

___. 2019c. *Asnad-e jonbesh-e showrai-ye Turkman Sahra (1356–1396), 2* [*Documents of the Council Movement of Plains of Turkmen (1978–2017), Vol 2*]. Sweden: Turkmen Study Center.

"Gonbad Kavus: Assigned to His Majesty for One Ounce of Crystalized Sugar" ["*Gonbad Kavus: Solh shod beh aalahazrat beh yek sir nabat*"]. 1979. *Ketab-e Jom'eh* 8 (August 23): 148–150.

Goodey, Chris. 1980. "Councils in Iranian Factories: The First Year." MERIP *Report* (June): 5–9.

Gorgani, Mansour. 1979. *Mas'aleh-ye zamin dar Sahra-ye Torkman* [*The Land Issue in the Plains of Turkmen*]. Tehran.

Gramsci, Antonio. 1971. *Selections from the Prison Notebooks*, edited and translated by Quintin Hoare and Geoffrey Nowell Smith. New York: International Publishers.

Hakimi, Abolhassan. 1952. *Eslahat-e melki va zera'ati* [*Land and Agricultural Reforms*]. Tehran: Jam'iyyat-e 'Amiyyun-e Iran.
Hamidian, Naqi. 2004. *Safar bar balha-ye arezu* [*A Voyage on the Wings of a Dream*]. Vällingby: Arash Förlag.
Hashemi, Abbas. 2001. "*Goftogu ba Abbas Hashemi (Hashem)*" ["Interview with Abbas Hashemi (Hashem)"]. *Arash* 79: 41–45.
___. 2016. "*Negahi beh 'Safar bar balha-ye arezu*'" ["A Review of *A Voyage on the Wings of a Dream*." *Prison's Dialogue* August 20, 2016. dialogt.de/2016/3550/.
___. 2021. "*Ghobarzadai az Durughha va Ettehamat-e Avamel-e Rezhim*" ["Dusting Off the Lies and Accusations of the Regime's Agents"]. *Shabnameh* (20 September 2021). http://dialogt.org/abbas-hashemi.
Hashemi, Fatemeh. 2009. "*Sabt-e amlak va mas'aleh-ye malekiyat-e khosusi beh ravayat-e asnad-e Majles*" ["Property Registration and the Issue of Private Property According to the Parliament Records"]. *Payam-e Baharestan* 2, 5): 399–411.
Holloway, John. 1998. "Dignity's Revolt." In *Zapatista! Reinventing Revolution in Mexico* edited by J. Holloway and E. Peláez. London: Pluto Press.
Holt, C. J. 1997. *Colonial England 1066–1215*. London: Hambledon Press.
Jafari, Peyman. 2021. "The Showras in the Iranian Revolution: Labour Relations and the State in the Iranian Oil Industry, 1979–1982." In *Worlds of Labour Turned Upside Down: Revolutions and Labour Relations in Global Historical Perspective*, edited by Pepjin Brandon, Peyman Jafari, and Stefan Müller. Leiden: Brill.
Jahani Asl, Mohammad Nasser. 2017. "Identity, Politics, Organization: A Historical Sociology of the Democratic Party of Iranian Kurdistan and the Kurdish Nationalist Movement." Doctoral dissertation, University of Victoria.
Jazani, Bizhan. 2009. *Enqelab-e mashrutiyyat-e Iran: Enqelab va hadafha* [*Iranian Constitutional Revolution: Its Forces and Objectives*]. Paris: Entesharat-e Sazman-e Ettehad-e Fadaiyan Khalq-e Iran.
Kamali, Mohammad Sharif, and Jamileh Arfa. 1992. "*Ezdevaj va khishavandi dar miyan-e Turkmenha-ye Irani*" ["Marriage and Descent Among Turkmens of Iran"]. *Aftab* 1, 2: 4–9.
Kar. 1979a. No. 3 (April 5).
___. 1979b. No. 4 (March 29).
___. 1979c. No. 5 (April 5).
___. 1979d. No. 9 (May 2).
___. 1979e. No. 12 (May 24).
___. 1979f. No. 13 (May 31).
___. 1979g. No. 21 (July 23).
___. 1979h. No. 22 (July 26).
___. 1979i. No. 23 (July 30).
___. 1979j. Special Issue (August 2).
___. 1979k. No. 29 (August 20).
___. 1979l. No. 30 (September 3).
___. 1979m. No. 32 (September 17).
___. 1979n. No. 35 (November 12).
___. 1979o. No. 36 (November 26).
___. 1979p. No. 37 (December 12).
Kar (OIPFG). 1980a. No. 40 (January 2).

___. 1980b. No. 43 (January 23).
___. 1980c. Turkman Sahra Special Issue 1 (February 11).
___. 1980d. Turkman Sahra Special Issue 2 (February 13).
___. 1980e. No. 46 (February 13).
___. 1980f. Special Issue on Leaders of Turkman Sahra (February 25).
___. 1980g. No. 48 (February 27).
___. 1980h. No. 49 (March 5).
___. 1980i. No. 50 (March 12).
___. 1980j. No. 51 (March 19).
___. 1980k. No. 53 (April 9).
___. 1980l. No. 54 (April 16).
___. 1980m. No. 56 (April 30).
___. 1980n. No. 59 (May 21).
___. 1980o. No. 60 (May 28).
Kar-Majority (OIPFG-Majority). 1980a. No. 61 (June 4).
___. 1980b. No. 72 (August 20).
___. 1981a. No. 101 (March 11).
___. 1981b. No. 108 (May 6).
Kar-Minority (OIPFG-Minority). 1980. No. 88 (December 11).
Kargar, Sadeq. 2011. "*Tarikhcheh jonbesh-e kargari dar Iran*" ["A Short History of Iranian Workers' Movement"]. *Radio Fardai* May 1. <https://www.radiofarda.com/a/f6_iran_1mayday_unions/16798549.html>.
Karimi, Esfandiar. 2013. "*Pasokh beh neveshteh-i gheryemas`ulaneh*" ["Reply to an Irresponsible Claim." *Kar Online* March 7. shorturl.at/CEH24.
Kasravi, Ahmad. 2013. *Tarikh-e mashruteh-ye Iran* [*History of the Iranian Constitutionalism*]. Tehran: Negah.
Katouzian, Homa. 1983. "The Agrarian Question in Iran," In *Agrarian Reform in Contemporary Developing Countries* edited by Ajit Kumar Ghose. London: Routledge.
Keddie, Nikki. 1968. "The Iranian Village Before and After Land Reform." *Journal of Contemporary History* 3, 3: 69–91.
___. 1981. *The Roots of the Revolution*. New Haven: Yale University Press.
Kets, Gaard, and James Muldoon. 2018. "Rediscovering the Hamburg Workers' and Soldiers' Councils," In *Council Democracy: Towards a Democratic Socialist Politics* edited by James Muldoon. London: Routledge.
Khajehnejad, Ahmad. 2020. *Ghobar-e sahra: Jang-e avval va dovvom-e Gonbad Kavus dar sal-e 1358* [*The Dust of Meadows: The First and Second War of Gonbad Kavus in 1979–1980*]. Tehran: Sujeh Mehr.
Khazaineh, Yahya. 2020. *A Tribute to the Late Dr. Barkley Moore (RIP) — US Peace Corps Volunteer*. Toronto: Self-published.
Khosrowshahi, Yadollah. 2019. *Bakhshi az tarikh-e jonbesh-e kargaran-e san'at-e naft* [*A History of the Movement of Oil Industry Workers*], edited by H. Ansari. London: Ansari.
Knüppel, Michael. 2000. "Turkmens of Persia ii. Language." *Encyclopædia Iranica*. iranicaonline.org/articles/turkmens-language.
Kor, Yousef. 2013. "*Piramun-e vaghay'-e 'kanun va setad' dar Turkman Sahra*" ["On

the Events Regarding 'Centre and Headquarters' in the Plains of Turkmen"]. *Kar Online* February 27. shorturl.at/mGK58.

Laclau, Ernesto. 1996. *Emancipation(s)*. London: Verso.

___. 2005. *On Populist Reason*. London: Verso.

___. 2014. *The Rhetorical Foundations of Society*. London: Verso.

Laclau, Ernesto, and Chantal Mouffe. 1985. *Hegemony and Socialist Strategy: Towards a Radical Democratic Politics*. London: Verso.

Lambton, Ann K. S. 1953. *Landlord and Peasant in Persia: A Study of Land Tenure and Land Reserve Administration*. London: Oxford University Press.

Lederman, Shmuel. 2018. "Hannah Arendt, the Council System and Contemporary Political Theory." In *Council Democracy: Towards a Democratic Socialist Politics* edited by James Muldoon. London: Routledge.

Linklater, Andro. 2013. *Owning the Earth: The Transforming History of Land Ownership*. New York: Bloomsbury.

Losurdo, Domenico. 2014. *Liberalism: A Counter-History*. London: Verso.

Luxemburg, Rosa. (1906) 2005. *The Mass Strike*. London: Bookmarks Publication.

Mahfuzi, Alireza. 1984. "Interview by Zia Sedghi." Harvard Iranian Oral History Project.

Maljoo, Mohammad. 2017. "The Unmaking of the Iranian Working Class since the 1990s." In *Iran's Struggles for Social Justice: Economics, Agency, Justice, Activism* edited by Peyman Vahabzadeh. New York: Palgrave MacMillan.

Mandel, David. 2018. *The Petrograd Workers in the Russian Revolution: February 1917–June 1918*. Leiden: Brill.

Mardom (Organ of the Tudeh Party of Iran). 1979. No. 95 (November 18).

Martin, John E. 1983. *Feudalism to Capitalism: Peasant and Landlord in English Agrarian Development*. London: Macmillan Press.

Matin-asgari, Afshin. 2017. "The Left's Contribution to Social Justice in Iran: A Brief Historical Overview." In *Iran's Struggles for Social Justice: Economics, Agency, Justice, Activism* edited by Peyman Vahabzadeh. New York: Palgrave MacMillan.

___. 2018. *Both Eastern and Western: An Intellectual History of Iranian Modernity*. Cambridge: Cambridge University Press.

Mentinis, Mihalis. 2006. *Zapatistas: The Chiapas Revolt and What It Means for Radical Politics*. London: Pluto Press.

Mirdar, Morteza, Javad Arabani, and Mojtaba Sultani Ahmadi. 2019. "*Tamalokkhahi ye Reza Shah dar Mazandaran: Angizehha va raveshha*" ["Reza Shah's Thirst for Land Ownership in Mazandaran; Motivations and Methods." *Biannual Research Journal of Iran Local Histories* 8, 1: 105–122.

Mofidi, Aid Mohammad. 2011. "*Mokhtasar tarikh-e ravabet-e siyasi Torkmenha ba hokumat-e markazi*" ["A Short History of Turkmens Relations with the Central Government"]. *Ulker Gonbad Qabus* March 7. ulker.blogsky.com/1389/12/16/post-111/.

Moghadam, Val. 1985. "Workers Councils in Revolutionary Iran: Balance Sheet and Prospects." *Against the Current* 3, 2: 17–24.

Muldoon, James (ed.). 2018a. *Council Democracy: Towards a Democratic Socialist Politics*. London: Routledge.

___. 2018b. "Council Democracy: Towards a Democratic Socialist Politics." In *Council Democracy: Towards a Democratic Socialist Politics* edited by James Muldoon. London: Routledge.

Naderi, Mahmoud. 2011. *Cherikha-ye Fadai-ye khalq, jeld dovvom: Enqelab-e Eslami va bohran dar goftman* [*The People's Fadai Guerrillas, Vol. 2: The Islamic Revolution and Crisis in Their Discourse*]. Tehran: PSRI.

Najmabadi, Afsaneh. 1995. *Hekayat-e dokhtaran-e Quchan* [*The Story of the Daughters of Quchan*]. Spånga: Baran.

Nizam al-Molk. 1968. *Seyr ol-moluk (Siyasat nameh)* [*Profiles of Kings (Letter on Politics)*], edited by H. Darke. Tehran: Bongah-e Tarjomeh va Nashr-e Ketab.

Nomani, Farhad. 2020. "*Naqsh-e dowlat dar qalabeh-ye sarmayehdari dar Iran*" ["The Role of Government in the Domination of Capitalism in Iran"]. *Naqd-e Eqtesad-e Siyasi*. <https://shorturl.at/ceglt>.

OIPF-M (Organization of Iranian People's Fadaiyan-Majority). 2010. "The Organization of Iranian People's Fadaian (Majority): 1971–2001." enacademic.com/dic.nsf/enwiki/2859167.

OIPFG (Organization of Iranian People's Fadai Guerrillas). 1973a. *Darbareh-ye eslahat-e arzi va natayej-e mostaqim-e an* [*On the Land Reform and Its Direct Consequences*]. OIPFG.

———. 1973b. *Barresi-ye sakht-e eqtesadi-ye rustaha-ye Fars* [*A Review of Economic Structure of Fars Villages*]. OIPFG.

———. 1973c. *Barresi-ye sherkatha-ye sahami-ye zera'i* [*A Review of Joint-Stock Agricultural Corporations*]. OIPFG.

———. 1974. *Barresi-ye sakht-e eqtesadi-ye rustaha-ye Kerman* [*A Review of Economic Structure of Kerman Villages*]. OIPFG.

"On Councils." 1979. *Nabard-e Khalq* (Organization of Iranian People's Fadai Guerrillas) 7 (July): 27–30.

Peterson, Brian. 1975. "Workers' Councils in Germany, 1918–19: Recent Literature on the *Rätebewegung*." *New German Critique* 4: 113–124.

Peygham-e Emrooz. 1979. "*Rahpeymai-ye avval-e mah-e Meh*" ["May Day Rally"]. No. 46 (May 2).

Peykar. 1980. "*Ettehad 34 showra-ye kargari va rahbari-ye e'tesab-e karkhanehha-ye Gilan*" ["Unification of 34 Workers Councils and Strike Committees of Gilan Factories." *Peykar* 49 (April 7): 3, 5.

"Plains of Turkmen was the Field of a Devastating Raid for Years" ["*Turkman Sahra, Salha Arseh-ye Takht-o-tazi Virangar Bud*"]. 1979 (April 10). *Ayandegan* 12, 3329: 5.

Popp-Madsen, Benjamin Ask. 2020. "From Workers' Councils to Democratic Autonomy: Rediscovering Cornelius Castoriadis' Theory of Council Democracy." *Critical Horizons* 21, 4: 318–334. <https://doi.org/10.1080/14409917.2020.1835040>.

Popp-Madsen, Benjamin Ask, and Gaard Kets. 2021. "Workers' Councils and Radical Democracy: Toward a Conceptual History of Council Democracy from Marx to Occupy." *Polity* 53, 1: 160–188. <https://doi.org/10.1086/711750>.

PSRI (Political Studies and Research Institute). nd. "*Rishehyabi-ye taharokat-e jaryan-e chap dar Gonbad*" ["Analysis of Leftist Moves in Gonbad"]. *PSRI*. psri.ir/?id=loparpb0ci.

Qorkhanchi, Mohammad Ali. (1903) 1981. *Nokhbeh-ye seyfiyyeh: Dar Tarikh va joghrafia-ye Astarabad* [*The Elite Swordsmen: On the History and Geography of Astarabad*], edited by M. Ettehadieh and S. Sadvandian. Tehran: Nashr-e Tarikh-e Iran.

Radio Zamaneh. 2023. "*Avval-e mah-e Meh, ruz-e jahani-ye kargar: Parvandeh-ye vizheh*" ["May Day, International Workers' Day: A Special Report." April 30. www.radiozamaneh.com/763012.

Rahnema, Saeed. 1992. "Work Councils in Iran: The Illusion of Worker Control." *Economic and Industrial Democracy* 13: 69–94.

Rappaport, Nina. 2021. "The New Industrial Commons: Worker-Owners and Factory Space." *Architectural Design* 91, 5: 48–55. <https://doi.org/10.1002/ad.2731>.

Rees, E.A. 1987. *State Control in Soviet Russia: The Rise and Fall of the Workers' and Peasants' Inspectorate, 1920–34*. New York: Palgrave MacMillan.

Safavi, Mohammad. 2017. "The Voice of the Workers: Iran's Labour Movement and Reflections on the Project-Seasonal Workers' Union of Abadan, 1979–1980." In *Iran's Struggles for Social Justice: Economics, Agency, Justice, Activism* edited by Peyman Vahabzadeh. New York: Palgrave MacMillan.

Salaman, K. 1980. "Turkmenha" ["Turkmens"]. *Ketab-e Jom'eh* 35 (April 21): 54–61.

Salour, Nasrin, and Sam Salour. 2020. "Council Power in the Iranian Labour Movement." *Tempest Magazine* November 19, 2020. <www.tempestmag.org/2020/11/council-power-in-the-iranian-labor-movement/>.

Sha'bani, H. 1972. "*Reza Shah va Amlak ekhtesasi*" ["Reza Shah and Exclusive Properties"]. *Khaterat-e Vahid* 14: 89–92.

Shafai, Ahmad. 1986. *Qiyam-e afsaran-e khorasan va 37 sal zendegi dar Showravi* [*The Revolt of Khorasan Officers and Living for 37 in the Soviet Union*]. Tehran: Ketabsara.

Shahidi, Hossein. 2007. *Journalism in Iran: From Mission to Profession*. London: Routledge.

Shamdanihagh, Ali. 2022. "*Faraz va forud-e nerkh-e dollar dar qarni keh gozasht*" ["The Rise and Fall of Dollar in the Past Century"]. *Euro News* September 13, 2022. per.euronews.com/2022/03/22/iran-money-currency-rial-vs-doller-us-100-years-economy.

Smith, Andrea. 2017. "Indigenous Feminism and Heteropatriarchal State." In *The Movement of Movements, Part 1: What Makes Us Move?* edited by Jai Sen. New Dehli: OpenWord.

Sorel, George. (1908) 2004. *Reflections on Violence*, translated by T. E. Hulme & J. Roth. Mineola: Dover Publishing, Inc.

Strangers in a Tangled Wilderness. 2015. *The Rojava Revolution: A Small Key Can Open a Large Door*. Combustion Books.

Subcommandante Marcos. 2001. *Our Word is Our Weapon*, edited by J. Ponce de Leon. New York: Seven Stories Press.

Tafreshian, Abolhassan. 1988. *Qiyam-e afsaran-e Khorasan* [*The Revolt of Khorasan Officers*]. Tehran: Atlas.

Taimaz. 1979. "*Yek rusta-ye viran-e Turkman Sahra*" ["A Ruined Village of Plains of Turkmen]." *Ayandegan* 12, 3326: 5.

"TV Debate between President Bani Sadr and OIPFG." 1980. *YouTube*. <www.youtube.com/watch?v=X4to0K-CFTw&ab_channel=niloupejvak>.

Vahabzadeh, Peyman. 2010. *A Guerrilla Odyssey: Modernization, Secularism, Democracy, and the Fadai Period of National Liberation in Iran, 1971–1979*. Syracuse: Syracuse University Press.

___. 2011. "SAKA: Iran's Grassroots Revolutionary Workers' Organisation."

Revolutionary History 10, 3: 348–359.

———. 2015. *Parviz Sadri: Namai az yek zendegi-ye siyasi* [*Parviz Sadri: A Political Biography*]. Vancouver: Shahrgon Books.

———. 2017a. *Iran's Struggles for Social Justice: Economics, Agency, Justice, Activism*. New York: Palgrave MacMillan.

———. 2017b. "Historical and Conceptual Preparations for a Multidisciplinary Study of Social Justice in Iran." In *Iran's Struggles for Social Justice: Economics, Agency, Justice, Activism* edited by Peyman Vahabzadeh. New York: Palgrave MacMillan.

———. 2019a. *A Rebel's Journey: Mostafa Sho'aiyan and Revolutionary Theory in Iran*. London: OneWorld.

———. 2019b. *Violence and Nonviolence: Conceptual Excursions into Phantom Opposites*. Toronto: University of Toronto Press.

———. 2022a. "*Iran 'Etnik' nadarad*" ["Iran Has No 'Ethnics'"]. *Naqd-e Eqtesad-e Siyasi* November 6, 2022. <https://shorturl.at/jkHO5>.

———. 2022b. *The Art of Defiance: Dissident Culture and Militant Resistance in 1970s Iran*. Edinburg: Edinburg University Press.

Wagner-Pacifici, Robin. 2017. *What Is an Event?* Chicago: University of Chicago Press.

"Why Did They Instigate the Turkman Sahra Catastrophe?" ["*Faje'e-ye Turkman Sahra ra chera berah andakhtand?*"]. 1979. *Peygham-e Emrooz* 20, 26: 1, 7.

Yeganeh, Cyrus. 1985. "The Agrarian Structure of Iran: From Land Reform to Revolution." *State, Culture, and Society* 1, 3: 67–84.

Zavareh`i, Davud. 1979. "*Gozaresh-e lahzeh beh lahzeh az ruydadha-ye Turkman Sahra*" ["By the Minute Reports of the Events in the Plains of Turkmen"]. *Tehran Mosavvar* 37, 11: 8–11.

Index

10 Nights of Poetry-Goethe Institute in Tehran (1977), 112–113
1953 coup, 36, 46, 48, 68, 70, 92, 99, 101, 108, 121, 151
1979 Revolution (Iran), 4, 24, 25, 37, 41, 51–52, 53, 79, 83, 85, 106, 109, 110, 113, 114, 115, 117, 119, 121, 122, 126, 128, 130, 131, 133, 142, 148, 151–152, 153, 159, 162, 167, 168, 170–171, 181–182, 208, 223, 229

Aba'i, Aba, 96
Abdulrahimpour, Qorban Ali, 138
Abrahamian, Ervand, 61, 65, 103
Afary, Janet, 32, 54, 60, 87
Ahangar (periodical), 173
Ahangari, Amir, 116
Ahangari, Bardi, 111, 128, 186
Ahmad Shah Qajar, 34, 35, 63
Ahmadzadeh, Massoud, 48–49, 77
Ahmadzadeh, Mastureh 137
Ajami, Haj Rahim, 113, 116
Alam, Assadollah, 96, 100, 102
Alamuti, Nuraddin, 102
Allamehzadeh, Reza, 157
Amanat, Abbas, 59, 64, 66, 103
American revolution (1776), 20, 22, 23–24, 129, 158, 221, 222
Ameli, Hassan, 189–190
Amini, Ali, 47, 71–72
ancestral / ancestrality (Turkmen lands), 2, 9, 10, 54, 55, 79, 90, 95, 101, 108, 110, 120, 122, 149, 164, 213, 215, 218, 222
concept of, 11, 160, 223–225
anjomans, 32–35, 37, 54, 184, 218
Aq Qoyunlu tribe, 82
aq saqal (white-bearded), 98, 117, 122, 125, 191
Aqa Mohammad Khan Qajar, 83

Arabs of Iran, 7, 103, 106, 168, 177
Arab Spring, 25
Arendt, Hannah, 7, 27, 28, 29, 30, 33, 158–159, 165, 221
councils, 11, 12, 19–23, 27, 53–54, 129, 181, 182
the social question, 23–27, 53–54, 123, 222
Arsanjani, Hassan, 71–72
Arts and Folklore Centre of Plains of Turkmen, 150
Arts Workshop of Iran, 150, 186, 205
Aryanism, 103
Arzanesh, Vali Mohammad, 120, 133, 138, 154, 175, 177, 179, 195, 198, 203
Ashraf, Hamid, 48, 49, 50
Assembly of Experts, 153, 175
assimilation
cultural, 9, 11, 81, 102–108, 191
of Turkmen councils, 4, 6, 26, 42, 155, 172, 206–213, 215, 221
Atabay. T., 138–139, 189, 192, 194–195, 210
Austria, 14, 15
Ayandegan (newspaper), 140, 147, 155, 173, 175, 200
Azad, Safar, 111
Azad University, 111, 114
Azerbaijan / Azerbaijani Turks, 7, 9, 10, 33, 34, 87, 88, 95, 103, 130, 153, 169, 177, 185, 186, 187, 214
Azadistan, 88
Azizi, Mohammad Qoli, 113, 116

Baghshi music, 150, 185, 186, 218
Baluchis / Baluchistan, 7, 84, 90, 100, 103, 106, 109, 121, 153, 157, 177, 214, 229, 230, 232
Bani Sadr, Abolhassan, 43, 151, 196, 199, 200, 204, 205–206
Baqer Khan, 34

Bar, Akhun, 111
Bardi Sowqi, Tavaq, 111
Bayat, Asef, 5, 38, 158
    critique of Arendt, 24–25
    on workers' councils, 36, 39–40,
        41–44
Bazargan, Mehdi, 43, 53, 131, 148, 154,
    170, 190
Beheshti, Seyed Mohammad, 151
Behlekeh, Gorkan, 113
Benjamin, Walter, 29
Between Past and Future (book), 12, 20
Blücher, Heinrich, 19–20
Bolshevik Party, 15, 18
    Bolshevik revolution (1917).
    See Russian revolutions
Britain, 14, 15, 91
Budesh, Juma, 118

capitalism in Iran, 54, 55, 62, 66, 70, 73,
    74, 77, 78, 79–80, 91, 99, 110, 144,
    178, 208, 218, 219, 223–225, 234,
    235, 237
    land capitalism, 73, 89, 92, 100–101,
        108, 165, 166, 208, 223
Carter, Jimmy, 50
Castoriadis, Cornelius, 19
Central Council of Federated Trade
    Unions (Iran), 36
Central Headquarters of Islamic Councils,
    210
Centre to Coordinate Workers' Unions,
    152
Chaqueri, Cosroe, 32, 33, 34, 91
CHCPT (Central Headquarters of
    Councils of Turkmen People),
    123–126, 127, 128, 129, 131, 137,
    138, 139, 142, 145, 146, 149, 150,
    152, 154–157, 159, 160, 162, 164,
    165, 166, 175, 177, 202–203, 206,
    207, 209, 210, 211, 213, 214, 222,
    230
Che Guevara, Ernesto, 48
Chiapas (Mexico). *See* Zapatistas
Civil War in France, The (book), 14
Cold War, 69, 70, 140, 183, 190
colonial / colonialism / neocolonial, 2, 5,
    7, 9, 10, 12, 31, 34, 35, 54, 55, 56,
    60, 78, 87, 90, 94–95, 105, 106,
    145, 219, 221, 223, 226
Communist Party (of Iran), 60
Confederation of Iranian Students-
    National Union, 49
Constitutional Revolution (Iran), 13,
    30–33, 35, 36, 37, 54, 61, 62, 102,
    218
    and Turkmens, 87–89
Coulthard, Glen, 224
councils
    3 conceptions of, 18–19
    Arendt, 11, 12, 19–23, 27, 53–54, 129,
        181, 182
    communism, 16, 18–19
    in Europe, 12, 13–19
    in Kurdistan, 40, 130, 153
    union/syndicate (Iran), 36, 39, 40–41,
        43, 236
    workers' councils (Iran), 37–46, 181, 221
council movement of Turkmens
    assimilation by Reconstruction
        Crusade, 206–213
    "first war", 135–144, 163, 167, 169,
        174, 183, 188
    Fishermen's Council, 2, 185
    formation, 116–119
    Gonbad Kavus Brick-Kiln Workers'
        Council, 185
    Rug-Weavers' Council, 117, 149, 185,
        193, 229
    "second war", 131, 192, 193–206
    structure of Turkmen councils,
        164–168
    women's participation, 191–193
    yashuli (elder) councils, 98, 125, 160,
        164
CPCTP (Cultural-Political Centre of
    Turkmen Peoples), 116–120, 122,
    123, 125, 126, 127, 128, 131, 134,
    136, 137–139, 142, 146, 149, 150,
    159–160, 163, 164–165, 175, 176,
    177, 178, 185, 186, 192, 193, 201,
    205, 206, 212, 213, 214, 218, 222,
    223
Cuba / Cuban revolution (1959), 48, 76
Cultural and Political Centre of Arab
    People, 168

Cultural Centre of Turkmen People–
    Bandar Turkmen, 120
Cultural-Islamic Centre of Turkmen
    People, 121
Cultural Revolution (Iran), 41, 43, 211
Czechoslovakia, 17

Dara'i, Fattollah, 142
Dardipour, Araz Mohammad, 136
Dardipour, Bardi, 175
Darvish, Mahmoud, 198, 206
Davaforush, Haji Ali, 32
De Abris, Alceste, 16
Debray, Régis, 48
Dehqani, Ashraf, 137, 207
democratic movements, 33, 162, 163, 215, 223
Democratic Party of Iranian Kurdistan
    (DPIK), 40, 52, 130, 168, 169, 189
Derazgisu, Seyed Ebrahim, 196, 198, 201, 204, 206
Dubček, Alexander, 17–18

Ebrahimi, Nader, 112
Emadi, Ghaffur, 116
Enferadi, Jalil, 37
Enqelab-e Eslami (newspaper), 199, 200
ethnic / ethnicity, 6, 9, 27, 56, 105, 107,
    109, 121, 127, 133, 152, 196, 213,
    216, 217, 220, 227,
    ethno-national movements, 6
Ettela'at (newspaper), 140, 142, 200, 204

Fadai/Fadaiyan. *See* OIPFG
Fadaiyan-e Turkmen, 113, 115, 116, 126, 204
Fallahi, Valiollah, 206
Fahim, Azhdar, 186
Farsiu, Zia, 49
Fatapour, Mehdi, 119, 120, 137, 138, 139, 140, 142
feudalism, 56, 57, 60, 61, 73
    and *Iqta'*, 58
Fire Without Smoke (novel/TV series), 112
Fishermen/fishery, 2, 32–33, 75, 90, 117, 157, 185,
    Shilat, 90
Freedom Movement of Iran (Nehzat-e
    Azadi-ye Iran), 148

French revolution (1789), 20, 23–24, 222
Galdi Goklani, Ane, 113, 205
Galdi Bidar, Morad, 205
Gari, Begmorad, 113, 116
Genkesh (periodical), 213
Germany, 14, 15, 16, 17, 19, 22, 29, 111
    Freikorps, 16
Gilan, 33, 35, 44, 87
    Jangali movement, 76, 87, 88–89
Goklani, Anin, 116
Goklani, Ghaffur, 116
Goli, Arne (Amin), 3, 114–115, 119, 185
Gonbad Teachers' Association, 114, 116
Gorgan, 81, 83, 84, 85, 86, 91, 92, 97, 98,
    99–100, 101, 107, 138, 145, 156,
    188, 196, 201, 204, 227
    Radio Gorgan, 111
Gorgan (periodical), 96
Gorgani, Mansour, 90, 92, 96, 100, 101,
    106–107, 137, 140, 144
Gorky, Maxim, 114
Gramsci, Antonio, 16, 106, 165, 221, 222

Hallizadeh, Halli, 205
Hamidian, Naqi, 119, 120, 123, 127–128,
    129, 138, 139, 140
Hashemi, Abbas. 119, 120, 136–139, 140,
    141, 147,
Hassanpour, Mahmoud, 117, 120, 147
Hemmat (organization), 32
Hosseini, Sheik Ezeddin, 121
Human Condition, The (book), 20
Hungary, 14, 15, 16, 22
Husák, Gustáv, 18

Iel Guyji (periodical), 150, 185, 213
Il Gün (periodical), 213
Incheh Borun, 139
Indigenous / indigeneity, 8, 10, 11, 22,
    24, 26, 76, 160, 164, 217, 219,
    224–225
Indonesia, 14
Iran Nation Party, 148
Iran-e Bastan (periodical), 103
Iranian Human Rights Society, 142
Iranian People's Fadai Guerrillas (splinter
    group), 207
Iranpour, Parviz, 202

Ireland, 14
IRGC (Islamic Revolutionary Guards
    Corps), 41, 43, 101, 130, 132,
    146, 147–148, 163, 168, 169, 172,
    174, 178, 186, 187, 188, 193, 194,
    196–199, 200, 201–203, 204, 206,
    210, 211, 221, 231
Ironworkers and Mechanics Union, 37
Islamic Associations (Anjomanha-ye
    Eslami) in workplaces, 42, 43, 151,
    210
Islamic Association of Teachers of
    Gonbad Kavus, 210, 212
Islamic Movement of Turkmen Youth, 126
Islamic Republic Party, 173, 176
isonomy, 23
Italy, 14, 15, 16, 17, 29
    Biennio Rosso (Red Years, 1919-1920),
        16, 29, 221
    Fascism, 16

Jabal Ameli, Bahman, 137, 179
Ja'fari, Hassan, 127
Ja'fari, Qasem, 179
Jafari, Peyman, 42, 43, 45, 46, 152
Jahanara, Mohammad, 168
Jajormi, Ebrahim, 186
Jamshidi Rudbari, Ferdos, 176
Jazani, Bizhan, 33, 48, 50, 75, 76, 88, 113,
    139, 161, 192
Johnson, Lynden, 69
Jomhuri-ye Eslami (periodical), 173, 178,
    200, 204
Jorjani, Hossein, 149, 202, 203
Journal of Turkmen Women (periodical),
    150

Kakwan, Kourosh, 142
Kar (weekly), 51, 117, 127, 135, 143, 147,
    170, 173, 176, 177, 181, 189, 192,
    200, 202, 203, 204, 206, 209, 210,
    211, 212
Karimi, Esfandiar (Fereidoun), 126, 147,
    176, 179, 187, 189, 194–195, 203
Kasravi, Ahmad, 32, 34, 35
Kayhan (newspaper), 142, 146, 148, 173,
    200
Keddie, Nikki, 69, 73, 74

Kennedy, John F., 47, 71, 85
Keshtgar, Ali, 141, 206
Khaledzadeh, Safar Gol, 192
Khalkhali, Sadeq, 170, 199–200, 201, 204
Khojeh Logarkaz village, 122, 164
Khomeini, Ruhollah, 41, 53, 114, 116, 121,
    130, 131, 132, 133, 135, 141, 147,
    148, 151, 152, 154, 155, 169, 170,
    172, 176, 177, 184, 187, 188, 189,
    190, 201, 212
Khoshru`i, 143
Khosrowshahi, Yadollah, 27
Khuzestan, 87, 88, 103, 153, 168
Khwarazmian Empire, 85
Komala (Revolutionary Organization of
    Toilers of Iranian Kurdistan), 40,
    52, 130, 139, 168, 169, 189
Komiteh (Imam's Committee, later
    Islamic Revolution Committee),
    116, 117, 121, 126, 130, 131, 132,
    136, 137, 138, 139, 142, 145, 146,
    147, 163, 165, 169, 172, 174, 178,
    186, 188, 192
Kor, Yousef, 117–118, 127, 194, 203
Kuchek Nazarkhani village, 146
Kurdistan/Kurds, 1, 2, 6, 76, 117, 119, 121,
    130, 131, 142, 152, 163, 168–169,
    170, 171, 172, 173, 175, 179, 183,
    189, 200, 207, 211, 232
    councils, 38, 40, 127, 130, 153, 184
    federalism, 52, 160, 168
    land, 153
    and OIPFG, 119, 171–172, 179, 189,
        191, 195
    and Turkman Sahra, 140, 182, 185,
        189, 195, 222

labour unions, 13, 14, 17, 33, 36, 37, 39, 96
Laclau, Ernesto, 26
Lambton, Ann, 57–58, 62, 65, 66, 68, 83,
    86, 98
land
    appropriation / dispossession, 11,
        55, 63, 64–68, 69, 73, 79, 81,
        89–93, 97, 99, 100, 102, 106, 108,
        110, 122, 123, 127, 145, 153, 156,
        157, 163, 164, 167, 215, 222, 227,
        230

Index

arbabi (large, private landownership), 59
commons, 54, 149, 220, 223, 224, 225
Exclusive (Royal/Pahlavi) Estates (Amlak-e Ekhtesasi), 65, 67–68, 90, 94, 97, 100, 156
gavband (land renting peasant), 61
iqta' (land assignment), 57–59, 62, 67, 101, 102
khaliseh (state-owned lands), 59, 60, 63–64, 65, 66, 91, 92
khordeh malik (proprietors of small lands), 61
khoshneshin (landless agricultural labourer), 61, 74
land occupation by Turkmens, 117, 121–122, 123, 124, 126, 127, 129, 133, 145, 149, 154, 159, 165, 230
muzare'eh (sharecropping), 60
nasaq (right of cultivation), 61, 77
Pahlavi Estates, 92, 99, 100,
property rights, 56, 58, 60, 61–64, 65, 72, 91, 126, 143, 221, 224, 225
ra'yat (peasant), 61
registry laws, 55, 56, 63, 64, 65, 68, 69, 79, 89, 90, 91, 92, 94, 97, 98, 99, 100, 101, 224, 227
tuyul (fief), 59, 62, 83
under Parthians, 57
under Sassanians, 57
under Safavid Empire, 59, 82–83
under Seljuk Empire, 57, 58, 82
vaqf (religiously endowed land), 66, 72, 59
Land Issue in the Plains of Turkmen, The (book), 90
land reform (1960s Iran), 11, 54, 56, 57, 61, 64, 68–74, 80, 81, 90, 108, 153, 188, 218,
   impact on Turkmens, 99–102
   PFG's analysis, 75–79
   réforme agraire, 70
Land reform (1980s Islamic Republic), 207–209, 212
Latin America, 48, 49, 75, 76, 218
Lenin, V. I., 16, 18, 19,
Letter on Politics (book), 58
Liebknecht, Karl, 19
List, Friedrich, 62
Luxemburg, Rosa, 19–20, 29–30
Madani, Ahmad, 168
Madarshahi, 132, 143
Mahabad, 152, 169, 186
Mahabad Republic (1946), 152, 168
Mahdavy, Hossein, 74
Mahfuzi, Alireza, 141
Makhdumi, Ayisha, 138
Makhtoom, Hakim, 116, 125, 126, 137, 150, 157, 175, 176, 194, 203, 204, 206, 222
making power, 223
Maljoo, Mohammad, 45
Mansouri, Javad, 204
Marighella, Carlos, 48
Marivan, 170
Marx, Karl, 14, 19, 27, 56, 58, 74
Marxism-Leninism, 48, 49, 52, 160, 183, 186, 212, 218
Marzban, Reza, 142
Mass Strike, The (book), 29
Matin-asgari, Afshin, 46
May Day in Iran (International Workers Day), 51, 96, 150, 151–152, 191
Mazandaran, 10, 63, 64, 65, 66, 67, 70, 84, 85, 90, 120, 125, 127, 131, 137, 138, 141, 146, 149, 176, 178, 186, 196, 198, 206
Meftahi, Abbas, 48, 49
Mellati, Bayram Bibi, 192
Mirza Kuchek Khan, 76, 88–89, 146
modernity (Iran), 7, 9, 30, 35, 54, 56, 217, 219, 224
modernization (Iran), 7, 11, 12, 13, 30–37, 47, 54, 55, 56, 59, 61–64, 70, 79–80, 90, 93, 102, 105, 110, 153
Modir Shanehchi, Mohsen, 137, 141
Mohammad Shah Qajar, 63
Mohammad Ali Shah Qajar, 31–32
Mohammad Reza Shah Pahlavi, 35, 36, 40, 46–47, 50, 51, 55, 67, 69–70, 71, 72, 74, 75, 92, 93–94, 95, 96–97, 99, 100, 101–102, 106, 108, 112, 114, 115, 121, 140, 151, 171, 172, 178, 188, 208, 218, 229, 234
Mohammadi, Ay, 111

Mohammadi Shopping Centre (Gonbad Kavus), 85
Mojahedin-e Khalq. *See* OIPM
Mombeini, Amir, 137
Mongols, 82, 85, 104
Montazeri, Hossein Ali, 201
Moore, Barkley, 85
Moradgari, Beik, 111
Mosaddeq, Mohammad, 46, 70, 99
Moshef, Abdolali, 125, 131, 206
Mostaz'afan Foundation, 109, 208, 212
Mother (novel/film), 114
Mouffe, Chantal, 26
Mozaffar al-din Shah Qajar, 31
Mozayan, Mansour, 100
Mussiyo, Ali, 32
Mussolini, Benito, 16
myth of general strike, 27–28

Nader Shah Afshar, 63
Nabard-e Khalq (periodical), 181
Naqadeh, 169, 170
Naqshbandi, Anaqelich, 115, 121, 231
Naraghi, Ehsan, 75
Naseraddine Shah Qajar, 60, 63
National Democratic Front of Iran, 177
National Federation of Trade Unions (Iran, 1921), 35
National Front of Iran, 55, 137
National Iranian Oil Company, 42
Nazer, Karim, 194
Negahdar, Farrokh, 139, 140, 141, 200, 203, 206
Netherlands, The, 18
Noor Mofidi, Kazem, 176, 198, 201
Nushin, Nazdordi, 202

Öcalan, Abdollah, 26
Oghuz Turks, 82
OIPFG (Organization of Iranian People's Fadai Guerrillas), 3, 6, 9–10, 11, 12, 13, 40–41, 80, 111, 113, 114, 115, 117–120, 122–124, 126–130, 131, 132, 135–139, 140, 141–145, 147, 148, 150, 152, 157–158, 160–161, 162, 163, 168–176, 177, 178, 179–180, 181, 182, 184, 185, 186, 187, 189–196, 198, 199, 200, 201, 203, 205–210, 212, 213, 214–215, 218, 234–237
  history, 46–53
  Kurdistan, 119, 171–172, 179, 189, 191, 195
  land reform analysis, 75–79
  minimum program, 180–184, 234–237
OIPFG-Majority, 41, 52, 171, 174, 191, 205, 209, 210, 212, 215
OIPFG-Minority, 41, 52, 171, 209, 210
OIPM (Organization of Iranian People's Mojahedin), 40, 43, 52, 114, 137, 141, 161
Omid Najafabadi, 133
On Revolution (book), 20
On the Land Reform and Its Direct Consequences (book), 76
On Violence (book), 20
Onsori, Kaka, 111, 116,
Organization of Iranian Workers, 36
Origins of Totalitarianism, The (book), 20
orientalism / orientalizing, 5, 7, 105, 106, 217–218
Osman Akhund, 89

Pahlavi / Pahlavi dynasty. *See* Reza Shah Pahlavi. *See also* Mohammad Reza Shah Pahlavi
Pahlavi, Ashraf, 100
Pahlavi, Gholam Reza, 122
Pahlavi, Shams, 100
Paknejad, Shokrollah, 178
Paris Commune, 13–14, 18
Paveh, 169–170, 178
Peace Corps (USA), 85, 218
Persian language, 7, 9, 105, 233
Persianization, 56, 102
Peshmak village, 122
Peygham-e Emrooz (newspaper), 113, 123, 139, 142, 147, 173, 200
Peykar (Organization of Combat on the Path of the Working Class), 40, 52, 114
PFG (People's Fadai Guerrillas). *See* OIPFG
Pishgam Youth / Student Organization, 128–129, 132, 139, 150, 156, 157, 175, 178, 185, 191–193, 195, 203, 206, 212

Index 253

Plenary Rural Union of Turkman Sahra, 166, 211
Plains of Turkmen. *See* Turkman Sahra
Plenary Union of Councils, 149
Podemos Party (Spain), 26
postcolonial, 7, 13, 56, 71
Prague Spring, 17
primitive accumulation, 56, 74
Puyan, Amir Parviz, 48–49, 75

Qabus Ibn Voshmgir, 85, 97
Qajar dynasty, 31, 34, 59–60, 63, 83, 87
Qajar, Nahid, 119, 120, 138
Qara Qoyunlu tribe, 82
Qarajeh, Yousef, 202
Qarna massacre, 170
Qavam, Ahmad, 151
Qezel, Abdollah, 205
Qezeljeh (Marjanabad), 100, 122, 167
Qorkhanchi, Mohammad Ali, 81, 98

Rabi'i, Ali, 151
Radinia, Abbas, 133
Ra`isi, Heshmat, 117–118, 119
Rah-e Kargar (Organization of Revolutionary Workers of Iran), 52
Rahbar, Mohammad Hossein, 100, 102
Rahnema, Saeed, 44
Rastakhiz Party of Iran, 36, 172
Rasuli, Ali, 137, 148
Reconstruction Crusade (Jahad-e Sazandegi), 155, 188–189, 194, 207, 208, 210, 212, 215, 221
Red Star (Setareh-ye Sorkh), 118, 127
Reflections on Violence (book), 27
repressive development, 7, 47, 54, 222
Reza Shah Pahlavi, 35, 55, 62–67, 69, 79, 83, 87, 89, 90, 91–93, 94, 96, 103, 105, 106, 107, 108, 227
Reza`i, Khalil, 137, 144
Reza`i, Mohsen, 198, 206
Rojava (Democratic Autonomous Administration of North and East Syria), 10, 26, 164, 219, 220, 221, 225
Rostow, Walt Whitman, 69–70
Rug-weaving Women's Council, 150

Russia, 5, 14, 16, 22, 27, 29, 31–32, 34, 40, 59, 60, 62, 83, 89, 182
Russian Social Democracy, 29, 32
Russian revolutions (1905, 1917), 13, 14, 15, 33, 218, 221
Russo-Persian wars, 31

Sadaqiani, Haji Rasul, 32
Sadeghinezhad, Eskandar, 37
Sa'edi, Gholam Hossein, 76
Safai Farahani, Ali Akbar, 48
Safavi, Mohammad, 38, 39
Safavid Empire, 59, 82–83
Sahabi, Yadollah, 175
SAKA (Revolutionary Organization of Iranian Communists), 37
SAVAK (Intelligence and Security Organization of Iran), 111, 115, 137, 142, 143, 145, 157, 172, 173
Same', Mehdi, 137, 141
Sanandaj, 131, 136, 140, 141, 169, 170, 174, 186
Sardar As'ad Bakhtiari, 35
Sattar Khan, 34, 35
Savaluni, Mehdi, 113
Secret Society (Anjoman-e Makhfi), 32
Seljuk Empire, 57, 58, 82
Shafiqi, Qorban (Arqa), 113
Shahnazi, Hakim, 205
Shamlu, Ahmad, 96
Shari'ati, Mohammad Baqer, 131
Shari'atmadari, Kazem, 187, 200–201, 205
Sheikh Khaz'al, 88
Shikak, Isma'il Aqa/Simko, 88
Shirmohammadi, Ashir Mohammad, 113, 116
Sho'aiyan, Mostafa, 22, 75
Showra (shura). *See* council
Siahkal, 37, 47, 48, 49, 51, 76
Sistan and Baluchistan Province, 90
Sistanis, 186, 214
Social Democratic Party-Mojahed of Iran (FEAM), 32
Social Studies and Research Institute, 75
Sorel, George, 27–29, 30
Soviet Union, 17, 23, 26, 30, 70, 83, 139, 140, 178

254 FOR LAND AND CULTURE

Speak Turkmen! (documentary), 157–158, 192
Spring of Freedom, 1, 2, 132, 144, 159, 168, 174
strike committees (Iran), 37, 44, 119, 151, 158, 181, 182
Sultanzadeh, Avetis, 60

Tabataba`i, Seyed Ahmad, 137, 141, 143, 149, 186,
Tagheni, Qelich, 111
Taheripour, Jamshid, 206
Tahmasp Shah Safavid, 82
Talebi, Mohammad, 137
Talebi, Taji, 116
Taleqani, Seyyed Mahmoud, 137, 140–141
Tatar Olya village, 149, 227–231
Tatari, Haji, 186
Tazeh Yol (periodical), 213
Teachers' Independent Association, 152
Tehran Mosavvar (periodical), 138, 173
Tobacco Protest (Iran), 31
Toomaj, Shirmohammad Derkhshandeh, 125–126, 137, 141, 143, 154–155, 156, 157–158, 175, 176, 177, 188, 189, 194, 202, 203, 204, 205, 206, 207, 218, 222
Truman, Harry, 70
Tudeh Party of Iran, 36, 40, 47–48, 51–52, 75, 95–96, 114, 148, 151, 190, 209
Tupamaros (*Movimiento de Liberación Nacional, Tupamaros*, or MLN-T; Uruguay), 48
Turkmen Islamic-Cultural Centre, 126
Turkmen Research Centre, 3
Turkmen revolt (1922), 88–89, 95–96
Turkman Sahra, 1, 2, 6, 9, 10, 25, 55, 81, 84–85, 90–91, 97, 102, 112, 114, 117, 119, 122, 126–127, 128–129, 130, 132, 145, 147, 150, 152, 153, 154, 157, 158, 159, 160, 162, 166, 171, 178, 182, 184, 189, 207, 211, 212, 213, 219, 222, 226, 227–231
    cultural assimilation, 106–107
    "first war", 135–144, 163, 167, 169, 174, 183, 188
    land dispossession, 92, 100–101, 106–107, 108, 123
    land reform, 99–102
    "second war", 131, 192, 193–206
Turkman Sahra Newsletter (periodical), 150
Turkmen Sesi (periodical), 96
Turkmen Teachers' Association, 113
Turkmen Women's Association, 149
Turkmen Women Centre, 192–193
Turkmenistan (periodical), 213
Turkmenistan (Republic), 82, 83, 84, 85, 89, 144
Turkmens
    Aqabay (Chuni), 86
    Atabay, 89, 98
    Chamur, 91
    Charva, 91
    Goklan, 86, 87, 92, 98, 112
    Jafarbay, 86, 89, 98
    Qajaq, 92, 94–95, 98, 100, 228–229
    Yamut, 86, 112
Turkmen towns and regions
    Aqqala, 92, 107, 113, 116, 125, 128, 134, 137, 166
    Bandar Turkmen (Bandar Shah), 67, 86, 107, 113, 116, 118, 120, 128, 134, 136, 137, 166, 185, 198, 202
    Bojnord, 84, 95, 107, 202, 204
    Gonbad Kavus, 84, 85, 86, 89, 92, 95, 96, 97, 107, 111, 113, 114, 115–116, 119, 120, 121, 123–124, 126, 127, 128, 131, 132–133, 134, 136–138, 141, 143, 146, 148–150, 155–156, 157, 166, 175, 178, 179, 185–186, 188, 191, 192–197, 198, 200, 202, 204, 205, 206, 210, 211, 212, 214, 218, 227, 228
    Gomesh Tapeh, 92, 96, 107
    Jargalan, 107, 144
    Maraveh Tapeh, 139, 140, 144
    Pahlavi Dezh (Aqqala), 107, 198
    Yalmeh Salian, 207

United States of America, 19, 20, 47, 50, 69, 70, 71, 74, 76, 151, 172, 190, 191, 211, 218, 235, 237
Unified Oil Industry Workers' Union, 152

Vahedi, Tavaq Mohammad, 141, 157, 186, 195, 202–203, 204
Wagner-Pacifici, Robin, 18
White Revolution (in Iran), 36, 69, 72, 75, 77
women's protest rally (March 1979), 147
women's status: see council movement of Turkmens
Workers and Revolution in Iran (book), 38
WWI, 17
WWII, 17, 67, 70, 88, 95, 151

Yelgay village, 122
yashuli (Turkmen elders), 94, 98, 122, 125, 160, 164, 218
Yeprem Khan, 35
Yugoslavia, 17

Zabolis, 90, 107–108, 134, 145, 222, 229, 230
Zapatistas (Chiapas Mexico), 10, 25, 26, 164, 219–220, 221, 225
Zavareh`i, Davud, 138
Zedong, Mao, 76
Zia Zarifi, Hassan, 48, 76
Ziyarian (Ziyarid) dynasty, 85